RE:GENERATIONS

RE:GENERATIONS

Canadian Women Poets
in Conversation

Edited by Di Brandt and Barbara Godard

Black Moss Press
2005

Library and Archives Canada Cataloguing in Publication

Re:generations : Canadian women in conversation / [edited by] Di Brandt, Barbara Godard.

Includes bibliographical references and index.
ISBN 0-88753-406-6

1. Canadian literature (English)—Women authors. 2. Canadian literature (English)—21st century.
3. Women—Canada—Literary collections. 4. Art, Canadian—21st century. I. Brandt, Di II. Godard, Barbara

PS8235.W7R44 2005   C810.8'09287   C2005-902693-6

Front Cover: Remedios Varo, "Tres destinos" (Three Destinies), 1956. Oil on Masonite, 90 x 108 cm. Private collection. Reproduced by permission of Anna Alexandra and Walter Gruen.

Back Cover, top: Phyllis Webb, "Cross Word," 2001. Acrylic and collage on canvas, 61 x 61 cm. Courtesy of Smaro Kamboureli. Reproduced by permission of the artist.

Back Cover, bottom: P.K. Irwin, "The Garden," 1961. Egg tempera, 15.5 x 25 cm. Private collection. Reproduced by permission of the artist.

Cover and book design: Karen Veryle Monck

Published by Black Moss Press at 2450 Byng Road, Windsor, Ontario N8W 3E8.

Black Moss gratefully acknowledges the generous support given by the Canada Council for the Arts and the Ontario Arts Council for its publishing program.

Le Conseil des Arts | The Canada Council
du Canada | for the Arts

ONTARIO ARTS COUNCIL
CONSEIL DES ARTS DE L'ONTARIO

We Are Alone

We are alone, who strove to be
Together in the high sun's weather.

We are bereft, as broods a tree
Whose leaves the river sucks forever.

We are as clouds, which merge and vanish
Leaving breathless the dead horizon—

We are as comrades, whose handshake only
Comes rare as leap-year and mistletoe morning.

Each one ploughing a one-man clearing
Neither one alive to see

In wider boundaries of daring
What the recompense might be.

Dorothy Livesay

Contents

Epigraph   *Dorothy Livesay*   **We Are Alone**

9   *Di Brandt*   **Looking Forward, Looking Back**

To Be a Writer Is to Interact with the World

15   *Karen Mulhallen*   **The Women Who Made Us:**
     The Loneliness of the Long Distance Poet, Miriam Waddington

19   *Jan Horner*   **"Beauty may live in small dry things:"**
     A Conversation with Elizabeth Brewster

26   *Cornelia Hoogland*   **Elizabeth Smart as Modernist Writer of 'the meantime'**

34   *Sharon H. Nelson*   **Anne Marriott: Treading Water**

50   *Rosemary Sullivan*   **Three Travellers in Mexico**

    Remedios Varo   **Los Amantes**

    P.K. Irwin   **The Dance**

    Lenora Carrington   **Ancestor**
     Monopoteosis

Mothering as in "Vital and Precise"

63   *Carolyn Zonailo*   **Foremothers: Four Modern Women Poets from the West Coast**
     Living in Exile
     My Body Is Also A Map

74   *Susan McMaster*   **Courage is a Transitive Verb**
     Courage/Coeur de Rage
     Howl

79   *Margaret Christakos*   **(Regenerations, or) Not asleep but not talking/in/A shared room,**
     or, A room of our own is a myth

86   *Janice Williamson*   **Adoptive Mothering, or the Art of Arching**

Wild Vein Through White Leaves' Ruff

95   *P.K. Page*   **Green, how much I want you green**
     Ah, by the golden lilies

97   *Elizabeth Brewster*   **On P.K. Irwin's Bright Centre**
     God As Maker of the Alphabet

99   *Daphne Marlatt*   **the force of the untitled**

103   *Penn Kemp*   **Triple Takes on Places of Their Own**

106   *Lola Lemire Tostevin*   **Semantic Memory**

109   *Betsy Warland*   **Suite of Red**

113   *Margaret Christakos*   **Uncomforted**

117   *Susan Holbrook*   **Who Will Make the Tears Wet for the First Time in a Hundred Years**
                                          Editing the Erotica Issue

119   *Lisa Fiorindi*   **Oatmeal Bath**

124   *Natalee Caple*   **from Imaginary Person**

Leap into Nothing, Joyful

129   *Di Brandt, Rebecca Campbell and Carol Ann Weaver*   **"Leap into Nothing, Joyful," or, Dancing with the Dead**

133   *Di Brandt, Dorothy Livesay,*   **Awakenings: In Two Voices**

149   *Claudia Lucotti*   **Estirando los limités: Translating P.K. Page in Mexico**

157   *Jana Skarecky*   **The Pictures Sing, A Composer's Musings Green and Gold**

Satya-gra-ha-ha-ha

169   *Betsy Warland*   **Phyllis Webb: The Spirit of Inquiry**

       Phyllis Webb   **Veiled Woman, Afghanistan**

177   *Nicole Markotic*   **"I am only a partial fiction": Phyllis Webb and the Prose Line**

184   *Aritha van Herk*   **"There's no reason for letting my mind lose its colour": Sheila Watson's Modernism**

192   **Contributors**

194   **References**

196   **Acknowledgements**

Looking forward, looking back

Di Brandt

*W*HAT IF we hadn't come to poetry, to literary writing, as women, threading our way carefully between rock and stone, competing for individualist masculinist privilege, daring public performance, mourning the loss of traditional feminine consolations, enveloping warmth of family, community, safety in shared silence? If there'd been a community of professional women already there, who'd made it, waving their banner of poetic achievement over us, generously, godmotherly, smoothing the paths for us in our trembling first attempts at artistic self-realization?

Re:Generations boldly announces a revision in Canadian literary history-making, a turning back to re-assess what happened in the century just ended: how in the midst of our feminist overthrowings of our mothers' and grandmothers' careful circumscriptions and prohibitions, in our solitary and united struggles for self-definition, surrounded by men and their large entitlements, we were not alone. We were not without company, not without guides and symbolic relations. We did not invent ourselves out of nothing: we were mothered, we were dreamed in advance, embraced in welcome, we were known.

Re:Generations represents, in this way, both defiance and celebration of canon-making in twentieth-century Canada. Our task, now, stepping out into a new century, is to shake off what no longer suits us, to gather in what does. We were alone, we were not alone. We were not taught by women professors, or published by women editors. We were not handed a women's tradition neatly bound in prestigious leather, nor fêted in women's salons. We were not looked after by housewives and assistants. Neither were we taught to see ourselves as entitled to public achievement and recognition, nor proffered public support getting there. No one suggested we were capable of professional lives. We wanted to do it anyway. We insisted on it. We pieced together our unbidden careers, our unforeseen poetics, surreptitiously, cunningly, in the cracks of faltering traditions, in the devastated battlefields of the old shattered order. We hopped rides on the new petroleum-winged technologies with their oversize promises and futurist optimisms. We put on trousers. We crossed cultural lines. We invented selves.

We were desperate for context, for reception, approval. We took what we could get from our male professors and colleagues: we fought their suppressions, misrepresentations, misunderstandings. We kowtowed to them, grateful to be given side seats in their great halls, their meeting rooms. We allowed ourselves to be seduced by them, sidetracked, undone. We rejected our mothers. We met secretly with each other, sisterly, in twos and threes, stealing time from our sanctioned, restricted other lives. We hammered out, flushed with red wine and emerging sense of new freedoms, our halting first steps toward a contemporary, a utopian futurist feminist poetics.

Once in awhile we stopped dead in our tracks, mesmerized by what we saw coming toward us on our rocky

9

solitary paths; older women, more experienced than we were, with weathered faces and ironic laughter, like H.D.'s Lady, newly written books shining in their outstretched hands. We wanted what they had. We didn't want to be like them. We didn't like to see the lines in their cheeks and foreheads: we didn't want to hear about the blood price paid to get them there.

We were ambivalent about them, they were ambivalent about us. We, their eagerly awaited protégées, were plotting to overthrow, betray them: they, whom we had envisioned as mentors, ushering us into gracious carpeted rooms for high tea, were instead craggy warriors, fierce with fight, keepers of small cluttered dusty studies, sharp eyed, weary, mistrustful, satiric, alone. They already knew what was ahead of us on the path. They were all evasion and red lights and warning.

We were busy with our complicated lives, our lovers, our children, our student loans, our grade transcripts, our curriculum vitae. We were ungrateful, angry on their behalf and ours. We were arrogant, daring, experimental, in the confident way young people are, in the way they themselves had been and still were. We didn't want their advice: we wanted to do it, everything, our own way, on our own.

They loved us. We loved them. They plucked us from our youthful distractions and illusions; they harnessed our libidinous energies, away from wispy, cinderella fantasies to astonishing, eye-opening, gut-ripping, flesh and blood womanly realities. They invited us for coffee. They inscribed their books to us with fond admonishments. They challenged us with their vaster experience, frank admissions, startling attention to detail, grand overviews, daring leaps between disparate realities, dazzling wordcraft.

Local/international, urban/green, primitivist/technological, progressivist/conservationist, objectivist/introspective, materialist/metaphysical, political/aesthetic, domestic/public, familial/collegial, utopian/dystopian, pared down/extravagant, passionate/ironic, heterosexual/ homoerotic—these were the fiercely debated stakes of early modernism, inherited problematically from the industrialist era and its romanticist opponents, who decried its cultural fragmentations and environmental ravages. These oppositional pairs came to be regarded, among modernists, as culturally imperative, and were often negotiated, particularly by male poets and critics, as either/or antimonies.

Women have always lived in dual, in multiple, realities. We never accepted masculinist views on the separation of nature and culture, self and other, progress and tradition, perhaps, as some of us have argued, because of our more extensive role in the labour of reproduction, which gives us the opportunity to mediate actively and creatively between these realities. In the hands of modernist women poets, newly released from traditional domesticities through education and travel, uneasily inheriting the privileges of colonialism, and more deeply inflected by a recently displaced and exploited gynocratic realm than has often been acknowledged, these oppositions melded creatively to become strange and wonderful new hybrids of experimentalism and conservationism. The vision of these adventurous women created the playing field that became the postmodern, and anticipated the millennial, ecopoetic post-postmodern. It is our rich inheritance.

Re:Generations marks a significant moment in Canadian literary history-making. We find ourselves, as women writers, in this new century, new millennium, organized enough, employed enough, well connected enough, to be able to honour our talented foremothers with public recognition and literary responses of our own. "Wider Boundaries of Daring"—the title of a conference and festival of Canadian women's poetry at Windsor in October 2001 where the conversations in this anthology began—is a line from Dorothy Livesay's haunting poetic lament, "We Are Alone," written in the 1930s. The poem looks forward to a time when the hard work of cultural renewal will yield happier "recompense" than the solitariness, exhaustion and bereavement she and her comrades feel at their darkest moments. Livesay's poem stands as a solemn reminder of how challenging the work of inventing culture can be, and the difficult circumstances in which Canadian modernism was born, straddled between two world wars, massive unemployment, pervasive racism, the most fledgling of literary scenes, minimal professional opportunities for women. It also commemorates now, the achievement of some of the enlarged possibilities so generously envisioned for their followers by Livesay and her contemporaries through their creative labours. It is true we no longer have to choose so definitively between career and family. Lifestyle and livelihood choices are legion. Publishing opportunities for women writers in Canada and internationally abound.

On the other hand, we do not share the sense of new, undreamed opportunities and futurist optimism which characterized modernism, despite its catastrophic beginnings in war, the shock of rapid social change and economic recession. The amazing hat tricks of petroleum culture, which brought unprecedented technological changes and prosperity to one part of the world, and poverty and exploitation to the rest, are coming to an end. We look forward to continued uprisings against large scale social inequities and escalating militarism from powerful countries in response to them. We fear the imminent convergence of diminishing energy supplies and ecocrisis. As economic opportunities shrink, so do affirmative programmes to protect women's access to equitable employment. Our literary presses are in dire financial straits despite large poetry audiences across the country and interested readers around the world.

Re:Generations is a collection of dialogues with our modernist foremothers, who set such high bars for creative accomplishment during the first half of the twentieth century, and who still inspire us with their writing today in the era of postmodernism and the post-postmodern. We present it in celebration of continuity between literary generations of Canadian women in a century that often discouraged it, and in a critical context that has to a great extent overlooked it. Reflections on the creative process, the poetry and creative non-fiction in the collection replace the venerable myth of artist as solitary seer into some empyrean realm with a different story, one occurring as lively conversations across generations and between art forms. Whether slipping into the skin or trying on the voice of an established foremother, sometimes even incorporating their words into a poem as in glosas, or collaborating with a friend or contemporary in multimedia works that marry words to music or visual image, or responding to the generative process of mothering or being mothered as these inform artistic practices, the texts in this volume testify to the dynamic exchanges that have created a vibrant tradition of women's poetry in Canada.

Works of celebrated modernist writers and painters are included here alongside the creative riffs on their art by the succeeding generation of poets who, as cultural activists—editors, publishers, conference and caucus organizers—have been facilitators of women's culture in Canada and are keenly appreciative of the enabling cultural work done by the preceding generation of women writers. In turn, they are nurturing further creative interactions and so foster the writing of an emerging generation. These writers also react against their predecessors and engage experimentally with different aspects of the modernist legacy.

The writers published in this volume, from young and emerging to sage and accomplished, are attuned to the nuances of intergenerational and intermedia transmission and cross-influence in both regional, national and international contexts. The texts also constitute an important contribution to the growing body of women's life writing in Canada with their reflection on the regenerative forces of the artistic process and present an inspiring portrait of influential community making among women writers, despite considerable institutional constraints.

We offer these texts as intimate glimpses into the specificities of literary transmission across generations for your inspiration, information and delight.

To Be a Writer Is to Interact With the World

Modernism in Canada: The Women Who Made Us

The Loneliness of the Long Distance Poet, Miriam Waddington

Karen Mulhallen

$\mathcal{W}$HEN I WAS asked to say a few words about the Canadian Modernist Female Example, I said that I had no time, only six months before the gathering of women of daring, and there I was spending the winter in Toronto going back and forth on an icebreaker across the harbour to the Toronto Islands to sit and write in a studio at Gibraltar Point, just around the corner from the Lighthouse.

But to deny is to release, denial brings affirmation and as I looked out of my studio window, or windows, for there were three in a row, I saw that the road from the east, from the eastern gap, curved toward my studio and the lighthouse at Gibraltar Point, and forked about one hundred metres away from my windows.

The fork was hidden by a group of evergreens, but the split roads emerged on either side of the trees, joined again and split again, where the northern part continued on towards Hanlan's Point and the barricade to the Island Airport.

Splitting, diverging, disappearing, wrapping, emerging.

Along these roads each day and increasingly as spring came and snow disappeared were solitary roller-bladers, couples walking their dogs, small groups, single birders with binoculars, and the odd fisherman. The men in the filtration plant emerged onto the road to Hanlan's Point as well, and the musicians in the portable studios on the beach played road hockey on the section that wrapped back on itself and became a circle.

Circling, wrapping

I was asked to say a few words about the example of Canadian Modernist Women Poets, and I thought after awhile back to the first poet whom I knew.

To know.

What is to know? How to count the ways in which we know? More than "knew of," and different than "had read," although both are also true of the poet whom I am trying to know.

Cooking Modernism, Postmodernism

The first Canadian woman poet I was aware of reading was the author of *Double Persephone,* in her first book and in a first edition which I bought in the University of Toronto Bookroom in 1960, a tiny book—hand-printed by John Colombo—which I later sold to a New York Book dealer, when twenty-six years later I carried it to New York, its glue dried out, but otherwise in what booksellers call "good—but not fine—condition," which then enabled me to buy kitchen cabinets for my derelict house in the Kensington Market District of the City of Toronto.

Even then there was value in Canadian women's writing.

But in 1960, I hadn't met M.E. Atwood, nor was she well-known, and of course she is neither modernist nor post-modernist, coming from that generation in Canadian Literature which might now be termed "Transition."

Transitions.

How can we know the transitions, the moderns, the post-moderns?

Transition: where the roads wrap or fork.

Retrospective Knowingness.

Of authors whom I read and was influenced by there might also be Jay Macpherson, whose *The Boatman,* in hindsight, seems to have been important for my own first book *Sheba and Solomon,* although at the time of my first book I hadn't read *The Boatman,* but knew it by its fame, its tight lyricism, its revisiting of conventional forms, its pleasure in rhyme. And there were Colleen Thibaudeau and P.K. Page, both of whose drawings and poems, like those of Kenneth Patchen, had a part to play in my early work, allowing me, even as I was getting to know the work of William Blake and bpNichol, to doodle and draw and sound and paint, to create a dialogue with aspects of self in mixed media.

Allowance, Permissions, Permissions by Example.

But perhaps to know is friendship, the overlapping shape of the daily, if not a shared world.

Drinking Poetry.

As an undergraduate I had been a student—a very poor student who never appeared at morning classes—of a highly respected Male Modernist Poet. This modernist was the German poet Walter Bauer, a pale man with a light fringe of hair and a preference for a beige trench coat, but of his life I had no idea. He did occasionally (and perhaps more often than I knew, since I saw him so infrequently) come into class with his poems. I remember one in which talking to us in his role as a teacher, he ended with the word "Trink," German imperative verb for "Drink." Yet I can't think that he had any influence on me, except in my predisposition in the first years of my own teaching to the wearing of beige trench-coats. And to a thirst for poetry, which has never left me.

But it is not about Modernist Male Poets that I was to speak anyhow. Yet in the way poets remain with us, and in the weaving of words who can distinguish the male and the female voice?

But perhaps this isn't true for you at all.

Cutting to the Chase

When I was a young graduate student at the University of Toronto, a dashingly elegant woman in a cape regularly arrived slightly late for "Early English and Renaissance Drama" classes with Professor Clifford Leach. She always appeared after the class had settled to silence, and always wanted to sit in the middle of a middle row. Now that I think about it, it was a pretty amazing group of students and included novelist Peter Such, with whom the woman in the cape appeared to have an intimate relationship, and the late film critic Arthur Zeldin, and journalist Barbara Amiel, although I think she scarcely appeared at class, since modelling for the Eaton's catalogue was an important source of her income, in those days.

I was befriended by the arresting woman in the cape, who had two young male children, and who had moved to Toronto from Montreal after the painful break-up of her marriage. She was living in a split-level house in the carefully-designed suburb of Don Mills. Her address as I recall it was 32 Yewfield Crescent. And her telephone number was 447-9691 . . .

My strongest memories of those days—aside from my own quite ordinary and inappropriate liaisons—as I struggled into a sense of myself—were the hours I spent on my way by public transport in all seasons, up from the downtown area of the campus, up Don Mills Road to Don Mills, and the rewards of that journey, which was my time spent in Miriam Waddington's home on that crescent.

Influence overtakes us unawares.

I was drawn to Miriam's vulnerability and her gift for friendship—she spoke of a whole generation of writers, Birney, Kroetsch, Layton, filtered in part through John Sutherland's magazine, *First Statement*. They were her contemporaries, and I had no idea what they might come to teach me, but I knew instinctively that her struggle as a mother, as a woman, and an artist, was something to which I should attend.

She brought with her as well her internationalism—she had studied in Chicago and at the New York New School of Social Work. She was a student of Otto Rank, and a close friend of the American art critic Harold Rosenberg. The books in her warmly furnished living room were international. The paintings on her wall were by Canadian artists, like Philip Surrey, and Inuit print-makers. And she was also an ardent nationalist.

At Miriam's, there was always dinner. There were always CBC types, and business types, and old friends, and her two children, and I felt privileged in her assumption of my presence. Visiting writers sought her out. And her friend and editor Bill Toye from Oxford, whose sensitivity and support were essential, occupied a position of privilege in her conversation.

Toward her modern split-level bungalow—she was my first friend with a contemporary house—I took the flotsam and jetsam of my life. I house-sat, and baby-sat, and shared the table. And I looked always at the native Indian baskets, and the Inuit carvings and the poets translated from Russian and Hebrew and German, and the books of art. Hers was a life lived with grace—although she was often querulous, and felt set aside as a writer, and as a woman—in a way that was new for me.

Influence overtakes us unaware.

One of the men, a young architect, whom I was dating at that time, went with me to Miriam's, and afterwards he asked me whether I had modelled my personality on hers—a remark that then surprised me, but not so now. At the time I wondered that he thought I too was demanding, insisting on intimacy, perhaps a complainer and a bit intrusive in my personal questions. I was horrified to think that this might be me. But now, older than she was when I first met her, single as she was, and having myself published many volumes of poetry, I have a sense of how put aside she felt, of how even her close friends seemed not to appreciate the seriousness of her art—one in particular remarked to me after an especially warm dinner party that he didn't read her poetry because he didn't want to read about Miriam's glands. (A turncoat at her table.) And I think too how difficult is this balance between the demands of art, the demands of making a living, and the demands of family.

Eventually I myself got a job at Ryerson University, and Miriam was contracted to the new university of York, at the Glendon campus—the academy is an important patron for the contemporary poet—and through my own brief marriage and its break-up we two continued to be friends.

Although my own mother had been a journalist and an amateur actress, and my father operated a movie theatre and produced a magic show—so my own childhood was peopled by professional actors and magicians—Miriam was the first practising female professional writer I knew, and the first poet, and the shape of her life has shaped mine in ways I could not then have anticipated. It is only now looking back that I realize the first lesson which she taught me was that writing is not an activity, it is a whole life. The preparation is constant; be vigilant.

Throughout the winter of 2001, as I sat in my room on the islands watching the snow fall, and the horses' muzzles against my window panes, the phrase 'The Whole Night Driving Home' kept nagging at me. It was several months before I realized that I had melded a book title by the postmodern poet Roo Borson, *The Whole Night, Coming Home* with an early book of Miriam's *Driving Home,* a book of her poems which I had reviewed for *The Canadian Forum* magazine in 1973. I had talked about her eroticism and about her poetry of place, about the land, Canada, as her ultimate lover. To be released is to enter the landscape:

however
far into northness
you have walked
when we call you
turn around please and
don't look so
surprised. ("Canadians" 176)

I talked about her dialogue between cities and nations and religions, about the richness of her layering, about her catching of the figure in the landscape, just as it disappears, like the paintings of Lemieux and Breeze.

Aphorisms the Poet Taught Me Driving Home

1. Poetry Is The Shape of the Whole Life
2. To Be A Poet Is To Eat Humble Pie
3. To Be An Artist Is To Function With All Your Receptors Open
4. To Be A Writer Is To Interact With The World
5. To Learn the Craft Is To Pay Homage To the Work of Others
6. To Be A Woman Is To Be Under Suspicion
7   Single Women Are Worrisome; Single Women Poets Are Dangerous
8. Books, Books, Books
9. Be Sociable, Friends Enlarge Us: Across Generations, Across Lifestyles
10. Poetry Is International
11. Poets Must Be Learning To Be Learned; Rilke, Klein, Yehuda Amichai, Anna Akmatova
12. Be Committed To Place
13. Poets Cook: National, International, Paintings, Chicken Soup, Soapstone, Sweetgrass
14. A Room Of Your Own
15. Keep Your Manuscripts: Think of Them As A Carved Chest
16. Be Prepared: The Female Voice Is Personal—Friends Might Be Wary Of Your Glands
17. Crave Recognition; Anticipate Rejection
18. Find the Ideal Editor—Audience
19. Participate In the Community Of Writers
20. Abandon Guilt—Give Yourself Permission To Yearn For Acknowledgement
21. Welcome the Next Generation

Miriam and I remained friends for a decade and a half and one evening she came to dinner at my home in the fashionable area near Summerhill on the edge of Rosedale. She was still living on Yewfield Crescent and had driven downtown to dine and my parents, who had come in from the country town where I was born in southwestern Ontario, were also at table. I remember nothing of the dinner conversation, but Miriam had left to go home and nearly an hour later the phone rang in my kitchen. Miriam asked to speak to my father. The rest of us sat in the dining area and heard him laugh, saying, I wish it were true, I really do. And then charmingly he wished her good night. A few days later she called me, thanked me for the evening and told me that she had dated my father in university, in fact she had taken a car journey with him to Niagara Falls—scene of many profound communions—not long before he met my mother, and conceived me.

So Miriam was in some senses the mother I almost had, and in many others the one I did have.

"beauty may lie in small dry things":
An Interview with Elizabeth Brewster

Jan Horner

My impression of Elizabeth Brewster is of a reticent and private person, but also of someone with humility and lack of pretension—despite her considerable accomplishments. She has published eighteen collections of poetry, two volumes of memoirs, and five books of fiction. Her *Footnotes to the Book of Job* (1995) was shortlisted for the Governor General's Award for poetry. She has been awarded an honorary doctorate by the University of New Brunswick, the E. J. Pratt Award and the President's Medal, and in 2002 was made a member of the Order of Canada.[1] Fred Cogswell has written that "her work from the very beginning has been essentially modern," but she herself is uncomfortable with the label "modernist" (*Dictionary of Literary Biography* 20). I believe at least part of this discomfort stems from the religious journey that has informed her life and especially her later poems.

JH: When I prepared for this conversation I tried to keep in mind the modernist impulse connecting Canadian women poets that is our particular focus here. I looked at the various understandings of modernism and there are many of them ...

EB: I don't think I had heard the word "modernist" until very recently because, of course, back then we didn't use it. People were modern because they weren't writing like Alfred Lord Tennyson, I guess. I'm not fond of labels myself, so I don't know if I fit into a modernist label or not.

JH: Could you say in what way were you aware that you were writing differently from Tennyson in theme and/or style?

EB: I think of Tennyson's language as consciously "poetic" in sound and word choice ("the moan of doves in immemorial elms;" "All night has the casement jessamine stirr'd/ to the dancers dancing in tune;" "When the face of night is fair on the dewy downs").

Not that I don't like some of Tennyson, especially parts of "In Memoriam" but I wanted usually to choose language for poetry that would also be suitable in prose. I suppose Robert Frost was something of a model in that respect, although twentieth-century poetry in general moves away from the lush late-Romanticisms of Victorian poetry. Perhaps there's a move away from Victorian "high seriousness," too.

JH: I did find something, an understanding of modernism that says it owes much to Classical style, that was put forth by T.E. Hulme in 1914. He said "the classical style is carefully crafted, characterized by accurate description and a cheerful "dry hardness" and furthermore that "it is essential to prove that beauty may lie in small dry things." I can hear a resonance of this in your work.

19

EB: I hadn't read that, but I can see it. I did take Greek and Latin at university, and so there's always that true classical influence. Also I was fond of the eighteenth-century, of Pope and people like that, and I suppose they're neoclassical, so there is that influence. Whether you would consider them as modernist or not ...

JH: I was thinking in particular of your fondness for Marcus Aurelius and his stoicism.

EB: Which would connect to the interest in the Classics. I did mention having read Marcus Aurelius originally I guess when I was in high school, when I was seventeen or so.

JH: Another hallmark of modernism is its tendency to use mythical, literary, and demotic allusions to disrupt narrative and to comment on it in a revisionary way. I can certainly see this at work in *Footnotes on the Book of Job* just in the sense that they are footnotes, and also because you're not so much trying to retell the story of Job as that your speaker is trying to come to terms with its meaning in her life.

EB: Job asks such basic questions, I guess, and the book is such a remarkable and beautiful book in itself. I suppose he is asking his questions of God, and I'm asking the same questions, maybe.

JH: I particularly noted the comment from the woman who said, when asked if losing her memory was disturbing, that "it was damned inconvenient," which both resonates beside Job's suffering in a wonderful way and breaks up the high seriousness of it.[2] Also there is something delightfully rather blasphemous about the speaker suggesting that God's incarnation is perhaps his answer to Job, that he went through that suffering himself.

EB: I'm not sure that I would go along with that. That was a suggestion that I think Carl Jung made, that incarnation might be an answer to Job. I'm not sure that it is but, however, there we are.

JH: But mischievously you do say that God may have wanted "baby talk from his mother after the cold music of the stars."

EB: Yes, that would fit in with incarnation, I guess.

JH: I know that you converted to Roman Catholicism at one point.

EB: Early. Later I converted to Judaism. So there we have it, Rhea ... which is why I was worried about the incarnation. [laughter]

DB: What are you now, Elizabeth?

EB: I guess I'm a Jew now.

JH: That's interesting because I thought that you definitely seem to be more drawn to the Old Testament.

EB: There was a working towards that in *The Garden of Sculpture* and *Burning Bush* and I think it will come out even more clearly in the new poems in *Jacob's Dream*. Even in writing the Job poems, I made use of the Jewish Publications Society translations with notes. I also like the Quakers but that was partly because George Johnston was a Quaker. [laughing] I called them "my Friends."[3]

JH: Your work as a whole seems so open to many mythologies and traditions of wisdom, the Bhagavad Gita, Gilgamesh, the Bible, the Tarot, Greek myth, and even in the poem on the Dalai Lama, Buddhism.

EB: That was just seeing him on television, of course.

JH: I certainly get a sense of a writer who is trying to come to terms with mortality and suffering and the nature of God.

EB: Asking all the questions and never really getting the answers, I guess.

JH: But I remember in particular one line where you said you find consolation in both the Tarot and the Bible and I wonder how you can place them together?

EB: I think because in a way ... if you thought of the Tarot pack not as something you're telling fortunes by but something that the character goes through, then it is a pilgrimage and the Bible is often a pilgrimage as well. The Tarot pack works through those different figures. The fool is the one who goes through the whole pack. You probably ran into that poem of mine where I saw myself as God's fool, so that ties them together in a way, doesn't it? There are archetypal images in both.

JH: I want to go back to T. E. Hulme for a moment. It was interesting to me to learn that his view of human nature was classical rather than humanistic or Romantic. He believed man is flawed though capable of improvement, rather than essentially good. This belief in turn is linked in his writings with a strong sense of God, which Alun Jones has said arose out of a "feeling of fear, isolation and wonder ... experienced in the face of the hostile Canadian landscape" (24). He apparently worked as a farm labourer and lumberjack on "the virgin prairie of Western Canada" in 1906 and 1907 (Hulme qtd. in Jones 23). You were perhaps not as impressionable as Hulme when you moved to the prairies—he was twenty-four—but what kind of impact did the prairies have on you when you went there?

EB: I've lived only in prairie cities—Edmonton and Saskatoon—so I missed the experience of "virgin prairie." *Sunrise North,* my Edmonton book, gives my first impressions of that city. I was certainly impressed by the cold of my first winter there. As I'm mildly claustrophobic, I liked the sense of space in, for instance, the drive between Saskatoon and Regina.

JH: Hulme's views made him receptive to what he called "geometrical art" or art that emerges from and portrays a hostile and antagonistic relationship between humans and their environment. This idea of geometrical art gave him a theoretical basis to support his interest in abstraction in poetry and art. Some would say he introduced or promoted an aesthetic that was impersonal or machine-like. In your poems, especially your biblical poems I do not so much sense an awesome and harsh physical or social world as I do a fearsome and not entirely benevolent god. And while modern, your poetic strategies tend less to abstraction than they do to narrative. Would you agree that these are important differences between your "modernism" and the modernism that Hulme promoted?

EB: The god of my biblical poems is sometimes fearsome, sometimes benevolent, sometimes unpredictable, maybe because the universe is. I'm fond of narrative—another likeness with Frost—also, of course, with poets from Homer and Virgil down through Chaucer, Spenser, Wordsworth, Browning, Hardy, etc.

JH: I love the way you end *The Burning Bush* with dreams. It seemed to me especially within the context of those Old Testament figures Jacob, Joseph, Dinah and Lot and Moses, that your speakers struggle to make sense of the world both in dreams and waking life and that what happens in those dreams are trials and challenges that both those who are awake and those who dream must come to terms with. Was that an intentional juxtaposition or did it just happen?

EB: I think the dream poems are written in a way parallel to the stories. You don't have a dream necessarily every night but I thought these dreams added up to a story. Probably you noticed the acknowledgement at the beginning that I'm grateful to Rabbi Pavey and his study group. Studying together was a journey. Many of these dreams were journey poems. So they added up more or less. Also, I needed some extra poems to fill the book. [laughter] There's honesty for you.

JH: It's interesting to me that you've had a career as an academic and a poet. And I wonder how you feel that they worked together. Has one fed the other, or have they been contrary poles?

EB: I have mixed feelings about that. I never really felt that I was a very academic academic. I'm not a natural teacher. I suppose that I've always been very fond of books and books are a large part of academic life. And my poetry connects with books, so that's semi-academic. And also sometimes my students taught me things so that may be academic too.

JH: You have worked for significant periods of your life in libraries and as you know I am a librarian. I'm curious about how working in a library affected your writing. I know that you became a librarian because you had to support yourself and academic positions were not necessarily open to women at the time. Was your ability to write lessened by working in a library or did you find inspiration there, or was your poetic output any less than it was teaching in an English department at a university? Were other factors more important to your ability to write at the time, factors such as frequent moves, personal relationships, family demands, encouragement from editors or other poets?

EB: Probably "other factors" were more important, as you suggest, though certainly I found books on library shelves which inspired me to write. Teaching was more demanding, but possibly more interesting than library work. A sabbatical year off from teaching now and then helped.

JH: A good deal of your work seems to be written in dialogue with other writers or other books or in response to them. There are your glosses for instance. I am particularly interested in the poems for Katherine Mansfield in part because I've been writing some poems about another woman of that generation who was perhaps flawed but also like Mansfield "spoke as the wind speaks, that cannot be captured." And I wonder, it doesn't seem to me that you have poems about Virginia Woolf or for Virginia Woolf.

EB: One of my early poems, "In the Library" is full of echoes of *The Waves*. I wrote an essay on Virginia Woolf and I didn't find myself writing an essay on Katherine Mansfield although I thought of doing it.

JH: And yet you do comment that Virginia Woolf thought she wore too much perfume (in "Wellington Revisited," *Spring Again 65*) which somehow made me more sympathetic to Mansfield.

EB: It was that love-hate relationship, rather like Dorothy Livesay and me. The Katherine Mansfield poems were all written at times when I visited New Zealand. And I read Katherine Mansfield early on. I think I was in high school when I read her short stories and I liked them. They had a kind of immediate appeal. When I went to New Zealand and visited Wellington the first of the poems came or was written about that. I thought her New Zealand stories were her best stories and perhaps there's a kind of parallel between Canada and New Zealand, that kind of a new world. I had always thought of Katherine Mansfield as an English writer but she was really a colonial writer, a New Zealand writer and those stories were her best ones. So I think all three of the times I visited New Zealand I wrote a Katherine Mansfield poem. The second time I went a conference of Canadianists was meeting in Christchurch and I went afterwards to Wellington. The third time I happened to land accidentally at the time they were having a Katherine Mansfield conference in Wellington and some people drove me out to Day's Bay, the location of those stories. I found that very interesting and wrote a poem about meeting these people and the Day's Bay thing. I really thought I should write an article about her but I'm really not a good article writer. The three poems are kind of a tribute—I really liked her work.

JH: Your comment about Dorothy, did you disagree about poetics or was it more personal?

EB: Both maybe ... I met Dorothy first at a Kingston conference in the mid fifties. I wrote a funny poem about that ("Exchange," *Spring Again* 10) and then of course, she was writer-in-residence in Fredericton when I was working at the Legislative Library. And then she was teaching Canadian literature in Edmonton when I was working at the library there. We were fairly friendly but also somewhat embattled. She had a strong personality and one had to battle her if one wanted not to be taken over. But I remember having an argument over the phone in which she said that poetry was always celebration and I said it wasn't always. Sometimes the poet got pretty depressed. I think I put that in a poem ("Minor Disagreement," *Sunrise North* 72-73).

RT: I just want to ask Elizabeth something that I was thinking about asking Miriam [Waddington]. When I first started publishing in the late seventies, when I encountered contemporaries who were also at that stage, there was this mixture of feeling encouraged by their presence and feeling competitive with them, and I wondered if you could comment on that. You've alluded to that in your relationship with Dorothy. Did you need there to be other women writing as well, or did you think of things in those terms?

EB: Of course I had encountered Dorothy's poetry fairly early in A.J. M. Smith's anthology. I think she won her first Governor General's award when I was an undergraduate. She published very early in life, when she was nineteen or so, something like that, so I was aware of her work long before I met her, and I liked her work. Actually I do owe her a debt. When I was in New Brunswick, I'd had these three little chapbooks published but I couldn't seem to get a book published, though I had all these things. I think I sort of got discouraged about this.

But it was Dorothy and Desmond Pacey together who told me I should get these poems together and I should send poems to magazines because then people would know about me. Publishers would not publish me unless they saw me in a magazine. Dorothy was quite encouraging in that way. I think she was encouraging more early on, if you know what I mean. I think she became more competitive. Margaret Atwood was in Edmonton at the same time we were there. I think she always felt Dorothy was in competition with her, was ready to push her down if necessary. Margaret, of course, was quite successful quite young.

RT: Would you ever have exchanged work in progress with Dorothy and had her input on it or did she send you her work, that sort of thing?

EB: I showed her things and sometimes she may have had some input. Although I think that our lines were a little bit different. For instance, there was at one point, when I had a longish poem and she thought I should keep only the first four lines and I said the first four lines are just leading up to the real poem. I needed more space. So I disagreed when I needed to disagree.

Margaret Atwood I also showed things to. Because she was so much younger and also very clever, there was not a sense of competition there.

JH: Did Atwood show you her work at that time and did you offer her your comments on them?

EB: No, Atwood didn't show me her unpublished work, though she did give me some of her books. I showed her my poems, and she did some of the arranging of the poems in Sunrise North and suggested that title instead of "Northern Sunrise." I liked her clever use of line breaks and probably picked up a bit of that technique from her.

JH: Have you acted as a mentor to younger poets?

EB: I've "inherited" some younger poets from Anne Szumigalski—they meet in my livingroom and read each other's poetry—but I don't especially think of myself as a "mentor" to them. *Jacob's Dream* was dedicated to them.

DB: Didn't I hear you say that P. K. was telling you early on to send your work to literary magazines, and P. K. remarked to you later that she didn't know where you got that from, since she wasn't sending out much work then herself?

EB: At the conference at Trent,[4] I read a brief paper about my first meeting with Pat Page and our early correspondence. I quoted from a letter of hers in which she sent me one of my own poems typed out and suggested that I send it to *Canadian Poetry Magazine*. (I did keep her letters and they are now in the National Archives.) Pat didn't come to the presentation and didn't say this to me. She had read my little essay on her. She probably had forgotten the advice. I think possibly she tended to think that everything started for her in Montreal, and rather minimized her earlier accomplishments. She was certainly writing lots at the time, whether she was sending it out or not.

JH: I was struck by your poems in *Wheel of Change* (1993) with their spectre of Quebec separatism: "The Land," "John the Baptist Day," and "First of July" in part because I wrote a poem in response to the 1995 Referendum which I called "No means Maybe." I think my poem is an emotional response and yours seem so much wiser, recognizing that all the angry words will "diminish into snowy silence." Even your poem about Canada Day seems to suggest that Canada may not exist forever? Still these poems seem uncharacteristic amongst the rest. Can you talk about how you came to write them?

EB: I thought of them as my Meech Lake poems. I suppose they were a response to the occasion. My earlier poem on the FLQ crisis was perhaps more emotional ("Another Sunrise: October 18, 1970," *Sunrise North* 71).

JH: Fred Cogswell has written that "the depth of the struggle expressed in [your] poetry has also, paradoxically, been obscured by [your] technical skill" (*Dictionary of Literary Biography* 20). W. J. Keith has said that your poems embody a "tension between the intensely personal and the deliberately objective" (*Oxford Companion* 141). My sense in reading your work is that you decided to let the power of the language and story in your poetry work on the emotions of the reader and kept your own emotional responses, which may have given rise to the poems, in the background. When you say that the poem about the FLQ crisis was more emotional, do you know why?

EB: I suppose the FLQ poem was an immediate response to the event. I think there is emotion in quite a few of my poems, but perhaps it is distanced by irony or some other way of cooling it down.

JH: In a number of poems you refer to writing the great or perfect poem. You have written: "Some time, I think,/ the perfect arrangement/ of words will come ..." ("Cloud Formations");

"Ten years from now/ I may write my great book" ("New Year's Day, 1978"); "And at long last I shall write/ the great poem I have not yet written ..."("When I am Old"); and "but in the end I don't want/the perfect state/...or the perfect poem"("16. Poetry and Politics"). I wondered if you are only being ironic here. And if you aren't, could you say what makes a poem great or perfect? Would you be able to recognize a great poem in your own writing, or can such assessments only be made by other people?

EB: The "perfect poem" or the "great" poem, or the great work? I suppose "great" and "perfect" are different. Some of Herrick's small poems might be described as "perfect" but not "great." *Paradise Lost* or Wordsworth's *Prelude* are "great," but probably not perfect. I think, especially as a young person, I would have liked to write something "great." My feelings about "perfection" might vary from time to time—from admiration to impatience. I don't know whether I could myself recognize whether one of my own poems was "great" or "perfect"—though I think some of the things I've written seem to me to be pretty good. I don't like "perfect" people.

JH: I am interested in the sequence of poems you wrote in response to Ezra Pound's *Cantos* in *Spring Again Poems* (1990), the book you dedicated to Livesay, P.K. Page, K. Smith, and Waddington. The question being, why Pound? Was it just that you happened to be reading or re-reading Pound's *Cantos*? What motivated you to read him at that time? As you point out it is easy to find his flaws—what in particular do you admire about him or his writing? Did it have something to do with his courage and the largeness of his project, not only aesthetic but also political? I think I wanted to ask you this because Pound is so much connected with Modernism, and therefore also wondered if you saw yourself in any way as his literary descendent. You didn't know him and probably didn't set out to emulate him, but did his writing make the way you write possible?

EB: No, I don't think of him as an influence on my poetry except in *Spring Again*. In fact, I deliberately avoided reading his poetry for many years, because (being of that war-time generation) I couldn't forgive him for supporting the Fascists. Of course, I had read some of his early poems in anthologies, but I didn't read the *Cantos* until that occasion. I went to a meeting of the League of Canadian Poets at UBC, bought a copy of the *Cantos* at the UBC bookstore, sprained an ankle so that I was more or less imprisoned in my rooms with only one book to read. I suppose I was attracted by the openness and inclusiveness of the technique. Also, the allusions to *The Odyssey* would have appealed to me, since I was fond of Greek and Latin poetry from undergraduate days. When I sent a copy of *Spring Again* to Miriam Waddington, she rather scolded me for seeming to overvalue Pound.

I think the twentieth-century poets who were an influence on me—aside from Canadians like Page, Livesay, Waddington, Klein, George Johnston, and F. R. Scott—were Robert Frost, Yeats, Eliot, Robert Lowell. Some of these people wrote poetry that was very different from mine, but Frost (modern but maybe no modernist?) wrote the kind of poetry I often aimed to write. Lowell's *Life Studies* encouraged my family poems in *Passage of Summer*.

JH: Can you say a little more about what appealed to you about the allusions to *The Odyssey* in Pound's *Cantos*? Was it that they were quoted in the original by Pound? Is there something in particular about classical poetry that appealed to you: its formal qualities, the beauty of the language, was it in particular the fantastic stories, or in the case of *The Odyssey* the character of Odysseus himself. Would you say, if pressed, that there were some classical poets you preferred over others? Did it have something to do with the fact that you studied classical poetry when you were quite young?

EB: I'm fond of *The Odyssey*. Did you see my poem in *Jacob's Dream*, "Images of Exile," which answers some of your questions? I suppose I liked the classical poets I happened to bump into: Virgil, especially Ovid, Catullus, Horace, Euripides, of the Greek dramatists.

JH: Yes, I did read "Images of Exile" and you do seem to depict a likeable Odysseus: resourceful, courageous, self-reliant, and undespairing—different from Tennyson's version of him that suggests more his irresponsibility and wanderlust, and different from feminist revisions of him. But the prisoner of war in the poem who clings to his tattered copies of *The Iliad* and *The Odyssey* makes it clear that you're not so much concerned with Odysseus as *The Odyssey* and the hopeful arc of the story over that long voyage and struggle to return home.

I'm going to jump back to twentieth-century poetry and Robert Frost. It's interesting that you mention him as an influence on you. I came across a recent book on Frost by Karen Kilcup that suggested that he had been influenced in his technique by earlier American women writers such as Lydia Sigourney, Sarah Orne Jewett, and Mary E. Wilkins Freeman. I wonder if you found that part of his appeal for you.

EB: I hadn't known Frost was influenced by earlier American women poets. I probably thought of him as in the tradition of plain-speaking poets like Wordsworth and another of my favourites, Thomas Hardy.

JH: According to Kilcup, Frost fared worse at the hands of academic critics because he was more sentimental or feminine in the sense of employing an affective or emotional voice in his poems while Eliot's and Pound's poetic voices were distant and intellectual.

EB: I heard both Frost and Eliot read at Harvard and would have thought of Frost as the more masculine of the two. I thought Eliot's poetry was more fashionable because more difficult; "Donne-ish" poetry was fashionable. I don't think I'd ever heard of Lydia Sigourney or Mary E. Wilkins Freeman. If I thought of women poets of that time, it would probably be of H.D., Elinor Wylie, or (in England) Edith Sitwell—or a "poetic" novelist like Virginia Woolf. Frost is more in the narrative tradition, perhaps.

JH: Why did you decide to dedicate *Spring Again* to Dorothy Livesay, P.K. Page, Kay Smith, and Miriam Waddington? They were your friends of course, but why this particular book?

EB: I can't remember if there was a particular reason. It was reasonable to link the four, who all belonged to an earlier generation (or half-generation) than mine. One does rather run out of people to dedicate books to: parents, early teachers, siblings, close friends. I made up the dedication in Victoria, I think, which was associated with Pat Page and Dorothy. I might have thought the "Nausicaa Cantos" should be dedicated to women.

JH: Can you talk about your relationship with Anne Szumigalski? Did you know her before you came to Saskatchewan? In the acknowledgements in *Burning Bush,* you say she read most of the poems in the book before her death? Was she an influence on you, personally and poetically?

EB: I had never heard of Anne before I moved to Saskatoon. Our friendship developed chiefly after I had retired from university. We got into the habit of having lunch together; and, as we were born in the same year, we had memories in common. We shared a group of younger poets, who met alternately at her home and at mine. That is where she read my poems, and I read hers. I think the chief influence would have been the encouragement to continue writing. Our poetry is very different. Her favourite Romantic poet was Blake, mine was Wordsworth.

JH: Did you find when you were in Saskatoon working at the university that it was hard to meet or get to know poets who were outside the academic community? Were you aware that Anne (Szumigalski) knew other academics besides you? Was the writing community divided between academic and non-academic writers?

EB: I was too busy teaching to be sociable with other writers when I was first in Saskatoon. I saw Anne frequently after I retired. She was friendly with Don Kerr and David Carpenter from the English Department, and with Hilary Clark who came to the Department around the time I retired. We were both friendly with Patrick Lane and Lorna Crozier. I don't think there was a division between academic and non-academic writers.

Notes

1 Elizabeth Brewster was born in New Brunswick, but since 1972 has lived in Saskatoon. In fact, she has lived in many places, having studied at Radcliffe College (Harvard), at King's College in London England, at University of Indiana, and the University of Toronto; and having worked as a librarian in Ontario, Alberta, and British Columbia. In addition, she lectured at the University of Victoria and taught creative writing at the University of Alberta before joining the English Department at the University of Saskatchewan, where she is now Professor Emeritus.

2 Elizabeth indicated later that she was actually quoting her friend Alice Caplin, who was in the early stages of Alzheimer's at the time.

3 Brewster here is referring to George Johnston, the Canadian poet. The Quakers are also known as the "Society of Friends."

4 Brewster is referring to the "Extraordinary Presence: The Worlds of P.K.Page," conference that took place at Trent University, October 24 to 27, 2002.

Elizabeth Smart as Modernist Writer of 'the meantime'

Cornelia Hoogland

$\mathcal{E}$LIZABETH SMART (1913-1986) wrote *By Grand Central Station I Sat Down and Wept* in 1941, during a nine-month stay in Pender Harbour, B. C. She lived alone in an abandoned schoolhouse, and later, with Maxie Southwell in a cottage on Garden Bay Road. Her daughter Georgina, born in August of that year, was the first of four children Smart was to have out of wedlock with the married poet George Barker. Although she had previously travelled far from her Ottawa-socialite upbringing, arriving in this remote location with little more than her books, clothes, *Remington* typewriter and monthly allowance, must have been difficult. In her journals Smart confesses that she decided to stick a pin in a map and go where it fell. Her affair with Barker, the war, and her unwillingness to tell her family about her pregnancy, were the probable reasons she felt driven to such an unlikely choice.

There is nothing unusual about visiting the places in which famous writers lived and worked—the English have turned such activity into a substantial industry. But for a young writer to discover that a relatively famous Canadian chose such a remote B.C. setting—my setting—as the site of her major work, was like the thrilling opening scene of a mystery novel. I'd already *met* Smart in her books, in her published journals (*Autobiographies* 1987), and in conversation with people who knew Smart when she was writer-in-residence in Edmonton in the mid-eighties. But among my strongest meetings with Smart and with *Grand Central* occurred in remote, barely accessible, Pender Harbour, B.C. In geographical setting; in place.

Although I call Pender Harbour *my place* it was as exotic to me as discovering the modernist generation of *Canadian* poets (I had studied Plath and Sexton) who preceded the one in which I'm immersed. I didn't use the term *foremother*, but I was nevertheless discovering and claiming a foremother of my own. Reading about Pender Harbour in Smart's journals felt like a discovery, and during the spring of 1989, three years after Smart's death, travelling her route up British Columbia's Sunshine Coast on my own (I had not travelled in this way, alone and without an itinerary) felt something like I imagined Smart must have felt. This sense of emulating her experience (however slightly) was the impetus for my poems about Smart. The bus stopped at Madiera Park and I began my search for Elizabeth Smart, poet and person.

Smart never mentions Pender Harbour in *Grand Central*, though she does mention the Californian coast. "He kissed my forehead driving along the coast ..." (*Grand Central* 22). But the textual cliff did not mainly refer to the Californian coastline nor to the one on which I perched, further north. Smart's cliffs and waves do not direct the reader back to the natural world, but, rather, to one situated in mythology and romance. In the context of

Grand Central—the narrator's love affair with her muse/lover—they allude to the classics and to myth. The kiss she describes above was imagined in terms of "the sword of Damocles" that "hangs above my doomed head ..." She pulls all the stops, writing "all through the night it is centaurs hoofed and galloping over my heart: the poison has got into my blood. I stand on the edge of the cliff ..." (*Grand Central* 22).

George Barker was the main focus of the love story in which Smart placed herself, in a relationship similar to Dido's with Homer's Aeneas (to whom, in Book Four, Dido writes in order to try one last time to persuade him not to abandon her). Smart writes: "By the Pacific I wander like Dido, hearing such a passion of tears in the breaking waves, that I wonder why the whole world isn't weeping inconsolably" (*Grand Central* 94).

At the time of my writing, however, my response to Smart's text might have situated me as her ideal or implied reader. The high drama of "I am over-run ... I am infested with a menagerie of desires ..." offered me a way to unleash a language that could give my grand feelings air and expression (*Grand Central* 23). My language was far more restrained than Smart's velvet-winged words; nevertheless I gained a way to talk about my own experiences as a young writer "infested with a menagerie of desires" of her own.

As much as I adored Smart's writing, failing to see or read the imagery of the British Columbian west coast in *Grand Central* was disappointing. Rereading my poems (a selection of which follow) fourteen years later, their strong sense of place seems to want to *show* Smart where she was, to make her *see* the local rocks and flowers she failed to mention. Perhaps it was my frustration with her seeming dismissal of the sand under her feet and the ocean before her eyes that caused me to begin my collection:

> Pender Harbour, B. C. Spent the first
> evening on the dock listening
> to geese honk their rubber bicycle horns
> over the marina. Those stick-to-the-point
> flights over Ontario, seriously Canadian
> as blanched carrots in the freezer.
>
> And wildflowers! Splitting
> out of rock, their little hooks into air. (*Marrying* 32)

My poems *talk back* to Smart. Not only did I want her to notice *where* she was, I wanted Smart to *see herself* as capable of being a writer who manages her hopes and her despair, and who *gets on with it*. Surely these strengths and abilities form the subtext of *Grand Central*. Smart's language and imagery didn't just soar into metaphoric heights; they also landed into what I call the *meantime*. The *meantime* was not only the days and months that Smart waited to be reunited with her lover. It was also the textual reality of her life; the significance and meaning she gave to words. Perhaps writing was a way of reconciling the gap between her fantasy and the everyday reality that didn't include Barker, but that did include "the small hard head jutting out near my bladder" (*Grand Central* 97). She instructs herself on the topic of filling in the less-than-miraculous months, days, hours and minutes, by suggesting she ignore or push aside the magnificent. "I will not think of the thing now. I have no time. When I have washed my stockings I will. When I have sewn on a button I will. When I have written a letter I will" (*Grand Central* 88).

At the time of my writing, I wanted to believe that Smart didn't just want relief, but that she wanted to infuse the domestic with the same intensity with which she infused her written text. "How can I find bird-relief in the nest-building of day-to-day?" she asks (*Grand Central* 23). But the overwhelming voice is that of a narrator "possessed by love," who screamed loudly for relief and release, and who did not seem to believe that she had "options" (*Grand Central* 39). She was "far, far beyond that island of days where once, it seems, (she) watched a flower grow" (*Grand Central* 23). Despite her denial, Smart did live the alternative to Barker; she lived a *meantime*. Her journal records her domestic activities, which included arranging flowers in tin cans. In my poems that follow, *Smart's fictionalized voice is presented in italics:*

> *I arrange everything.*
> *The borrowed furniture and on the high*
> *stilted balcony dozens of silver tin cans*
> *of narcissus, dafs and hazel. More yellow*
> *on the newly painted door.* (Marrying 42)

I attempted to infuse my poetry with Smart's passion, but directed toward the place—the natural world—of Pender Harbour. In Smart's voice I wrote:

> *I head down to the beach, and in the wreckage*
> *see what a night's storm can effect.*
> *Over the sand, hundreds of gulls peck-walking.*
> *Flapping ineffectual arms and screaming*
> *through surf that pounds*
> *the words back up my throat, FLY IDIOTS FLY*
> *and a cloud rises above the sounds growing*
> *quieter. I feel better. Head bent*
> *as far as Francis Point, picking up shells*
> *and the split-open conch* (Marrying 39)

It's true that Smart's wait for George, her desire for George, her belief that she would die without George, are uncomfortable thoughts to read today, but the quality of her waiting is significant. She not only nourished and gave birth to a child during her wait, but she wrote her novel, *Grand Central*. The meantime was her flesh-and-blood experience as well as the language-building of "day-to-day." In Smart's writing and in Pender Harbour I saw that the miraculous is most comfortable in the day-to-day, in the mundane, in the nest-building that, like empty vegetable tins, can be arranged to hold flowers. Or the empty pages of a ten-cent scribbler that can hold a good story.

Fourteen years later, I don't want my early literary efforts stranded in the realm of personal discovery. Elizabeth Smart was hard to find; modernist female writers were largely ignored in my university curricula. So I place my efforts in the larger historical context of the continuity of writers, of women speaking to women, of women learning from women. What I and the women in this volume are attempting is not just to make the private public, but to articulate what of the private can become the public, shared, tangible foundations of our work and growth as writers. Many women have been making literary connections with their literary foremothers privately, in small volumes. In my poems and this essay I insist on the importance of *place* as a meeting ground between past and present writers. In Pender Harbour I discovered my place included the ability to travel alone, and being alone, in turn, allowed me a fuller experience and articulation of my relationship with the place. I had something to show to, as well as to learn from, Smart. In *writing back* I showed Smart (as it were) something of her own investment in the place in which she wrote and in the solitude she experienced. It was in the "leafrot in the mottled shade of cedars" that I met the brave, solitary Smart whom she failed to write into her own text.

The generational links created by writing backward and writing forward can make our collective story stronger. I believe this volume helps mark those intersections of individual and collective turning points. Since Smart, the private voice has gone public in ways that confirm Smart's genius, and that confirm her foremotherly gift to our generation of writers of widening the boundaries of what is permissible to write.

◆ ◆ ◆

In the poems that follow, *Smart's fictionalized voice is presented in italics* alongside the narrator's voice which appears in conventional type.

It was spring. I was in love
and needed a place to have my baby.
Circled the map with a pin and pierced
Pender Harbour. Barely accessible,
boats calling just often enough.

Anyway, with mother's hysterics and war
there was no room in Ottawa for bursting
with either child or happiness. Plus, his wife.

Night won't settle. Hills smudge
with coal from earlier fires, and light shimmies
the water as if the artist's unhappy
with too thick a night. So there's none.

◆ ◆ ◆

High-heeling it
off the Union Steamship at Irving's Landing,
my body's cells charged
with Allenbury's basil soap,
red carnations and dresses, sherbet,
R & J at the Old Vic.

Blitz what went before!
Impossible to be poor. But
will the wild clematis compensate?

I'll keep the fires
in, peel potatoes in good time.
Knit booties.

◆ ◆ ◆

In the schoolhouse all the windows
visible at the turn of my head.
Each frame fills with a green
discontent that pours
over the little half table where I write.
The panes are painted yellow but the house
is green as water. Layer on layer
of maniac things up between the cracks,
waiting in the washtub, dead
at the outhouse door. Until
my correct cells in garters and hat
scream for their rightful places.

I head down to the beach, and in the wreckage
see what a night's storm can effect.
Over the sand, hundreds of gulls peck-walking.
Flapping ineffectual arms and screaming

through surf that pounds
the words back up my throat, FLY IDIOTS FLY
and a cloud rises above the sounds growing
quieter. I feel better. Head bent
as far as Francis Point, picking up shells
and the split-open conch

that you kept on your worktable.
Its candid blue wrapping into itself reminding
that the watery lip of the world
is blue   blue and how, just when
you could have snapped your case, gone off,
you stayed.

✦ ✦ ✦

I was furious and disgruntled when those two young girls
came knocking at my door and sat wasting my evening,
 interrupting my wait …

…girls flopping over the bed that waited
for him, picking up books for his hands, drinking
coffee hoarded for him, smoking his cigarettes,
and then, Lord save us, hollering to their boys
whistling below, leaning out the window
that couldn't hold, full as it was of desire,
braiding my stripped life into a ladder to let him up
or me down. I don't know which but it's my window
and sitting at it steadies the room until
his appearance up the path. Then quick as stones
they run off kissing their youths, trampling
trilliums, delicate flowers. It doesn't matter.
As long as they're out of the days I wait
for life to start. My pretty room. My sonnet.

✦ ✦ ✦

He comes after a long rain
the sudden sun on every wet thing so fierce
the compost in its gleaming wire-mesh
begins to percolate. And underneath
my fussing with sheets and drinks
hums the unplayed strings of a room
bursting for dancing.

In bed at night that old image
of strong capable woman surfaces.
My hair falls like grief over his face
thinking he sees me as braver
than Jessica. Surely
it won't work against me.

30

Roll onto my back
to ease the cramp, ask
G to rub and his fingers sink into the joint
where pain's sharpest. Asleep
under his hands if it weren't for the baby
kicking up like wind off water and

the field tomatoes heaped below the window.
Spiked with rain. Smelling of feverish decay.

❖ ❖ ❖

I wake to the ship's whistle marking
his passage, and Maxie, warm milk
in hand, urges me to sleep for the good
of the baby, but I refuse.

Next day I send
Maxie home. Tramp the hills
for bracken ferns and bulbs I know will die
in a formal garden.

There lay all the difference. You could
have had any of fifty varieties of the best
domestic sort, but you wanted
the costly bear-grass whose white stars
trail like comets over the fields
every seven years.

It isn't just handing G back to his wife—
it's that my whole life seems to back up
like the view at the pass. That rocky cut
through events.

e.g., giving up my dress allowance
(a lady has to think of her looks) for books
and Barker. Gone the silver dinners,
summers at Kingsmere.

❖ ❖ ❖

Walking as far Oyster Bay led to sleeping
like a baby. Woke only once. Pelting rain
but I rolled over, secure. Wood on the porch
stacked high as my shoulders. Innocent days.
No need to lock up, nothing intrudes.
Not a desire. And yet I'm always putting up
the best of the crop, hedging
against cold, things getting out of hand.
And the worst, the time of not loving.

I used to sleep without pillows
or sheets, to be free in case
I should ever be wrecked on a desert island
or be too poor to own them.

You knew that when he came
you'd spare nothing. Indebting yourself
with neighbours, the grocer
you owed for the rest of your life.

This moment. Lavish.
The resin wrung
from wood when it's tossed on the fire.

◆ ◆ ◆

You couldn't keep your hands off. Crimson,
magenta, palest white; gathered into jars
on the verandah, rows of them
in vases on the sill; some you found
growing on leafrot in the mottled shade
of cedars. Everything giving way,
nothing to lean on. Yet through snarls
of tree and wild, unsettled growth—
alyssum, dame's violet. Motif
of the mortal world

that string of cut-out carnelian hearts.

◆ ◆ ◆

To coax warmth into this house
I get down on my knees. Blow and blow
till black and cooling coals
break red.

◆ ◆ ◆

Small wonder you came to Pender.
Field trip you spent your childhood
leaning toward from your dormer window
the winter you spent in bed with a leaking heart.
Days scratching little plays, learning the seed
catalogue: sedge, beachgrass, rushes.

This place. Chosen as deliberately
as you chose George.

But then to keep on with it
when you didn't know why you weren't together,
when life swelled your hips and brambles
spilled over the vegetable beds.

♦ ♦ ♦

Each time, I got better
at seeing him off at the gate, the harbour;
all the exits. It took days
to rid the chair, cup, windowlight
of his image.

And then the long-in-the-meantime
learning chair, cup *over again.*

Notes

I am indebted to Ted Rowcliffe for his generosity in sharing his research on Smart during the writing of this paper.

Anne Marriott: Treading Water

Sharon H. Nelson

$\mathcal{A}$NNE MARRIOTT (1913-1997) was an extraordinary communicator who integrated political awareness and humanist sensibility in her writing and acted on them in her life. Her work, which spans fifty years, includes eight books of poems, one book of short stories, and numerous film scripts and newspaper columns from periods during which she worked as a script-writer for the NFB and CBC and as a journalist. Her long poem *Calling Adventurers* won the Governor General's Award in 1941. In 1981, her collection *The Circular Coast: Poems New and Selected* was nominated for the same award.

Women of Anne Marriott's generation experienced structural sexism and misogyny as part of normal, everyday life. As Anne Marriott was well aware, these social constructions and prejudices limited their careers, their publishing possibilities, and their incomes. I first met Anne Marriott in October 1981 in Vancouver at what proved to be the founding meeting of the Feminist Caucus of the League of Canadian Poets. At that meeting, a group of women writers discussed acting to ameliorate the negative public presentation of women's writing in Canada; the exclusion of women's writing from academic texts, anthologies, and classrooms; the paucity of reviews of women's writing and the tone and tenor of the reviews that were published; and a system of structural sexism in grants, awards, and appointments that favoured men over women and disadvantaged women writers in every way, including financially (Nelson 1982). Anne Marriott had come to that meeting not only because she believed that her own work and career had suffered from sexism but to right a wrong. She was prepared to act with women writers of different generations and at different stages of our careers to improve the situation of women's writing and to try to end discrimination against women writers.

After a very promising start and a Governor General's Award, Anne Marriott did not have a book published between 1945 and 1971. This hiatus was not due to domestic responsibilities or childrearing. She did not withdraw from writing or from literary life during that period. In fact, Marya McLellan, her daughter, remembers that throughout her childhood and adolescence, her mother continued to write and to meet other writers for discussions (McLellan 2003). During what was definitely not a fallow period for her, Anne Marriott continued to publish poems and stories in magazines. She was actively engaged with writing and with other writers, as Fred Cogswell remembered. He was adamant that domestic duties did not prevent Anne Marriott from writing and spoke about meeting often with her and other writers to discuss poems. During that time, he remembered, she was active on the literary scene and deeply engaged and committed as both a writer and an editor. Fred Cogswell published Anne Marriott's chapbook, *Countries,* in 1971 and thus launched a second series of book publication

(Cogswell 2003).

If not domestic and personal responsibilities and commitments, what accounts for the hiatus in book publication that affected Anne Marriott among other women writers? In the decade immediately after World War II, even established women writers in Canada experienced difficulty achieving publication of books of poems. Though writers like Anne Marriott and Dorothy Livesay, for instance, continued to publish poems in magazines, neither achieved book publication for a decade or more after World War II despite previous strong publication records. For these writers, there was no self-imposed "silence" or "failure to produce" but rather a cultural phenomenon of silencing overtook their publishing careers. The lack of book publication was related to cultural problems experienced generally by women in post-war society.

During the war years, many women experienced a change of circumstances, a broadening of horizons, and new social and economic mobility. This was accompanied by a sense of community while they worked in support of "the war effort," an effort which often was tied to notions of social justice. On several of our infrequent meetings, Anne Marriott and I talked about some of her experiences during this period. She told me about her shock and dismay on having realized that the values Canadian troops were supposed to be defending in Europe were not to pertain in Canada. She mentioned in particular the termination of social relationships due to the continued acceptance in some circles in Toronto of overt anti-Semitism. In post-war culture, men were cast as heroes for whom room had to be made, and women were cast as consumers who were to "retire" from jobs and public life to make that room. Women moved from the paid work force and participation in public life to consumerism as a public duty, often at great personal cost.

This shift came about in response to a determined effort on the part of western governments, especially that of the U.S., to create a consumer society and a consumerist culture that emphasized strongly defined gender roles and households confined to nuclear families. If the nuclear family could be made normative for a household, the resulting rise in the number of households would increase potential sales of consumer items. The valorization of the nuclear family undermined the support systems provided by extended family and community relationships. In combination with the uprootedness of industrially managed life and strong gender stereotypes, these trends isolated people, especially women, and destroyed support systems.

In this cultural milieu, women writers such as Anne Marriott, who continued to display interest in issues of social justice and who chose to write for publication, did not easily find book publication for their work. A book is a public statement and appears in the public sphere from which women had been cast out. In addition, as Gwladys Downes pointed out to me, on the west coast, about the time that women writers might have recovered some ground, TISH took over as "the west coast voice" and made it difficult, if not impossible, for west coast poets writing outside that movement to be heard (Downes 2003). Anne Marriott's poems did not see book publication. Much of her work was out of print and uncollected, until a new wave of feminism, in which Anne Marriott participated, sparked renewed interest in women's writing and opened publication space for women writers.

My long poem "Silencing," addresses the situation that first brought me, Anne Marriott, and a number of other writers together. Below are sections of "Silencing" that describe some of the experiences of women writers that are pertinent to that meeting and to Anne Marriott's career.

Silencing

1

A WOMAN WRITER, SIMPLY BY VIRTUE OF BEING A WOMAN AND A WRITER,
IS A RENEGADE AND A SUBVERSIVE, YET WE READ WOMEN'S WRITING
AS IF IT HAD BEEN WRITTEN BY RESPECTABLE MEN.

My mothers who are lost have been denied
their majority. They are not Major Figures.
They lie uneasy in narrow graves

fitted to contain them narrowly.

They do not take
so much space
as a man.

If you listen carefully, you will hear them.
They stalk, clanking their bracelets and bones.
They scream, laugh and tell jokes, are ribald and bitchy.
They grin widely, reveal imperfect teeth.
They smack their thighs. They cackle, crackle,
crack their knuckles, tighten their hands into fists.
Their lines spill out, spill over, spill forth, released
like bellies from girdles, midriffs from stays,
thighs from the tight lines of garter belts. They are released
from the tyranny of pantyhose, from speaking Prose.

My mothers who are lost stamp their lines in rhythm,
spit words out of books in all directions,
commit the sin of inelegance. They are noisy as an army.

My mothers who are lost scream at us.
Nothing is sacred to them. They will not be stilled.
They are in pain. Their pain is visible, tangible,
woven into words that betray it. They tell us:

We have been here before you, my dears;
we know the score.
We know the meanings of "Literature,"
the convenient historiographic lies that obtrude
so that when we speak clearly,
what we say cannot be heard.

The study of Literature,
a bloated politics of meaning,
prevents you from seeing;
biographical detail stops you from hearing;
and history, the cloak of those who define
the growth of their own power over time,
is murderous in its uses;
like cotton wool stuffed in a mouth or down a throat,
innocuous in itself, nursery furnishing,
it chokes our voices as it block your ears. . . .

2

IF A WRITER DOES NOT PRODUCE WHAT IS CONSISTENT
WITH THE IDEOLOGY OF THE DOMINANT CULTURE,
NO ONE WILL HEAR HER VOICE.
IF A WRITER PRODUCES WHAT IS CONSISTENT
WITH THE IDEOLOGY OF THE DOMINANT CULTURE,
SHE MAY CHOKE ON HER OWN WORDS.

I contemplate their narrow graves,
the narrower grave prepared for me,
contraction of the female form to fit
a narrow shelf,
contraction of the voice to fit
constriction of the soul. . . .

. . . so that we take the smallest spaces,
speak in the smallest voices,
barely audible,
sometimes
not audible at all. (*The Work of Our Hands* 28-32)

Another of my poems, "Circus Animals On The Commons/Green," mentions Anne Marriott among other writers and gives some idea of the effects on women writers and women's writing of male hegemony over language.

Circus Animals On The Commons/Green
for Rachel Loden

Two women of an age, we share
a politics, a consciousness,
the literate rebellion of a time,
(the heady scent of hyacinths?) a clime,
a climb out of the guarded crypts.
"Climacteric," the guardians suggest.
(Actually, they sneer, but we/won't speak of this.)
And we, fatigued, heavy-lidded, anguished, bored
with hearing, yet again, (again? again? my dear!)
misogyny in different tones that shift,
and modulate, and drift,
and infiltrate the very marrow of our bones
would gather up our words—our skirts?—and go
silently? on tiny, slippered feet?
But no! We don't. We're duty bound,
three-ringed? multi-purposed?
spiralled certainly, we women of the book,
accosted by *The Student Prince* or other such
lines and lies that culturally echo, "speak to me
only with thine eyes," who Pledge, weekly,
the literary furniture that occupies

our mothers' houses and the houses we
cannot help but occupy.
Oh Miriam, Edna, Dorothy, Anne:[1] who knows
what passes now (soft cloth against mahogany;
soft tongue against soft palate in an agony
of language and of silences),
passing (softly, softly, deftly), passing and surpassing
(the elephants parade; clowns tango, masquerade
as emperors, or ice cream vendors, while acoustic waves
beat on shores; and burning tigers jump through hoops;
and acrobats walk high wires where we spiral,
suspended by the bits in our teeth), tiring
"for such a pretty head" to think. The dead
flail in evanescing, frothy waves of poppy red,
wag their tongues, would speak out of our mouths;
but we, dutiful as daughters, censor what they've said. (*Other Voices* 2000)

"Courage is roped with hunger, chained with doubt," Anne Marriott wrote in "The Wind Our Enemy," her famous 1937 poem about the dust-bowl conditions of the Prairies during the Depression first published in 1939 (*The Circular Coast* 68). Anne Marriott's courage as a writer, and in particular as a woman writer working in a misogynist era, is striking. Her poem "September 29," which appears in the title section of *Letters From Some Islands,* shows the woman, the writer, the hunger, and the doubt. Set at mid-autumn, it is the sixteenth in a series that moves from high summer through the end of a year. Presented here alone, "September 29" does not reverberate with the resonances provided by the fifteen poems that precede it in the series. Seeing it in isolation is like seeing a single thread in a tapestry and trying to envision the art that supports and defines it and of which it is a supporting and defining part.

September 29

I write now to myself
(Did I always? to
the image of myself in you
the imaged, longed-for you?).
No one but yourself
will comfort you
the counsellor said
(but that was long ago).

God will comfort you
my friends here say
true
but I crave another comfort
arms and skin
warmth against the breasts
I am empty
and so cold.
When I was a child

```
never quite good enough
I ran from the house
to the chestnut tree
on the Victoria lawn
ringed its trunk
with my spindly arms
watched its gentle hands
stroking the air.
Can I find a comforter
in bristly spruce? (Letters 56)
```

A first stanza that alone might have been read as confessional changes completely with the addition of the second. Though the details in the second stanza are as personal as those in the first, they broaden the perspective and the subject by raising questions. Is faith childish? Is a disembodied spirituality useful? Is it useful to a woman in need? How are we comforted?

The poem that begins with doubt about the whole project of writing moves on through doubt about the whole prospect of comfort, from either a distant and disembodied source or from "nature." Though the gentle hands of the chestnut tree are conflated with human/female comfort and the "bristly spruce" is conflated with human/male comfort, the question is left open whether either can provide comfort to an adult woman. Clearly the tamed trees of the urban landscape and their personification are the stuff of childhood. The comfort of the natural world, one purported salve for doubt and lack of community, is bristly at best.

While the poem insists on physical being and on the being as physical, its tensions revolve around questions rather than answers, doubt rather than faith. God's comfort, however true, is apt to leave one empty and cold. When writing is an entirely private, confessional act, it fails to ask for or to achieve any interpersonal or social function, and thus, in the terms stated in this poem and generally in Anne Marriott's oeuvre, it too fails to provide comfort. The poem itself succeeds because the apparently confessional tone and details are used to suggest and imply significant social, spiritual, and philosophical questions. These are questions, moreover, to which the poet offers no answers, though the poem suggests where one might most usefully seek comfort.

The combination of intellectual truth-seeking with spiritual quest and their relation to our existence as physical and social beings is at the core of Anne Marriott's writing. In a complex and resonant poem, "Sketches," rich with literary and Biblical allusion, she uses eyesight as a metaphor for vision:

Sketches

for John Brook

```
My father sat by my sickbed
when I was seven
read from the prophet
Write the vision!
But I was born myopic
my vision broken.
I make only sketches
guessed-at, uncertain.

Reality is not here
always elsewhere
the friend far away
```

(dear friend, sharer)
clearer than this friend
near.

    These parks and houses
    island
    even the dark sea
    are only shadows
    that loom   turn brilliant
    pass like a sunset.
    Is there no solid land
    we can grasp so firmly
    our fingers
    cannot be unloosed?

Through a glass darkly
read my father
read
love never faileth.

    Until the light
    bursts through the broken glass
    I will write love
    to this friend whose hand puts down
    the same words of joy and pain
    as my hand.
    I will write love
    to any friend
    whose mind locks even a corner into mine.
    I will write love—
    and praise
    for every word we write
    that goes down true. (*Islands* 24-25)

"Sketches" is the final poem in a series, "The Danish Sketches," that forms the opening section in *Letters From Some Islands.* Like many of Anne Marriott's poems, it is clearly intended to be read in concert with others in a group of texts that are interdependent for full effect and meaning. Anne Marriott often wrote large, multi-sectioned poems and groups of connected poems that range broadly over complex issues that encompass the personal, political, social, and ethical. The effect of such poems is cumulative, and often the narrative element itself is structured by the imagery over the whole of a series, where images appear and repeat. In addition, as Jean Mallinson pointed out in her "Introduction" to *D'Sonoqua,* Anne "Marriott's precise descriptions have a symbolic double focus" (Mallinson np).

The symbolic and multiple foci of "precise descriptions" coupled with the connected nature of the work produce a complexity and richness difficult to accomplish in short poems and that do not show well in excerpts from larger works but come through strongly in the totality of Anne Marriott's oeuvre. So does her generosity of spirit as well as her appeal to readers to respond in kind, and a lifelong struggle to see what was true and to act on it with humility and charity, as we see in her poem "Breughel In The Museum Of Fine Arts, Vienna," which begins:

"Pieter, all across Europe/I've been looking for you/(never knowing it)" (*Islands* 63-64). While it is often resonant with the language and imagery of spiritual quest, Anne Marriott's oeuvre also demonstrates a strong, ongoing commitment to humanist and humanitarian Christian values, as "Breughel In The Museum Of Fine Arts, Vienna" shows. The poem ends:

> The tour parties clump close around me
> it's a hot day
> their heat increases it
> their furnace breath burns my breath
> how I hate them!
> Then I look at you and am ashamed.
> Your world is crowded with people
> ugly and innocent
> you painted them drinking
> grieving and greedy
> jostling off the edge of your canvasses
> and I see you loved them all.

Anne Marriott combined a broad knowledge of liturgy, hymnology, and Old and New Testament texts with a wide, often hands-on knowledge of plants, geography, geology, and food. This hands-on knowledge and the images that grew out of it enliven her writing and elicit the reader's trust. Though the images often are organic and the language sometimes deceptively simple, the central theme of Marriott's work is spiritual hunger. Such a theme is not fashionable in a consumer culture, which ours increasingly became during the course of Anne Marriott's working life as a writer. Nor does Anne Marriott's writing support the image, retailed wholesale after World War II, of woman as male-centred, passive, or a physical object. The persona in Anne Marriott's poems is physically present and is concerned with the details of the physical world, and in fact insistently lives in her body, but she is not diminished or spiritually or intellectually confined by the physical or by this physicality. Throughout Anne Marriott's oeuvre, the persona she represents is actively in search of spiritual, intellectual, and social sustenance, which are connected by vision and language through the physical. Often some integration of these elements of human existence form the ground on which Anne Marriott's poems are constructed. Though her resonances often are literary and Biblical, her reference points are also social and political in the broadest sense of that term.

Even in Anne Marriott's earliest work, *The Wind Our Enemy* and *Calling Adventurers,* there is a strong commitment to Canada as a concept that is emblematic of cooperation among diverse communities and as a physical, geographical space. In *The Wind Our Enemy,* Anne Marriott combined grounded images and language rooted in hymnology to communicate complex themes and political insights. In this perhaps more than in other of her multi-sectioned poems, it is difficult to sense the breadth and scope of the work or its meaning or intention from a short section, but the directness and vibrancy of the language and images are visible.

> The wheat in spring was like a giant's bolt of silk
> Unrolled over the earth.
> When the wind sprang
> It rippled as if a great broad snake
> Moved under the green sheet
> Seeking its outward way to light.
> In autumn it was an ocean of flecked gold
> Sweet as a biscuit, breaking in crisp waves

That never shattered, never blurred in foam.
That was the last good year . . . (*Circular* 61)

The diction and imagery together provide an almost palpable joyousness and suggest not only the fields of ripening wheat but a well-run, gracious, and welcoming home redolent with the scent of baking biscuits, that homeliest of home baking. This is an image of the land domesticated and tamed in a way the sea is never tamed. With the ominous reference to the breaking waves and the invocation of that which shatters and is blurred, the mood of buoyancy changes, and with it the direction of the work. The celebratory tone of the opening lines is underscored by the unexpected reference to shattering and then undercut by the final line of the stanza, which is also the final line of the section, and all the more ominous for that and for its trailing dots.

Throughout Anne Marriott's writing there is mention of and movement towards illumination. In the first section of *Letters From Some Islands*, "The Danish Sketches," the opening stanza of the first poem, "Dinner In Copenhagen," ends:

> *Light explodes everywhere   light*
> *a warm language*
> *everyone can understand.* (*Islands* 11)

The light with which and towards which Anne Marriott's poems move is not the cold light of logic divorced from physical, human warmth. Nor is it the "true" light emanating from a disembodied godhead. Rather it is light as "a warm language" where language is communicative and welcoming and represents a kind of home. Anne Marriott's poetry is distinguished by this illuminative vision and vision of illumination embodied in, to use Jean Mallinson's words again, "precise description" that "everyone can understand" (Mallinson n.p.).

"Living Under Water" is the title of the opening group of texts in Anne Marriott's last book, *Aqua*. In this group of connected poems, the second, "To Come To Your Shore," shows some of the complex winding and binding of thought, literary and Biblical resonance, and directness and elegance of imagery and prosody which are the hallmarks of Anne Marriott's work. Like many of Anne Marriott's poems, this one, almost breath-taking in directness, intensity, and reach, reads as a much richer work when it is viewed in the super-rich allusive context in which it appears in its sequence.

To Come To Your Shore

The only way I can come
to you and to your shore
is by grief
walking over it like a bridge
across the dark inlet
its supports wavering
in the flood tide
or by swimming through the black seas
to your shining island
(but I could never swim).

Grief is like an animal hit by a truck
writhing on the pavement.
Grief is like the thick closing in
of the suffocating tunnel

collapsing in a nightmare.
Grief is a crucifixion
agony
too terrible for any simile.
(But the only way, some say,
to a resurrection,
to coming to you). (*Aqua* 12)

The work in *Aqua*, like much of Anne Marriott's writing, references and resonates with water imagery. One of the final poems in this final collection, "After A Meeting Of Poets," contains the lines:

For myself? All that I ask
is that when I have to leave
there'll be a survivor
with a space for me
talking and scribbling in his brain
insisting he recall
my life's essential act:
I wrote poems
as
did all of
you. (*Aqua* 81)

I hope that my poem "Treading Water," a poem dedicated to Anne Marriott and about her life and writing, will serve as a response to those lines.

When she was in her 70s, Anne Marriott was disabled by a stroke that severely limited her mobility and her ability to speak or to use language. The last time I saw Anne before her stroke, she expressed serious concern that she was not getting appropriate care or treatment and that ageism and sexism were in part responsible. "Treading Water" in part explores foreshadowing in the imagery that appears in Anne Marriott's poems and in part references water imagery throughout Anne Marriott's oeuvre. "Treading Water" also celebrates Anne Marriott as poet and gardener, social activist and jam-maker, and as a woman writer of enormous courage who throughout her lifetime confronted issues that continue to confront us.

Treading Water

For Anne Marriott

1

The lake has tried to swallow you,[2]
the wind to knock you off your feet.[3]
Not raging, but determined, you resist,
fight back hard, with all your strength,
more strength than you guessed you'd need.

Eyeball to eyeball with death,

mute for a time, unable to muster words
(what has the poet against certain death but words?),[4]
you stare, an old woman
redolent of the smells of hospitals,
barely able to swallow now,
but tough as this land you loved, and catalogued,[5]
charting its coast, its bays, its coves, its vast interior:
an old woman, everything gone but one good eye,
strong enough to outstare death—this time.

2

Recovery from stroke is . . . slow.
One   moment—at—a—time.
One   muscle—at—a—time.

The young and hale don't know
the price of each
small motion.

Come on, dear; you can do it.
They try   jollying us   along.

That eyeball,
bulging now with life,
speaks volumes.

Deaf to any but the speaking voice, the girls
(they are women, but so young,
we think of them as girls)
don't read the flashes of that speaking eye,
know only the almost-helpless flesh;
still, they sense the will,
a force to reckon with.

3

Hair needs washing!
Oh, they keep you clean,
and comfortable,
by their own lights:
dry not wet,
cleaned not dirty,
bed adjusted,
straw in a cup close enough
for the hand that works to reach.

Cold comforts,

but comforts,
nevertheless.

That's all there is at this stage.
That's all there is now.

The eyeball that outstared death
glares otherwise,
glares: *"No!"*

Aqua

Agua

water:

knowing

how not

to drown.[6]

4

The great aquifers, clean and clear,
boil just below the surface of the rock.

Parched, you lick your lips. Words roil
just below the surface of your tongue,
a gathering sound you cannot find,
a place you can no longer go.

This nightmare you once wrote,[7] who dreamed,
like Joseph, of plenty,[8] given freely,[9]
and a lifetime of oceans, islands; who loved
the damp, coastal climate; your blood
rushing seaward, in full flood, away from drought.[10]

Though you understood the flat interior,
its dry seasons, you craved water:
sweet or salt, cascades and falls,
undertows, streams, lakes, seas,
darting, flashing in the sun,
rolling in to shore,
whatever shape or form,
phosphorescent,
luminescent,

life springs
from water.[11]

5

Before the current flood of elegant words,[12]
facile language, frothing metaphors,
a tide of euphemism that covers,
like new, unblemished skin, the same old sins:
greed, cupidity, and, of course, plain selfishness,
you spoke, a stubborn, headstrong woman who had seen
a thousand miles of prairie
spoiled; a once-luminous country
parched and drying in its soul,
failing to sustain life for want of care:
a fate worse than drought.

6

New research finds that hunters
do not eat more meat than others,
that we survive, as species, and by tribes,
not by selfishness and brutality
but by mutual aid and reciprocity,
the culture of the circular coast you loved.[13]

7

Anne, my Anne,
who sent red currant jelly across the continent,
the fruit picked with your own arthritic hands
in the garden you so loved
because I have no currants in my own:
where have you gone, if not home,
into the pages of your texts?

In the flesh, I missed you by ten days,
an ill-starred trip, and when you'd gone,
before I flew across this continent,
this land you loved to hoe and rake and plant,
in my small plot, I put eighteen tulips in,
eighteen bulbs, the choicest I could find,
a promise for the Spring:
eighteen, *chai,* the Hebrew sign for life,
and planting bulbs as close as I can get
to an understanding of eternity.
Late-flowering Apricot Beauties

I feared might not bloom
came up, each and every one;
not one was eaten;
not one rotted in the ground;
and each bore a flower on its stalk,
delicate in colour and in shape,
and strong enough to stand against the wind
without the aid of stake or twine.

Between the earliest blooms of spring
and early summer's blooms to come,
open and generous, they shone,
the only blooms in the garden then,
a sight for hungry eyes. (*This Flesh* 32-38)

"The Marks Of Our Single Species" is a phrase I borrowed from Philip Morrison's review of Steven Pinker's *The Language Instinct* (Morrison np) to serve as the title of the final poem I offer here. This poem is intended to broaden the scope of this appreciation to encompass themes that appear throughout Anne Marriott's life and work.

The Marks Of Our Single Species

Because you are so far
distant beyond hands' reach,
more than arm's length:
an ell   a cubit   biblical *pi?*
these arithmetic metaphors,
measurements of separation,
are grounded in the certain knowledge
that I cannot reach you
without crossing deep water.

The bridge between us, a tenuous link
between an island and a continent,
has been under construction for years;
sometimes it's closed to a single lane,
and not much passes;
any minor breakdown escalates
to a major obstruction
to the smooth flow of traffic;
communication stalls,
grinds to a halt.

Language takes us anywhere,
across bridges
whether the flag's up or down,
whether there's safe crossing,
whether there's any bridge at all.
We wait our turn for safe passage

47

across deep water,
rest, uncertain, on the bridge,
at the top of its arch,
the mid-point of its span.

The air is heavy;
the atmosphere is tense;
we may at any moment
overbalance, plunge,
eyes first, into that medium
where we drown easily, fast:
the medium of drowning,
the medium of life.

Sources of life: light and water;
each sterile without the other.

Sources of life: language and vision;
the brain hard-wired for communication.

Pen and brush, both once a feather,
reversed, become two implements,
the brush, an extension of the hand,
finer, more delicate in its touch;
the pen, an extension of the tongue;
two tools that share a single purpose,
diverging from a single object,
arising from one need:

commune   communication   community

Hillel the Elder said:
do not separate yourself from the community.[14]

alienation: isolation:

cut off
without a line

speech a liferaft
for those who would not drown,
each syllable a bridge,
a touch,
a hand;
therefore: ensure

the speaking voice is clear;

complete lines;

work images;

conclude arguments;

ground metaphors;

close circles;

define meanings;

build solid footings,

strong bridges;

keep the lifelines

always

coiled. (*This Flesh* 75-78)

Notes

1 Miriam the Biblical prophet, Miriam Waddington, Edna St. Vincent Millay, Dorothy Parker, Dorothy Livesay, Anne Sexton, Anne Marriott.

2 See Anne Marriott's "The Lake," *Aqua* 83-84.

3 See Anne Marriott's *The Wind Our Enemy*. The concept of ruach adonai, the divine breath or wind of life, may be useful in reading Marriott.

4 See Anne Marriott's "After A Meeting Of Poets" in *Aqua* 80-81, and "Sketches" in *Letters From Some Islands* 24-25, especially the final stanza.

5 Anne Marriott began cataloguing the landscapes and geography of Canada in her earliest works, *The Wind Our Enemy* and *Calling Adventurers*. Her work is full of images of the elements of physical geography, especially coastlines.

6 These lines reference my poem "Making Waves": "the sensuousness of words/is the only death by drowning/poets know" (*The Work of Our Hands* 61); "waves of sound/. . . wash away meaning/. . . drown conscience" (62); "supple sounds/sweet on the tongue/betray" (67). The last time before her stroke that I saw Anne Marriott, she told me how much she appreciated this poem and asked me to read it to her. She told me also that she had read it many times herself and that it had contributed to her work on the poems that eventually were published in Aqua.

7 In "Aqua xii," Anne Marriott asks: "what if I lose/the power to swallow?" (*Aqua* 33), and in "Crying in Sleep": "Drowning, I fought for breath,/screaming/I woke" (*Aqua* 68).

8 The dream references Marriott's *The Wind Our Enemy* as well as *Genesis* and *Deuteronomy*. Pharaoh dreamed and Joseph interpreted the dream and implemented "a reserve for the land against seven years of famine" (*Genesis* 41:36).

9 *Deuteronomy* 15 provides a discussion of lending to those in need, and especially in relation to the 'sabbatical' year. Verse 10 advises: "You shall give him freely, and your heart shall not be grudging."

10 Water imagery recurs throughout Anne Marriott's work. See for instance "July 9": "All my life/blood has rushed saltily in my veins/like sounds of water" (*Letters From Some Islands* 46) and "All of us come in water from the womb" and "that easy element/their aqueous mother" ("Aqua v," *Aqua* 25).

11 See also the final stanza of Anne Marriott's "Sketches" in *Letters From Some Islands,* and above, and "Aqua v" (*Aqua* 25).

12 In an early work, Anne Marriott refers to personal letters as "Tying homes, lovers, lives together/With visible, precious words" (*Calling Adventurers* XI 7).

13 The material in this section is based on an essay by Samuel Bowles and Herbert Gintis, "Is Equality Passé? Homo reciprocans and the future of egalitarian politics" (*Boston Review* 1999). See also Marriott's "Breughel in the Museum of Fine Arts, Vienna," final stanza, in *Letters From Some Islands* (64).

14 See *Pirke Avoth* II:5: "Hillel said, Separate not thyself from the congregation; . . . and say not anything which cannot be understood at once, in the hope that it will be understood in the end;" in *Sayings of the Fathers*, or *Pirke Aboth* (33).

Three Travellers in Mexico

Rosemary Sullivan

*T*HREE MONK-LIKE, sexually ambiguous figures sit in castellated towers. A soft light shines in each room, focused from a different interior source. One figure is a painter, one a writer, and one sits drinking from a cup of wine. Each is independent, each unaware of the other. Yet, hovering in the air, a barely visible spindle connects the three figures to a distant star. The artist described this as "a complicated machine from which come pulleys that wind around them and make them move (they think they move freely) ... [but] the destiny of these people ... unbeknownst to them, is intertwined and one day their lives will cross" (Kaplan 181).

The artist is the great Spanish-Mexican painter Remedios Varo, and three lives did eventually cross, pulled as if by synchronicity to act out the narrative of her painting, three women who, independently, had carved the same artistic vision. It was a magic meeting, the meeting of P.K. Page, Remedios Varo, and Leonora Carrington in Mexico in 1960. They were antic, hilarious, and deeply committed to their art.

What was that friendship like? We are so used to the traditional scenario of the young woman artist taken under the mentorship of the older male artist. Each of these women had had that kind of experience in their youth, when they played the muse at the centre of an artistic circle—Carrington and Varo for the surrealist circles in France; Page for the *Preview* poets in Montreal. What would it be like to glimpse inside the process of imaginative cross-fertilization when it is taking place entirely in the context of female friendship? I have a reason for wanting to know this. P.K. Page has been one of the most important influences in my life.

Page is among Canada's foremost writers: author of twelve books of poetry; a novel *The Sun and The Moon*; short stories, one of which, "Unless the Eye Catch Fire," has been made into a play and a film; a travelogue, *Brazilian Journal*; and three books for children. But under the name of P.K. Irwin, she is also a painter. A number of her works can be seen in the National Gallery of Canada.

I first met P.K. in 1974 when I moved to Victoria, B.C. She had just published an article called "Traveller, Conjuror, Journeyman," in which she described art as magicianship; the point of art is to alter our way of seeing (Page, *The Glass Air* 208). I liked this, but it was her voice, so candid and playful, that made me want to seek her out. I still remember that first visit. Her suburban home looked ordinary on the outside, but entering it was like walking into an exotic mind: on the shelves of her living room there were Mexican candied skulls and gaudily painted trees of life, Mexican paper flowers and Australian bull roarers, and her walls were filled with her own paintings—one was of strange strings of dancing vegetation reaching towards the sun through scarlet air; another of stippled silver moons. We became friends after that visit. We used to trade our dreams. I recall her telling me of her dream about two dogs—they were Irish setters, but golden in colour. Above their eyes as they stared up at her was a third blue eye which was human. The thought of the dream was: if their third eye is human, what is our third eye? She could play wonderful linguistic games: "There is no difference between *there* and *here* except for an irrelevant, inconsequential 't.'" Once she said to me: "If the world is a plant, perhaps you are a nodule of growth." For me P.K. is one of the searchers, ahead of the rest of us, throwing back clues. She encouraged me to believe I might one day become a writer.

She also introduced me to the paintings of Leonora Carrington and Remedios Varo and spoke of their time together in Mexico. Intrigued by that friendship, I decided to go to Mexico in search of them.

Buzzed through by an attendant guard, I walked into the Galería Arvil in the Zona Rosa in Mexico City. For its twenty-fifth anniversary exhibition, Arvil was featuring works by Carrington and Varo. I knew these paintings from books but this was the first time I had seen them in the flesh as it were. How to describe their impact on me?

Leonora Carrington's paintings had titles like "Monopoteosis," "Hierophant," "Reflections on the Oracle," "Penelope," and "Took My Way Down, Like a Messenger to the Deep." They seemed to move in a vortex of light that pulled the viewer in and I had a sensation of *bouleversement,* being turned on my head—I was travelling into the paintings drawn by a will stronger than my own. What was she telling me about light, space, time? And beside her was this other strange myth-maker. Varo canvases were filled with complicated alchemical mechanisms, creatures of inverted heads and alembic bodies, heads emerging from walls. One painting was called "The Lovers." A couple, holding hands, had faces of mirrors and they were lost in each other's eyes. Their magnetic attraction was so great that it rose as a whirl of steam from their blue matching clothes, then condensed as water drowning their feet, and the space around them was mysterious, black and stippled with falling light. Another was called "Farewell." The lovers had separated and were just visible disappearing down adjacent corridors, but their shadows, still tied to their feet, stretched back to take a last kiss. This woman was telling stories and she had lived deeply.

Varo had died in 1963 at the age of fifty-five, but I was able to meet Leonora Carrington. Her New York and Mexican galleries had tried hard to discourage me, insisting that she now refused all interviews, but the fact that I was carrying greetings from Pat (as Leonora called P.K.) meant that she kindly invited me without hesitation to visit her. The portrait of their friendship was as delightful as I had expected. This is the story.

When P.K. Page arrived in Mexico City in 1960 as the wife of the Canadian Ambassador, it is not likely that the Canadian embassy had seen her kind of woman before. She was forty-four, and already a successful writer, with a novel, several books of poetry and a Governor General's Award behind her. Because her father was an army officer, she grew up in Calgary, Winnipeg, and Saint John, New Brunswick. Determined to be a writer, she set off at the age of twenty-five for Montreal, where she worked days as a filing clerk and nights writing. Soon she found her way to the *Preview* people, the poets and painters who collected in F.R. Scott's living room to put out their progressive literary magazine. Scott was a charismatic lawyer—he would become famous for single-handedly taking on the reactionary government of Maurice Duplessis—and the best minds collected around him. The wartime context of their debates gave everything an edge, though they were mostly young people trying to find out if they could write. In the early fifties, working as a scriptwriter at the NFB, P.K. met Arthur Irwin, a magazine editor who had been hired as executive director and chair of the board. Shortly after their marriage—she was thirty-five— he joined Foreign Affairs and was posted to Australia. They had just completed a four-year posting in Brazil before they arrived in Mexico. For P. K., Brazil had been a dazzling experience, a flamboyant world of Doric palms and flowering jungles, and she had turned for the first time to painting to fix the whirl of images. In Mexico, because of her, the ambassadorial residence on Montes Carpatos was suddenly filled with artists.

One evening after a dinner party, P.K. found herself recounting a strange experience from her childhood. She and her mother were standing looking from the living room window of their home and suddenly found themselves staring into the eyes of a completely terrifying creature who was watching them. "It looked," she says now, "like current descriptions of aliens: round dark eyes like disks, pointed chin, narrow with languorous hair, soft like a baby's, as if it were under water almost" (Sullivan, Interview with Page). The creature was not threatening, but it frightened her. She turned to her mother, who had also seen it, and her mother quietly closed the blind. Little did she know who was in her audience as she recounted her story that night. Leonora Carrington approached and said: "It sounds totally true." Others would have dismissed the story as fantasy or eccentricity. For Leonora this was elementary stuff, but it had verisimilitude. They became immediate friends.

Carrington was by then already famous in Mexico. She had just had a one-woman show that had filled the Belles Artes national gallery and was revered as the country's leading surrealist. P.K. remembers her as tall and narrow, with exquisite eyes. "I always used to say she could slip through a crack in the door, as if she had one finger and one toe less than the rest of us, her physical self was so narrow." One detail of her past life that everyone knew was that she had been the lover of Max Ernst, the don of European Surrealism, but this is the least remarkable thing about her.

Carrington was born in Lancashire in 1917, the child of a wealthy industrialist. A fleet of servants ran the family residence, Crookhey Hall, and a Jesuit came Sundays to give mass in the family chapel. Her Celtic mother was a remarkable beauty; when she took Leonora to make her debut at the court of King George V in 1934, she advised her rebellious young daughter to look decorative and added, "You'd better be careful or you'll be an old witch before you're twenty-five." Leonora decided she'd rather be the witch. After being sent to finishing school in Florence, followed by school in Paris where she spent her time drawing and climbing out of windows to escape, she convinced her parents to allow her to study art and enrolled at the Amédée Ozenfant Academy in London in 1936. A friend invited her to dinner with Max Ernst, a married man of forty-six. The encounter was electric. They fled to Paris.

They had three years together, but it was a terrible time to be romantic lovers. Ernst was arrested twice—by the French in 1939 as an enemy alien and then again by the Vichy regime in 1940. Leonora fled across the Pyrenees to Spain but the psychic pressure of Ernst's double internment was leading to disaster. In Spain she began to spiral out of control, under the pressure of fear. She was institutionalized in Santander and her experiences of shock and drug therapy were so horrendous she came to call them "death practice." Her parents sent her nanny from England to fetch her. Convinced their intention was to ship her to hospital in South Africa she persuaded her keeper to take her shopping in Lisbon. A lady, she explained, could not travel without gloves and hat. Demanding to stop at a café to go to the bathroom, she slipped out the back door and fled to the Mexican Embassy where an acquaintance, the poet-diplomat, Renato Leduc, agreed to marry her so that she could get out of Spain. In New York, she found that Ernst had become involved with Peggy Guggenheim. In 1942, she set out with Leduc for Mexico City where many refugee artists were settling. Established in the abandoned Russian Embassy, she wrote the whole experience in a story called "Down Below," possibly one of the most lucidly hallucinatory accounts of madness that has been written. "At least when you go mad you find out what you are made of," she says laconically (Sullivan, Interview with Carrington).

In Mexico, which offered citizenship and help to refugees the rest of the world wouldn't take, she met the painter Remedios Varo. Varo's escape had also been spectacular.

Born in Catalonia in 1908, Varo had joined the surrealists in Paris where she had become the lover of the noted surrealist poet Benjamin Péret. When the Nazis invaded in June 1940 and hoisted the swastika atop the Eiffel Tower, Varo fled with eight million other refugees in cars, on bicycles or pushing wheelbarrows, towards the unoccupied zone in the south. She eventually joined Péret in Marseille. A New York group called the Emergency Rescue Committee had set itself up three days after the Nazi occupation of Paris with the express purpose of saving as many of Europe's leading intellectuals and artists as possible. A thirty-two-year-old Harvard-trained classicist, Varian Fry, was sent to Marseille in August 1940 with $3000 strapped to his leg and a list of names which had been composed in New York. He established a safe house called the Villa Air-Bel to begin the rescue mission. Péret was famous enough to earn a spot there, which required establishing one's credentials as an intellectual worthy of attention.

The committee wrote frantically to the U.S. to raise the fare for Péret and Varo—the price of saving the life of one escapee was $350. The process moved at a snail's pace and, while food became more and more scarce, the secret police searched the premises for signs of subversion. It took well over a year to find safe exit, but passage was finally secured for Varo and Péret from Casablanca in November 1941. Still they had to get to North Africa. Péret negotiated with a black-market operator to take them across. Luckily for them their money was stolen on the docks before they found the fishing boat, since it was discovered that the black-marketeer they had hired was a psychopathic killer who had murdered the previous refugees he was meant to save; twelve bodies were found buried in his backyard. Varo and Péret did finally reach Mexico at the end of 1941. They had thought of the U.S., but the Americans refused Péret refuge because of his political record. Under the progressive government of President Lázaro Cárdenas, Mexico offered automatic citizenship to all Spanish refugees (15,000 came) and protection to any members of the International Brigade.

From the moment of Remedios's arrival she and Leonora became intimate friends, seeing each other nearly every day, studying alchemy together and exchanging dreams.

By 1960, Remedios too was famous. She had been commissioned to do a mural for the new Cancer Pavilion of the Medical Centre and her paintings were selling well. She still kept her surrealist roots, writing an essay in 1959 called *De Homo Rodans*, a pseudo-scholarly treatise on the origins of man and of the first umbrella. She and Leonora were treated with awe as two eccentric geniuses. Their antics owed something to the old surrealist sense of play. When she had a party, Remedios would search the telephone directory under psychiatrists and, finding a likely name, call doctor so-and-so, daring him to come. The meals she and Leonora put together were famous: for example, serving rice coloured with squid's ink as caviar. Remedios's sense of humour surfaces in paintings like "Vegetarian Vampires who keep Animals as Pets."

To me these two women offer a model of women's friendship, rebelling against all constraining conventions and using humour as their weapon of choice. One of Varo's most amusing paintings is called "Woman Leaving the Psychoanalyst." A robed female, her mask sliding from her face, is shown departing from a stone building; in her hand she dangles a shrunken head. Varo explained: "The patient drops her father's disembodied head into a small circular well ... [which is the] correct thing to do when leaving the psychoanalyst ... the basket she carries holds yet more psychological waste." The psychoanalyst's name is Dr. FJA, a reference to Freud, Jung, and Adler (Kaplan 155). They were even able to make the erotic funny. Perhaps rebounding from her Ernst encounter, Leonora could say: "If you have to, get on with your genital responsibilities, but I won't be the Lady of Shallot." When André Breton asked her to participate in an exhibition of eroticism in 1959, she described her intended contribution: "A Holy Ghost (albino pigeon) three meters high, real feathers (white chickens', for example), with: nine penises erect (luminous), thirty-nine testicles to the sound of little Christmas bells, pink paws ... Let me know, Dear André, and I will send you an exact drawing ..." (Warner 11). She came to dislike the heroic myth of artistic genius, the grandiose gesture: "Painting is like making strawberry jam—really carefully and well."

When Leonora discovered that P.K. could speak her language, she immediately invited her to her studio. At that time P.K. had progressed in her painting from gouache to oil, but was finding the process unsatisfactory. Leonora insisted she try egg tempera, giving her her own private recipe. When P.K. responded that she didn't know how to use it, Leonora replied: "Find out." P.K. developed her own technique, putting on expansive swaths and then scraping and cutting through, loving it immediately because it dried so quickly she could touch it. "It was my idea of bliss." They would race around Mexico in P.K.'s car, negotiating the gloriettas where the traffic merged from eight different directions, hunting gold leaf and pigment. P.K. also helped Leonora with the production of her surrealistic play *Penelope*, assisting in the labour of making papier-mâché sets, costumes, and masks for the characters that included a fabulous and omniscient rocking horse and an oracular nurse dressed in her true character as a cow goddess.

In her own version of surrealism, Leonora used everything to advantage for humorous or provocative purposes. When P.K. walked into her studio one day, she discovered her working on a "thing." She had found some boards lying around and knocked them together, painting them black and boring holes in them. Over the holes were absurd little titles. She said: "You put your fingers through the holes. In one hole there was the sharp end of a thumb tack, in another face cream, in another soot," P.K. explains. "It took courage to put your finger through those holes. You realize how vulnerable the blind finger is. Grown men refused Leonora's experiment."

P.K. remembers their times together as often hilarious, especially a dinner party at Leonora's house. Leonora had phoned that morning to complain that the other couple who had been invited were insisting on bringing a Dr. Stern with them. Leonora was always uneasy with people whose imagination stopped at "too low an octave," and a stranger at her table was disconcerting. The only Stern she knew was a Mexican urologist. The dinner was quite respectable by Leonora's standards: the toilet paper and ketchup bottle that usually graced the table had been removed. Wringing her hands anxiously Leonora launched into a string of questions about urology over dinner, until her guest interrupted indignantly: "Leonora, do you know who you have at your table? Only the greatest violinist in the world, Isaac Stern." The conversation then turned somewhat awkwardly to art and someone asked if Stern liked to play for himself. He responded that he could only play for an audience. Asked if he could not go into a room by himself and play for the sheer joy of it, he replied that he could not. Both P.K. and Leonora were horrified. Why do you paint, he asked, if not for an audience? P.K. remembers one of them saying: "*For God*, which was a fairly pompous reply but we meant for ourselves or perhaps a higher being." Isaac Stern replied that anyone who could say that was a "liar." "By this time," P.K. explains, "I was filled up to my gullet with red wine and, outraged at his comment, I picked up my glass and threw it over my shoulder. It went through a window behind me and crashed on the cement entrance way downstairs." As a rhetorical response to the maestro's condescension, Leonora thought this a brilliant gesture. The next day Leonora sent Stern a bouquet of flowers, telling P.K. that, though Stern would miss it, there was a message in the flowers. Each flower had a meaning. She had looked it all up.

There were many other antic parties. P.K. recalled the embassy reception held in honour of the dazzlingly beautiful Maria Felix, considered the Sophia Loren of Mexico. When she warned the house staff of the actress's imminent arrival, the news spread like a brush fire and suddenly brothers, sisters, cousins, nieces, all the staffs' extended family, arrived at the doorstep to see the star. The head butler had a nose bleed at the shock and bled all over his white gloves so that he had to borrow his subordinate's which were three sizes too big, making him look like a good stand-in for Mickey Mouse. At another party given for Kathleen Fenwick, Curator of Prints and Drawings at the National Gallery of Canada, P.K. remembered that one of the invited artists was Remedios Varo. The Canadian society columnist, Zena Cherry, had just arrived from Italy sporting the latest fashion in shoes. Instead of heels, the shoes had fixed wheels. Remedios was beside herself. For years she had been painting wheeled shoes on her figures, and she was desperate to have the shoes. The more cocktails she drank the more importunate she became until finally P.K. turned to Cherry and said: "Oh, give her the damn shoes. Can't you see she needs them?" Cherry remained poker-faced and left the party.

P.K. was deeply fond of Remedios, but they could not communicate verbally, Remedios's flights of poetic Spanish being too hard for her to follow, but according to Remedios's husband, Walter Gruen, Remedios came to depend on P.K. and her husband Arthur Irwin. The legacy of her wartime experience had left her terrified of governments and deportations, and she always believed that Irwin would save her when the worst inevitably came to the worst.

One thing the three women had in common was their interest in space, time, and other dimensions, and in the spiritual. They were questers. They talked of Jung, whose work they were reading together; about levels of awareness; about things that seemed vital and absolutely essential. One of the paintings Remedios did at the time, called "The Phenomenon of Weightlessness," would later be used by the physicist Peter Bergman for the cover of his book *The Riddle of Gravitation*. Working intuitively, she had got the phenomenon exactly right. They also conducted their own experiments. P.K. remembers the three of them lying naked on a bed, laying their hands over each other's backs to determine at what distance from the body they could feel the pull of the magnetic field.

Each was different: Remedios more allegorical, perhaps intellectual, and fascinated by mystic disciplines: one painting called "Spiral Transit" evokes the medieval notion of an initiatory rite or The Call. Leonora would explain that her paintings were based on hypnagogic visions, not on dreams. To a Freudian who once claimed she was not adjusted, she replied: "To what." She was also the most feminist. In the foreword to the catalogue of one of her exhibitions she wrote that there are gaps in our understanding, wisdom covered up, and "the Furies, who have a sanctuary buried many fathoms under education and brain washing, have told Females they will return, return from under the fear, shame, and finally through the crack in the prison door ... [give us back] the Mysteries which were ours and which were violated, stolen or destroyed, leaving us with the thankless hope of pleasing a male animal, probably of one's own species" (Carrington, "Commentary" 23). P.K. was the most verbal, interested in the pressure of interiority and the idea of symbolic patterns. In retrospect she would describe her time in Latin America. "If Brazil was day, then Mexico was night. All the images of darkness hovered for me in the Mexican sunlight. If Brazil was a change of place, then Mexico was a change of time. One was very close to the old gods here ... [where] objects dissolved into their symbols ... Coming as I do from a random or whim-oriented culture, this recurrence and interrelating of symbols into an ordered and significant pattern ... was curiously illuminating ... The dark Mexican night had led me back into myself and I was startlingly aware of the six dimensions of space" (Page, *The Glass Air* 212-13).

But none of them easily ascribed to systems. P.K. remembers that Leonora introduced her to the writings of Gurdjieff, but she also told her that when she was asked to a Gurdjieff group in Mexico, she found she couldn't stand it, all the people sitting around looking so poker faced. She had finally got up and stamped—just one leg— and recited: "You can tell by moulds that their flesh hangs in folds / You can tell by their smell that there's blood in the well." She told P.K. this with laughter in her eyes. They had asked her to leave. P.K. believed that Leonora would have been unable to follow anybody else's lead. "She's such an original. She'd probably have to go her own way."

But she felt Leonora did lead her, "into places that nudged you into remembering that you knew those places almost, couldn't quite get your hands on them, but they weren't totally foreign. She activated some part of my imagination and mind that normally wasn't activated in me. She knew that we are not whole and we want very much to be whole. She's not like the rest of us. She would say 'Despise nothing, ignore nothing; create interior space for digestive purposes.'"

They had often talked about transmutation, how to change the core of your being. "Once she asked me: 'What does it mean to you if I say: Going backwards very, very fast, counter-clockwise, into a small black hole.' It didn't mean anything to me at all. She said: 'That's the way you get back into your body when you've been out.' I believed her of course, that she could get out of her body. I think we're very gross matter. The finer matter is there, but only a few people can get at it, and a few of us have glimpses sometimes. Life demands that we stay with the gross matter. But Leonora was very strong. You know the finer matter is as strong as adamant. It is the gross matter that bleeds."

In 1962, Remedios Varo died suddenly and unexpectedly of a heart attack. "Everything came to a blinding halt when she died," P.K. said. "I remember we called on her husband Walter [Gruen] and there was a circle of chairs in the room. Walter wasn't there. Nobody knew anybody else and nobody knew how to get out of that room. So there we sat. It was as if Remedios had done that to us. Frozen us somehow." She remembered the funeral, trudging up the hillside, the day wild with a ferocious wind, Gruen planting a tree on the grave. "It almost sent Leonora into hysterics," she remarked, "the idea of those roots going down into Remedios's grave."

I met Leonora Carrington in her spartan home in the Chimalistac district of Mexico City where she had been living since the 1940s. She immediately put me at ease by discussing the new "corset" she had just bought at Price Choppers in Florida—it was the kind train porters use for a weak back. As I sat at the kitchen table where Dr. Stern had sat, she reminisced about those days in the early 1960s. "Pat had a wonderful eye, a very textured visual sense. She used egg-tempera with detailed precision. And she had a textured verbal sense, too." Once I remember her sitting down to a particularly unappetizing dish of rice and calling it 'congealed blood.' Nothing more needed to be said." But our talk soon took a higher note as we began to speak of Jung. "He was absolutely right about one thing," Leonora said. "We are occupied by gods. The mistake is to identify with the god occupying you." She, for instance, was possessed by Demeter, the mother, so obsessed was she with her two sons. "They are adult, have nothing to do with me, and yet I am still tied umbilically." "Who occupies you?" she asked. When I said I did not know, she replied: "My guess would be Diana, the huntress. Identity is so mysterious. What, after all, are we? Identity is not the issue: our machine-mentation. I am. I am. I am. But is this so? The problem is not ego, but the mannequins. I have one for the gallery, one for each of my sons, one for my cat." At one point I found myself talking about Timothy Findley's *Headhunter*, about a woman who believes she has allowed an evil character to escape from a book. "Entities do enter our lives," Leonora said. "One I experienced was malevolent. It has happened six or eight times since I was very young. It was a thing without shape or boundaries, amorphous. It comes as a sound. It was voracious, sucking, a sucking force and inside this entity were millions of other entities, equally voracious, crying desperately, one of which was me. As in hell." "That sounds evil. What must evil be?" I asked. "An absence of attention. That is the only thing I can think of," she replied. "The only thing we can do about evil is pay attention." Such was a quiet afternoon with Leonora Carrington.

Varo and Carrington are well known in Mexico and Europe. Leonora told me that the privilege of Mexico is that, there, the artist is free. P.K. says the Anglo-Saxon approach is that if you're an artist you're suspect, no good, at best a conversation piece. But in the small space accorded art here, P.K. Page is recognized as an essential figure. When she reads from *Hologram*, her brilliant book of glosas, a Spanish poetic form from the fourteenth and fifteenth centuries, she is clearly one of our great poets.

Remedios Varo, "Los Amantes" (The Lovers), 1963. Mixed media on bristol board, 75 x 30 cm. Private collection

P.K. Irwin, "The Dance," 1962. Egg tempera, 36.5 x 32 cm. Artist's collection.

Leonora Carrington, "The Ancestor," 1968. Oil on panel, 60 x 40 cm. Private collection.

Leonora Carrington, "Monopoteosis," 1959. Oil on panel, 72 x 92 cm. Museo de Arte Contemporaneo, Monterrey.

Mothering as in "Vital and Precise"

Foremothers:
Four Modernist Women Poets from the West Coast

Carolyn Zonailo

 𝒩o one writer creates in isolation. The poets we resonate to who have gone before—from other cultures, centuries or generations—as well as those elder poets we may be fortunate enough to meet when we are young, become the warp and woof from which a literature is woven. I began my literary life at a liminal time for Canadian poetry. As a young poet, I was able to meet and know modernist poets writing in Canada, and also the generation who followed right after the modernists poets, those who helped to bring Canadian literature to international recognition. I am a poet writing in both the twentieth and twenty-first centuries, during a time when Canadian poetry has "come of age," as it shifted from modernist to post-modernist, and now into a new millennium.

I am very grateful for having known the poetry, and the women behind the poetry, of P.K. Page, Dorothy Livesay, Marya Fiamengo, and Anne Marriott. These women poets were my foremothers, four modernist women poets in Canada, living on the west coast, and dedicating their lives to creativity and to poetry. Their example, their friendships, and their literary works have lived within me for the past quarter century, since my first seminal meeting with P.K. Page in 1976. It was in meeting, knowing, and listening to the poetry of these four women that I was able to claim my own voice as a poet and as a woman. They all gave more of themselves and their art than it is possible for me to articulate. By their lives and by their bodies of literary works, they have helped to weave the living tapestry of Canadian literature.

I began writing poetry when I was a teenager in Vancouver, where I was born. While still in high school, I discovered a collection of poetry entitled *The Modern Poets: An American-British Anthology*. From that time on, I was an eager reader of modernist poetry, in addition to the more traditional literature courses I was taking at school. In the final year of my undergraduate studies I decided to combine academic work with writing, and to finish my degree in creative writing. I submitted a portfolio of poetry and went for an interview at the University of British Columbia's creative writing department. The poet who was the department's poetry professor told me that my work was good and he admitted me to the programme. But he also informed me that my poetry was "excruciatingly female." He said this to a young woman just entering her twenties. I was shocked by his response and decided to continue my B.A. and M.A. studies in literature rather than in creative writing.

In 1976 I attended the writing summer school at the University of Toronto which was organized by Gerald and

Arlene Lampert. There I took a poetry workshop with P.K. Page. This was very unusual, as P.K. did not often teach during that part of her literary career. In fact, I think it was her first experience teaching poetry. This short workshop was of enormous importance to me. While at the summer school, I wrote the following poem for P.K. Page:

> Walking along a crowded
> Toronto street
> this poet
> looks like any other
> middle-aged woman
> striding to market
> in a contemporary world
>
> But she is the crossroad
> of the four paths
> the ancients knew
> In her mind are all
> the unsolved riddles
> of the past
> As she walks
> she answers them
> one by one
> poems dropping from her purse
> like loose change   (*Giant Canadian Poetry Annual* 1977)

P.K. Page was elegant, artistic, and a brilliant poet. I was twenty-nine years old when I met her. I was juggling M.A. studies, teaching work, and a poetry career-along with my personal life as a mother, a wife, a daughter, a sister, a friend. Although I had encountered outstanding teachers and professors, most were male. And, although I had read the modernist poets and attended readings by many contemporary American and Canadian poets, something was still missing. There was a piece of the puzzle that was crucial for me to find, in order for me to stand on my own ground, as a poet, a woman, and a Canadian writer. In meeting P.K. Page I at last found a female role model. P.K. was in her late fifties and coming more fully into her own as a poet than ever before. She has continued to blossom, grow, develop and publish, from her mid-fifties, well into her eighties. When I first encountered P.K. I was immediately struck by her. She was, quite simply, beautiful. When she performed in public she had a distinct speaking voice; her clothes were dramatic, as were her large, silver jewelry pieces. There was nothing apologetic or retiring about P.K . She was feminine in an expressive way and forceful as a poet. P.K. lived very much in the world of the imagination and confirmed the poetic, the imaginal, the artist's vision, despite the other life roles she actively participated in.

The workshop I took with her was comprised of only five or six students. P.K. was candid and open. She explained to us that she was neither teacher nor scholar, but rather a poet and artist. Meeting P.K. in this intimate forum became a turning point for me: through this woman poet I finally understood how I, too, could combine my personal life, in which I lived out many roles as a woman, with my poetic life, which I had embraced from very early on.

I remember being transported into that distinct world of poetry when P.K. Page gave an evening poetry reading during the summer school session. She read the poem "Phone Call from Mexico." She spoke to the audience about how personal and difficult the subject matter was for her. P.K.'s reading of the poem was dramatic, memorable, and moving. Here are excerpts from this poem, which introduced me in an intimate way to the incomparable work of P.K. Page:

Over the years your
voice weeping
telling me you are old
have lost your mind
and all the winds and waters of
America
sound in your words

I see your house
a square-cut topaz set
within a larger square
tangle of garden
walled
Brick walks
wild dahlias
raspberry canes and dogs
Raised ladies' flowerbeds
crammed with mignonettes
lobelias
little red-eyes
all the buzz
and hum of summer
. . . .
A phone call
will not do
cannot give comfort can
not thorns extract
nor antidote
force down
Over this distance
cannot touch your hand

What impressed me most about P.K. Page at the time of taking the workshop with her, was her insistence on the value of the poem itself. Both poet and artist were alive within her, bringing her experiences and ideas vividly into language or painting, but it was primarily as a poet that P.K. affirmed the life of the imagination.

She gave simple writing exercises to the class members—ones that I continued to use when I taught workshops to students in schools. P.K.'s poetry—crafted, visual, expressive—became an influence in my work that until writing this essay, I had really taken for granted. One exercise that P.K. gave the students was to take a single word that had both concrete and emotional content, and to build a short poem around that word. In 1985 my book, *Compendium,* was published by Heron Press in Vancouver. This book contains short, lyric poems that use language in a tightly compressed metaphorical way, perhaps partly inspired by those writing exercises given by P.K. Page. Several of the poems from *Compendium* were later set to music by classical composer Mark Armanini and performed live and broadcast.

P.K. Page was the first "real-life" Canadian woman poet who inspired and encouraged me. She embodied all the modernist American and British women poets I had read on my own, but had not met in the flesh. P.K. Page wrote to me, when I was still a young poet, struggling with the artistic process and coming to terms with my own poetic voice. Here is a sample of P.K.'s supportive encouragement:

I'm much impressed by your book. Read it on the ferry coming back. Some excellent poems and those curious cool pieces of prose. I sense a big talent in you. Today the new poem. Beautiful. I'm so pleased if in some way I helped its release. And thank you for responding so warmly to my new work ...

In 1977, I founded Caitlin Press in Vancouver. After the first year, I managed the press along with poet Cathy Ford and editor Ingrid Klassen, and then in later years by myself. It was the first literary small press in British Columbia, founded and run solely by women. We published poetry chapbooks, and books of poetry and fiction. I sold Caitlin Press in 1991, and the press was relocated to Prince George, where it became the literary small press of northern British Columbia.

In 1978, I joined the League of Canadian Poets and attended my first annual general meeting in Montreal. Ken Norris, Cathy Ford, and I were the youngest new members. F.R. Scott was at that gathering, as were other well-known Canadian poets such as Louis Dudek, Milton Acorn, and Miriam Waddington.

It was a wonderful experience to be in Montreal, the city of poets. By then I had published my first two poetry chapbooks. At one point in the course of the weekend, Dorothy Livesay came up to me, cupped my face in both her hands, and began talking to me. She told me I was a beautiful young poet—and then she began to argue with me about my poems! That was Dee, generous in her support, her passion, her willingness to argue poetry. I never met Dorothy, ever, at one of her own poetry readings, or at formal or informal literary events, when her passionate being was not a hundred per cent present, and open to anyone who needed her.

Whenever I think of Dorothy Livesay, I always hear her lyric poem, "The Unquiet Bed" echo within me. This poem epitomized Dorothy—she was more than just a poet, activist, mother, wife, friend—she was a force.

Dorothy Livesay was a powerful and outspoken personality. She had travelled, taught, founded a literary periodical, been active in Canadian politics, and published her poetry throughout her whole life. Dorothy was not afraid to talk about sexual desire, or about literary ambition and rivalries. Once I sat with Dee at the Governor General Literary Awards where Earl Birney was addressing the audience. Throughout the formal ceremonies, Dorothy kept up a running diatribe against Earl Birney. As a much younger poet, I was both shocked and entertained by Dorothy's behaviour. But what Dee really did during that event was treat me as an equal, at the same time as she challenged the status quo, and this helped me to learn to question, take risks, and not to be afraid to be myself. And the passionate sexuality expressed from a female point of view in her mid-life poems was liberating, provocative, honest:

> The woman I am
> is not what you see
> I'm not just bones
> and crockery
>
> . . . .
>
> the woman I am
> knew love and hate
>
> . . . .
>
> the woman I am
> is not what you see
> move over love
> make room for me

Dorothy actively mentored and encouraged other women poets. She was generous with her opinions—whether solicited or not! But she was also generous with her time, and with her talent. She had a sure lyric voice in her best poems, some of which were unabashedly "female."

As woman poet role models, P.K. Page and Dorothy Livesay were certainly very different from each other, both in their lifestyles and their poetry and their politics. For me, as a younger woman poet by more than thirty years, but also from the west coast, I could not have asked for richer, more fertile poetic ground in which to grow my own work. Dorothy, as outspoken feminist and political activist, was at the other end of the spectrum from P.K. who lived in a different social class and who never defined herself as a feminist.

Around the same time that I joined the League of Canadian Poets, and met Dorothy Livesay, I was also introduced to Marya Fiamengo. Patrick Lane told me there was someone he wanted me to meet, and he took me to Marya Fiamengo's West Vancouver home. It was filled with books and had incredible art on the walls, many of those works were paintings by Joe Plaskett, her lifelong friend. And Marya was a jewel at the centre—larger than life, brimming over with ideas, with hospitality, and with poetry. Marya became a close personal friend. As a woman poet twenty years older than me, she was an inspiration. Marya's encouragement, along with her critical ear, helped to keep me writing, despite a very difficult period in my life when other responsibilities threatened to overwhelm me. Marya had a real passion for living; it was expressed in her love of ideas, her love of teaching, entertaining, and her love for her country.

Marya was a professor in the English department at the University of British Columbia. Many times over the years I read to Marya's classes—it was always obvious that her students loved her teaching and her presence. Marya Fiamengo published several collections of poetry, plus numerous reviews of poetry books. She was a fastidious reviewer—always trying to maintain a critical ear, balanced with encouragement for younger poets. She often read me the reviews aloud, and I read the poetry books along with her. Marya shared with me her Dalmatian heritage, in her poems as well as in her stories and anecdotes.

Marya Fiamengo loved to travel across Canada giving poetry readings; she was an ardent federalist and a proud defender of our country. During the years when I was a partner with graphic artist and poet Ed Varney in the small press The Poem Factory, we published poetry broadsides and chapbooks. One of the poetry broadsides we published was the articulate poem by Marya Fiamengo, entitled "Hobotnica (The Octopus)." Marya's parents were from Dalmatia. Her father and uncle were fishers, as was her son later on. They became part of Canadian society, whereas Marya's mother never assimilated into her new language. Marya translated for her mother, and wrote poems that reflected her dual legacy, representing her Dalmatian heritage and her own country, Canada, where Marya was born.

In the poem, "Hobotnica (The Octopus)," later reprinted in her book *White Linen Remembered,* Fiamengo's visual and economical use of language brings to life her mother's youth, back in Dalmatia, catching an octopus for the family's evening meal. It is written with tender love and an eye for the details of living. Here is an excerpt from the longer poem:

> I recall
> my mother
> leaning
> on a withered
> wooden fence.
> Her kerchief
> like the fabric
> of her country
> torn.
>
> She speaks
> of her youth.
> How as a very
> young girl, a child

almost
she walked
to the sea
at the end
of her garden.

Walked to where
in the clear
water swam
the octopus, the innocent
hobotnica.

She dips
a dazzle
of white linen
into the pristine blue
of the Adriatic
making a blaze
of whiteness
enticing the pink
and white
sea creature
into its milky
folds.

Artless
he swims
into the crystal
cream of its weave.

Triumphant
she holds him
fast.

Ties a swift
knot.
Takes him home
for the family
evening meal. ("Hobotnica")

By the 1980s, I had published several chapbooks and also full-length poetry books. I was running Caitlin Press, serving on the national council for the League of Canadian Poets, and raising my two children. I helped to found the B.C. Book Prizes and the Federation of B.C. Writers. It was a full life—both on the home front, and with my own poetry; and on a national level, traveling, doing work for literary organizations, and giving poetry readings. The legacy of P.K. Page, Dorothy Livesay, and Marya Fiamengo was alive, and thriving. They had shone a beacon of light for me to follow—giving me the affirmation I had needed—that is, that it was possible to balance the life of poetry with that of being female.

In the 1980s in Vancouver, I was part of an ongoing poetry workshop. We were all women, we met once a month at each other's homes, and we workshopped our poetry together. Among the women who were part of this poetry workshop over the years, were Jean Mallinson, Elizabeth Gourlay, and Anne Marriott. It was a great privilege to work with Anne Marriott on such an intimate, creative level. She was definitely a sustaining force for me. Here was a woman who had raised children, had a fulfilling marriage, written all her life, and who was what Jungian analyst Jean Shinoda Bolen would call "a juicy crone!" Anne was enjoying a re-entry into her own writing, a second flowering in her later years as a widow. She was intellectually alive and growing—writing, traveling, savouring the poetic process.

Anne Marriott was a writer with a diverse range of work. When she was not writing poetry, in her middle years, Anne wrote journalism, scripts, a collections of short stories, an unpublished children's novel, among other writing projects, not all of which saw their way into publication before her untimely stroke. Anne Marriott possessed a creative energy that spilled out in several directions. For some years, poetry took a back seat to "living." Anne devoted those years to raising three children and to her marriage. She also lived in Ottawa and Montreal, and worked for the National Film Board writing film scripts. The poems Anne Marriott worked on during the years I took part in the writing workshop with her were marvelous poems. I remember fondly being able to share in their creative birthing. Anne Marriott was definitely both a poet and a human being—her humanity shines through in the poems. Anne had many dimensions and aspects to her sensibility and to her writing.

Anne Marriott was working on the poems that would be later published in *Aqua*, by Wolsak and Wynn, Toronto, 1991. We workshopped several poems from this collection, including the long title poem, and shorter poems including "Sunken Cities," "The Lake," and a personal favourite of mine, "Living Under Water."

Although Anne lived in several parts of Canada and her award-winning second book of poems featured a poem about the prairies, Anne Marriott was born in Victoria. As I was born in Vancouver, we both expressed a love for the west coast, for camping and enjoying the sensuous beauty of the coastal landscape. I could readily identify with the poems that Anne Marriott was writing and workshopping with us in the writing group. I, too, also wrote long poems and so it was fascinating to share with Anne in the process of the long poem "Aqua" as she fine-tuned and revised it. This poem records a time of psychic journey, through the story of a camping experience in the wilderness she and her husband took together. Growing up on the west coast, the sense of wilderness and coastal remoteness was also a part of my own poetic sensibility; in all, Anne Marriott was a poet whose work spoke eloquently to me, from an older west coast poet to a younger one.

Looking back, I now see those later poems by Anne Marriott as having a sense of prophetic feeling—her last years of silence are somehow eerily evoked in these 'watery' poems, that contain such a degree of awareness of the depth of the unconscious mind. Here are excerpts from "Living Under Water":

First the plunge (escape)
sinking down into the cold
green, surprised perhaps
how cold the green is
and how dark
growing darker as it deepens
almost black
when one gets to the secret sea-bed.
One sees at length
scraped out on a stone
between the barnacles
by some earlier diver
There shall be no light here.

. . . .

A flash of phosphorescence
can make it seem worthwhile
for a few minutes, and the quiet
and seclusion (what one came down for)
then one happens
to drift upward
see the shadow of a ship.
Forgotten pictures form
behind watery eyes:
sunlight in cobalt sky
over golden fields, sparkling—
but deadly now. Beached
one could only gasp and shrivel.

This process cannot be reversed. (*Aqua* 14-15)

Writing this essay has made me more aware of the tradition that informs my writing. As an expression of gratitude for the creative example of my Canadian poetic foremothers, I include in closing new poems from a poetry manuscript in progress, entitled "the moon with mars in her arms." These are poems written at the mid-life stage P.K. Page was in when I first met her. My new poems reflect both personal experience and current world events. As always in my work, I strive to move from the intimate to the archetypal, and from the concrete to the visionary.

By way of introduction to these poems I want to add a fifth "foremother." I never met Pat Lowther, a woman poet who was also from the west coast. Lowther is from a generation in between myself and the modernist poets I have identified in this essay, but she was also an influence on my writing. Pat Lowther wrote intensely about the coast and directly out of her own personal perceptions, with breathtaking clarity. Unfortunately, Pat Lowther was killed before I joined the League of Canadian Poets, and I never had a chance to meet her or hear her read her poems to an audience. She had just begun teaching at the creative writing department of the University of British Columbia, shortly before her death. Had Pat Lowther lived, and had I been just slightly different in age, I could possibility have encountered her as the poetry professor, when I was still a young woman developing my own poetic voice. That, however, would have been a different story than the one I have told here.

Living In Exile
Carolyn Zonailo

But we were wrong and the map was true
and had we stood and looked about
from our height of land, we'd have had a view
which, since, we have had to learn by heart.

(P.K. Page "The Map")

We are living in exile, the snow deep
and icicles like swords of barbarians,
frost covering the window, intricate lace,
the air so cold it burns my lungs

70

cutting deep into airways too sensitive
to breathe in this frozen land. Through
weeks of winter we have lost our bearings,
the compass needle set to a northern point,
the afternoon sky already turning away from blue—
but we were wrong and the map was true.

This is the exact spot we were meant
to inhabit, arriving—despite the blinding storm—
to this place, to call this home, forgetting
where we came from or want to travel to.
It is here and only here, at half past midnight
when it is below twenty degrees out
and the fields sleep under their blanket of snow,
the dairy cows housed in their barns, walls cracking
with frozen night sounds, minds resting from doubt.
And had we stood and looked about

the land as it lay around our white, wooden
farmhouse, circa 1880, in the darkness
of this January night, the sky so clear with stars,
everything frozen and still and silhouetted
under the light of a full moon glistening,
the snow glistening, the sparks that flew
from our wood stove briefly suspended in the air
as if brightly frozen—we would have held
each other in a warm embrace and felt new.
From our height of land, we'd have had a view

of the Trout River, a layer of snow over ice
with footprints down the middle of the river
where we had walked earlier in the daylight.
Living in exile, we have made love in the heat
of summer, in this same slow, shallow river.
We thought we longed to stay, as in the start,
in bodies that would be forever young, in seasons
that were not winter, in places that were
not exile, but homes created by family and art,
which, since, we have had to learn by heart.

Huntingdon, Quebec, 1992-1997

My Body Is Also A Map

Carolyn Zonailo

The first time I almost left my body
I went quietly. You dropped me
at the hospital ER
and drove to the airport
to catch a plane.
It happened so quickly
I forgot to cry out loud or protest.
There were no angels hovering.
Later on, during the weeks it took
for my lungs to expel stale air,
unbidden messages came to me
at unexpected times, in various ways.
Once I was standing
on the metro platform, people
all around, the loud roar
of the train entering the station
when suddenly a voice spoke.
And still later, when I was walking
uphill in pale, spring sunshine,
forcing myself to breathe and walk,
again a voice assailed me.
I got used to hearing messages,
prayers, whispers of mortality.
I even learned to breathe again
and gradually lost the sensation
of being underwater and drowning.
I came back to live in the climate and air
humans have long since adapted to.

I began to understand the map
my body had become—this road
leading to a known destination
or a secret passage of the heart;
another artery leading out toward
the cosmos, immortality, and the limits
of knowledge. After all, the body
is where we live, it can be read
like the palm of one's hand
when placed face up
in front of a skilled practitioner.

The second time I was even more
nonchalant, doing the dishes
en route to the emergency room,
taking time to organize household chores
on my way to the other world.
Curious how calmly it happened,
like a camera running everything
in slow motion, each gesture distinct.
There were no voices, messages, glimpses
of heaven or hell—in fact the whole thing
as if another one of life's daily tasks—
straightening up, I'll be back soon,
tonight's dinner is in the fridge.
The road map of my body leading
to the common place, the everyday,
the quotidian feat of staying
incarnated. As if it's all that simple,
the internal compass pointed "to life"
rather than "to spirit." And then
a slow recovery, no messages to guide me
as the known was definitely left behind,
the map a crisscrossing of valleys,
mountain peaks, unnamed rivers,
the everyday become a wilderness.

This is the first poem
I have written since then,
when the map veered off
into unknown territory,
the sheer sides of mountains
sheets of rock, the valleys green
and lush beyond springtime,
the river a dazzling golden colour.
Here is a poetic utterance
spoken like a primal scream
from a poet who lives in a place of exile,
in a body that is also a map.

Courage Is a Transitive Verb

Susan McMaster

THERE WAS A point when every book I bought or borrowed was by a Canadian, a woman, a poet. Just kept gravitating that way. P.K. Page, Elizabeth Brewster, Dorothy Livesay, Miriam Waddington, Phyllis Webb, Mimi Mandel. What they said seemed to cut right through all the guff. Directly. Speak *to* me, not around me. It didn't surprise me that they were a full generation older. My mother was (and still is) the most intense and remarkable conversationalist I knew, the most intimate and creative—though in the way of daughters I'd stopped telling her everything when I hit about age fifteen. Now here, in these explosive paper packages were women like that, women I could talk to in my mind, listen to for hours, whose spoken voice I could hear right through the covers. In the middle of masculinist romanticism (barbed and Marxist or sappily pedestaline, it all seemed unattached to me), someone said what it actually felt like. I began to carve out my own words. Started a magazine—*Branching Out,* a national feminist arts and literary bi-monthly published out of Edmonton from 1973-80—that some of them generously contributed to. Amazing. Elizabeth Brewster, who actually lived down the street, took the time to say kind and heartening words about my first crude efforts and where I might arrive if I kept at it for twenty years.

So I continued to sing. Somehow, no matter how I strove to match the genteelly abstracted and rigorously unconstructed ideal poem presented in my university courses, my own verses kept falling into that old folk-song form, the quatrain. Sometimes they even rhymed. Ah, but that was alright, Jay Macpherson's did too, she of the snake poem— "Come all old maids who are squeamish / and afraid to marry snakes. / Don't clutter your lives up with boyfriends: / the nicest girls marry snakes ..."(Macpherson 22)—which I still recite in full at gentrifical parties.

Somewhere along the line I discovered P.K. Page was also P.K. Irwin, the artist. With no talent myself for drawing, still I saw every word in vivid visuals—the letters themselves, the colours and images that cloaked and expanded them. Her "filled pen ... eager to draw again ... the rarely glimpsed bright face / behind the apparency of things" made the link for me between what I saw in my mind's eye and how I could express it (Page 102). Later I met Anne Szumigalski, who mixed her words—fragments, whole paragraphs of conversation—with music, dance, theatre, any medium that came to hand, all built on an unshakable structure of powerful, interlinked diction: "shrapnel has torn the man's rib's apart / there is a shabby wound in his breast / his mouth opens innocently upon a cry" (Szumigalski 112). And later yet I found the work and wisdom of Elyse Yates St. George— "This one, we say / will not accept the pen / but rams us hard, twisting this way and that, worrying / herself wild"—another poet-artist who moves between the modes without seeing a real difference (St. George 74).

74

Which made sense to me. The lullabies I made up for my babies were poems too, weren't they? The books I stapled together in the absence of any big-name publisher rushing to rescue me from the soda counter required art and hand-crafting and all that stuff. Already I knew, from my artist mother, that you can make anything with your hands if you figure out how to do it and work hard enough. And that the best sound is overlapping voices full of vitality, agreement, laughter, the next story—the voices of friends and lovers in full conversational flight. The joining of things together seemed and still seems natural to me. And joining in creation the best.

What did they mean to me three decades ago, these Modernist women, as I now see they can be called—passionate, open, searching, considering, rejecting, declaring meaning and importance everywhere? Declaring in full-throated, clear sentences the vital need to record and weave the babel of communications blanketing and stuffing our ears into some kind of sense?

They meant making. Not sitting and waiting for someone to tell you what it was all about, but to declare, to find, to search for that integration yourself in whatever corner and with whatever tool came to hand. My mother was deaf in one ear, so I learned about gestures, reading faces, turning *toward* not hunching away or covering your mouth with a hand. These poets, not poetesses (and yes, that word was current then), were not all pretty in an era when prettiness was the essential survival trait, the highest female value. They grinned and didn't care. They faced you straight on. They stomped and ranted and lusted and exulted without apology, showing—proving—that the doing, in and of itself, meant and means something. All of it—word to word, ear to ear, heart to heart, dishpan hand to dishpan hand. And they wrote about it, the whole kit and caboodle, not just the "poetic" parts. They refused to speak in the respectful and abstracted intellectual mode then fashionable. Their words were as narrative and pungent and humorous as my mother's ever-changing red soup. Elizabeth Brewster: "I have never taken any drug / stronger than aspirin. / I have never been more than slightly drunk. / ... / If I wanted to be fucked / I should probably choose a different word. / (Anyhow, I am not quite sure / whether it is a transitive or an intransitive verb, because it was never given to me to parse)" (Brewster 87).

They talked about children and domestica as if they mattered. Miriam Waddington: "Last spring I wished / for myself a full-grown garden ... I hacked away in my backlot / to the heart of North America / (virgin stone dammit) until my hands / trembled with failure; then I cried / as bitterly as a nine-year-old" (Waddington 118); or Phyllis Webb: "at five o'clock today Alex four years old said / I will draw a picture of you / at first he gave me no ears and I said / you should give me ears / I would like big ears one on each side / and he added them and three buttons down the front ..." (Webb 118).

They addressed men in sexy ways I'd never even mouthed—but loved. Dorothy Livesay: "Let your hand play first / fanning small fires / over arms, the breasts / ... till the whole body flowering ... / shudders wildly out," and "The hard core of love / is only muscle, thrust," and "The record of all our nights / is on these sheets" (Livesay np). Yeah!

Lots of pain and dark: Mimi Mandel: "I hear the doors clang shut / the constant turning of keys / the turning of people in sleep / and the closed lock of my heart turns" (Mandel 22). But then I felt that too.

Lots of anger. Phyllis Webb: "Sprouts the bitter grain in my heart / green and fervent it grows ... / Even the crows ... / scream and collect the glittering fires / of my hatreds, dispose this desperate love, / my fury, amid the sinister leaves" (Webb 72). And P.K. again: "Go out of your mind. / Prepare to go mad. / Prepare to break / split along cracks / inhabit the darks of your eyes / inhabit the whites" (Page 101). Well of course.

But mostly vitality. Mostly thinking it mattered. Above all, paying attention. Courage to speak out, to speak the truth, that came half from unfailing love and half from rage—the coeur de rage. Grabbing whatever medium came to hand—cloth, flour, soap carvings, children's leftover paints. And the most secret and available of all, words scratched on scraps of paper while ironing or shopping, tucked in a pocket.

I've gone on to mix words and music and art and even dance and theatre from time to time, always holding tight to the belief that mine and these other mothers taught me in the power of meaningful content, in the danger and exultation of true speaking, in the need for work, hard, hard work. In taking what comes to your *own hand* and *making* with it.

With courage. Because, sometimes, speaking even one true word can save a life. *Envoi*

The poem I read as my entry piece into the League of Canadian Poets in 1988 was "Courage / Coeur de rage," half silence—sign and gesture, the poetry of the deaf—and half song, whisper, shout. I wrote it thinking of my mother, and at that reading dedicated it without a moment's pause to Elizabeth Brewster, who was there in the audience, as she had promised she would be, paying attention. "I'm interested in these," she wrote in response to my unpublished poems in 1971, "but I can't tell whether you're a poet yet, or not. Come back in twenty years." Demanding meaning in return. Later, my mother used the skill of her own hand to imitate my gestures (in pictographs drawn loosely from American Sign Language) for the page, so the poem could be published in the radical feminist and multicultural Canadian magazine *(m)Öthêr Tøñguès*. This year again it's been published in *Line by Line,* by Heather Spears. In the intervening decades I've performed it as wordmusic in a trio of voices with First Draft poet Colin Morton, and recently as a bassoon/spoken voice duet with Dave Broscoe; another version with five musicians will soon appear on the next Geode Music & Poetry CD. The piece won't lie down and shut up. I offer it to this gathering of words as a tribute, and thank you. And accompany it with a more recent full-throated yell in "Howl"—another kind of thank you, for the free voice.

Courage / *Cœur de rage*

Susan McMaster

A tribute to my mother, artist Betty Page—
in words and *silence,* GESTURE *and stillness,*
eye and ear. Ottawa 1985/99

Voice	Gesture (ASL, freely interpreted)	

(Performed together. Blank spaces indicate silence [left] or still hands [right]. Each line is two slow beats.)

Voice	Gesture	
	COURAGE	COURAGE
	COURAGE	COURAGE
See our age.	C OUR	AGE
See		OUR AGE
Our age—*ou rage.*	HOUR	STORM
Our care—core—cure.	CENTRE	CURE
Curse! *Orage!*	CURSE	*ORAGE*
	CURSE	*ORAGE*
If oh you are gone—	O YOU R	NOT
	O YOU R	NOT
what our-less cage.	OUR NOT	CAGE
Bring back are—		R
what arc, grace.	ARC	GRACE
	ARC	GRACE
How to choose among so many? DO NOT KNOW		
Seize the page.	GRASP	BOOK
All lines are self-limned . . .	WRITE	PAGE
Courage—	COURAGE	
Heart's rage!	COEUR	DE RAGE
	(double-handed gesture)	

HOWL

Susan McMaster

I heard you howl
from the shaft to the roof
a whistle or train
foghorn
storm
O it rose till it knocked at the beams
you threw your mouth
open to the sky
eyes closed only sound
vibrating like bone
as the mountain fell
o - o - o - o - O - O
and so wide at the end
the air rushed in
walls shook and caved
cracks rent stone
wind rushed through
wind blew me down
while you stood and blew
were blown by sound
blew and the walls
shook and stood
stood and stand
and nothing fell
in the end not you
nothing but me
blasted to all fours
hooted to the ground
the wind blew out
you rocked and stood
and stood
and stand
rocked off your feet
rocked empty
dumb
still you stand
as silence sucks in

(Regenerations, or)
Not asleep but not talking/ in/ A shared room
or
A room of our own is a myth

Margaret Christakos

ART ONE

Have you seen the new film by Catherine Breillat, *A Ma Soeur?* Its English release title is *Fat Girl*. This film is astonishing. There are three central figures, a mother and two adolescent daughters. The mother, played by Arsinee Khanjian, is stylish, aloof, sexually contained and evidently content with her curt businessman husband. They are on the classic French summer vacation. There is no surfeit of fondness between the mother and her two daughters. The mother is clearly apart from them, an adult, almost another species, whose gaze only flickers over the surface of the daughters' bodies and judges them according to image. The older daughter looks very much like her dark-haired sensuous flamboyant mother; she accepts the script that it is time for her to be initiated sexually and actively pursues the attention of boys, for her own pleasure, but *chiefly* to humiliate her younger, fat sister, who is brainy, wry, ironically self-loathing and the constant companion, indeed the charge, of her older sister. Their relationship is extremely s & m in the manner of many young girls' friendships. Highly competitive with one self-effacing but prescient, submissive, pandering to and flattering a vain clueless dominant, who is the more dependent on the terms of the attachment for a sense of self. Without the object of humiliation she would herself have to address her own imperfection. She is like the mother because the other girl is not at all like the mother. She is liked by the mother; the fat girl is a wretch and therefore condescendingly adored by both for this abject subjection. Several scenes show the fat young girl stuffing her face with food and the sister and mother looking on approvingly. Poor wretch, that is the only way she can find comfort, or love, because no one will love her, except for us, we love her, the poor wretch.

In this movie the fifteen-year-old sister does indeed bag a boy, an attractive college-aged playboy who reads the situation immediately; this pretty virgin will put up a fight, but is fuckable. There ensues a scene in the middle of the film in which the girl has snuck the boyfriend into her room, and they are making out in her bed. The younger sister is in this room, in her own bed on the other side of the room. The older sister orders her to go to sleep, to not eavesdrop. She has told the sister she will "give herself" to this boy. During an extended scene in which the most mundane script of sentimental rape occurs, the helplessly awake younger sister writhes and stifles the contradictory field of her reactions under a pillow: shock and desire, grief and scandal, anger and embarrassment, and we are thrown back onto the contradictions of our own voyeurship.

It would seem that it deeply matters how close one is to the subject to feel what is at stake.

It would seem the degree of detachment and attachment we feel to our sisters and mothers is not the product of one emotional shift or achievement or trauma.

Each of us has both ogled and rationalized away the damage done to another woman, for fulfillment of the romantic script.

Now this film ends with the most astounding and brutal scene, in which, of this classic female triad, the good fat ignored sister does not turn into a slender princess and marry the prince and move to the castle, instead she is the only survivor of a horrendous attack. You must see the film before I talk more about it, but its effect is to smash a script. Perhaps the mundane is the site of real violence. Perhaps when we speak in the uninterrogated plots of the everyday we are supporting the deepest violations among us.

PART TWO

The reason I want to talk about mothers and daughters now is that we are talking about motherhood and the idea of lineage, that we are dancing at the base of a belief in the natural order of passage from mother to, in this case, daughter. But when has a transfer of daringness ever been the character of mother-daughter passages?

Are we not much more experienced in the disavowals of daringness from one generation toward the preceding generation?

Generally we do not see our mothers as daring except in how our received notions of their lives dare us to live, or in this case, write, differently. Mothers are not generally sexual creatures upon whom we can affix our adoring gaze and eroticize, which I think is what happens when we take literary heroines. They are more like the wildly daring older girl cousin, related to the family but apart from it, the first adventurers from the extended family into the world, whom we watch having known them as young teenagers and whom we've watched grow to full-fledged women. I think I have been attracted to women writers who are either two full generations back or who are part of a staggered generational distance, like Brossard and Mouré and Scott, who are sexy and daring and radical because they are not maternal figures to me. I watched them emerge onto the scene. I am not inclined to smash them down, as I admit I would a mother figure. I am inclined to want them like inaccessible lovers, though, rather voyeuristically and voraciously.

But this *is* the voraciousness of the daughter toward the mother, isn't it, to desire her, to want to become her? This seems a suitable point of entry for a discussion of influence, for the flux of desire inherent in this relation between generations does not move in one direction. There is much talk about the daughter's disavowal of the mother, but what of the mother's avowal of herself to herself, which may come in a form of disavowal of the daughter, or an avowal of the daughter not to any other, but to herself? To autonomy, agency, independence, self-possession?

I think these really are questions of the relationship between the daughter and the mother-artist. Since we are discussing literary lineage, we can centrally discuss the contradictory scenario of the mother-artist's need for independence, space, time, etc. When I was in my early twenties, a young artist, I chose to have an abortion; after this very difficult experience my mother actually came to Montreal to see if I was all right. She tended to me in a way she had not since I was a very little child. No, it's not true, I couldn't remember her ever just being present to tend to me; there were always the siblings and of course her full time job out of the house. And she did not look after me in Montreal, she just came. But it was significant that she did come.

Today, I have three children. My daily lived sense of my four-year-old daughter replaying so much of my own physical and emotional self is very very tender and allusive all the time now. It is as if I have myself running at my feet, which I do not feel at all with my two boys. They are of me, but she seems to be both herself and me. There is a physical resemblance between us, but it is more of a memory I am replenishing of how utterly sentient I felt in my own body when I was that young. When I was a girl, waiting in many ways for my mother. And because she was not there, becoming an understudy to the real understudy, my older, fatter sister.

You know as well as I do that it is almost blasphemous to use that word, fat. So unlike the word today, *wide*. What if the conference was Fatter Boundaries of Daring? I am trying it out, trying to figure it out.

Also recently I am conjuring the subject of where my writing voice comes from. From my first writings to my present work, but particularly my first book, *Not Egypt*. A book I disavowed and have revisited, and now see more fully. Partly this is the question under discussion here: what are our influences?

As a child I was not read to. I was put to bed and left, like most kids in the 60s. In the space of not being read to and dreading the onset of sleep in darkness, itself very frightening, which produces an erotics of nostalgia in itself, there is also the strategic response of motion. Gail Scott wrote of this predicament in *Main Brides:* "Precisely at the moment the body sinks into sleep, this starts, this panic rising from the stomach, waking her again. No amount of self-willed resistance seems to stop it. As long as conscious, she can maintain order in her mind. But at the point where wake concedes to sleep, that inner voice she's fighting to keep down, with such plucky determination, surfaces, crying: 'I'm betrayed, I'm abandoned.'"

But I was not really ever alone, either. I did not have my own room. So in my case, a connection of daring the onset of sleep was through masturbating (otherwise I thought I would die), but with extreme constraint, for my sister was across the room on the other side of a commode (which was placed there to represent a wall), and also I was aware of my mother alone on the other side of the wall. A twin awareness of their bodies alone, one to either side, for my father slept in the basement and my brothers slept in their room which my own did not border. I was always really ashamed about the failure of my parents' marriage, but now of course I know it is really a very common thing for couples to stop sleeping together. No one likes to talk about it and besides it is held to be better for the children to stay together no matter how painful the marriage becomes. So every night, I would lie there not sleeping, terrified my lungs would freeze, feeling a surreal separateness from yet connectedness to my mother and my by-now sound-asleep sister, both very present in my self-comforting, or rather represented the condition of shame passed down.

I wrote some really strange unconscious things in my first book *Not Egypt* about this scene. The female narrator is addressing a male lover who has abandoned her, and after summarizing this boy's potential for violence, she depicts him dancing in a nightclub with his arms outstretched. But: "A cold wind takes back this image. And darkness: seals the muscular pact in your neck." Then his torn torso becomes a wounded organic-architectural structure inside of which or whom the narrator finds herself:

> She sees in the long join, she finds herself, her body, discomfitting naked with lovers at night, searching the entranceways back to her child self, that body she rocked desire in and out of, that soft skin she touched every night to locate self in a household of contradictions. What are the things she places alongside those lips, what are the memories she reproduces in this adult bed, this new ridged vagina she finds in her, me, in you, these structures ... This place her body she knew as [... a] wound in darkness touching itself, and in this she had to locate pleasure, her pleasure in touching, but always the site of the wound which could not convince love and abhorrence from each other's spasm. (*Not Egypt* 78-79)

Also I grew up watching TV, endless episodic, serial sit-com TV, in the basement, on a couch, with my father and brothers and sister, waiting for my mother to come home from work. She was never home for dinner, which I and my sister took turns making. It was a typical girlhood of the late 60s and 70s, when mom had found a room of her own by getting the hell out of the house, having to in order to help support the family, and the rooms of the house were in spite of her. She did not get to be the artist. This is an important influence on my work.

Here is a quote someone just sent me from a promo blurb on a press release about an upcoming reading by Anne Carson: "As members of human society, perhaps the most difficult task we face daily is that of touching one another—whether the touch is physical, moral, emotional or imaginary. Contact is crisis." Supposedly Anne herself said or wrote this, but two things strike me about it. First, the person who forwarded it to me is someone I very badly want to touch and should not because I am partnered; and second, that of all of the women writers whose work I like, Anne Carson's has seemed to me to be the most cerebral, the very least about touch. Maybe because she knows contact is crisis.

Crisis is the site of daringness unfolding to action.

Feminism is in crisis because feminism has broken through and now we as its subjects must act. This is why wider and boundaries and daring as the three terms under discussion here keep puzzling me so. From my book *Not Egypt:* "The relationship is a triangular web sewn into the hollow between brains, directly behind the bridge of the nose. Light sifts through it as if a screen hovers, half-pulled." (22)

Yes, this gathering of women and texts is a web and a screen and a hollow and more than a half of something. It seems so self-restraining. It keeps revoking its own possibilities, like a dazzling leap stifled mid-air by the sudden thickening of the air itself.

I keep hearing it as the Wider Daring of Boundaries. As in: To dare a boundary to shift, perhaps to attenuate (like a stretched elastic band) or to thicken (what—like a wound scabbing over and then dropping off? Not pretty but organic and usually successful) or to change consistency, from hard to soft or soft to hard (like forms of cooked and cooled sugar) or to smudge (like evidence of crime messed up, tampered with, to exonerate or complicate traces of consequential action) or to fold back on itself, to invoke and revoke its own reason for boundarying the thing or action it was there to do …

𝒫ART THREE

Revisiting my own influences, I will start with a beautiful tall strange green-eyed woman with wide hips and long skirts who loved the poetry of Musgrave and MacEwen and Marie-Claire Blais. It was 1980 and I had never had a best female friend. This strange beautiful woman dared to roll her green eyes at me from across the boundarying desks of Frank Davey's "Intro to Cdn Poetry" class at York University. I had lived in the same house in Sudbury, Ontario for seventeen years. "And never having seen the body of mother, sister, grandmother, come these inhibitions about writing anything down …" (from my *Other Words for Grace*). I was going to be a visual artist. Frank would read some poetry aloud from *15 Canadian Poets* and then would ratchet his gaze to the large window filled with hedges and sky and gap out for five minutes or so, with the centrifugal intensity of an absinthe drinker. My tall wide-hipped friend would write ardent notes to me and escort me out to the vast field beside the Fine Arts building and compare the modernist minimalist sculptures moored there—which relied largely on thrust and rust for graphic drama—to Celtic runes and witches' covens. Her speech was never natural, it was always "poetic" and strayed frequently to sex and desire and the intense complications the conjunction of these two terms would effect. She was seducing me but not seducing me. Her mystical hypochondriacal poetics converged with the new body-centred video and performance art I was being introduced to, of Suzy Lake, Lisa Steele, Yvonne Rainer, General Idea, Joseph Beuys' allegorical body of felt and fat, Eva Hesse's wax and vellum drawings and sculptures, Frida Kahlo's paintings, plus, after for some time trying to talk boys into it, I finally at age seventeen had sex.

I have to admit I didn't get the animistic forests of Musgrave's work. I sublimated my difference from my friend in ecstatic surrender to Cohen's *Beautiful Losers,* to Ondaatje, and to the idea of the rightness of sex and the body and intense interiority sharing the same room in the house of writing.

By the summer of 1981, I knew text would be central to my art, visual, time-based or otherwise, and lucky for me bpNichol was the second year Poetry instructor. This wide-haired, velour pyjama'd man would dare to place a box of donuts and 2 cans of Coke beside him for the 3-hour afternoon class—now I know it was the year he had a newborn daughter and was probably sleeping very little—but he never looked out the window. He was about presence, and process, language as a bodily act of the voice in the telling, the telling in the voice, of motion, (e)motion, and the moment, the writerly duration of the hours, the sounds that make up words, and unstating the obvious. About putting the I in sentience. About lineage and place. He dropped about a hundred names a class. Stein, Joyce, Bissett, Ginsberg, Marlatt, Warland, Brossard, Dewdney, Coach House Press. He made strong connections to the performance and art worlds, especially Michael Snow, Weiland, of course the Four Horsemen, Gerry Shikatani, Susan McMaster, Karl Jirgens, Meredith Monk, Laurie Anderson, Robert Wilson. The PostPartum Document. Connections to the art of Diane Arbus, Cindy Sherman, the Guerrilla Girls, Nancy Spero, Irene Whittome. I'm pretty sure he in some way introduced me to Kathy Acker's work. It seemed as if the culture was literally teeming with smart original writers whose influences and interdisciplinary expressions were web-like and whose engaged experimental formalism and subjects of interest cross-generated new, ever more inquisitive, work. The palpable relevance of gender to the writing act, making both art history and social representation grounds for unwriting and rewriting gave me purchase on the fullness of my own voice. Also lullaby and song and noise. There were tremendous poetry marathons at downtown clubs and many poets performed new work for the occasion, and like a James Benning film or a Chantal Akerman film, much of it tested the endurance of the listener. The experience for both performer and listener was actively immersive and interrogative and often very fun or weird or both.

(I have not mentioned who I should mention.)

But in my third year the elf-like enthusiast of Canadian modernism Eli Mandel would bring in a book of poetry a week and shake his glinting wide eyes and gleam "Astonishing!" He would gaze at all of us and then repeat "Astonishing!" Phyllis Webb's *Wilson's Bowl* was one of these books. He was so damned excited about the work of his contemporaries! Among those he mentioned a lot were Waddington, Atwood, Page, Marlatt, Wah, Barbour, Kroetsch, and then Kamboureli and Tostevin. Universities are rarely the site of this kind of advocacy. Male professors do not typically recognize the unquestionable authoritativeness of female writers. At that particularly fertile moment, though, when virtually all the Creative Writing teaching posts in youngish and monied departments were held by men, they were at least a good sort of truly curious men who read and took into account the innovations of work by Canadian women poets of the day, and I would say that this was due to the strides made by the idea of Canlit itself through in part the generation of modernist women writers we are speaking about here. A feministic platform had been planked. The specificity of the gendered subject, individualistic voice, locality, the body, personal history, sexuality, the landscape of the line made white women's textual explorations central to the "new" and "avant-garde."

In 1983 the university also had money to bring in writers, bimonthly visits with wine and dinners and extended contact, a salon-type atmosphere where writers were treated as valuable guests and students could mentor to the thriving culture-in-the-making of contemporary producers. Erin Mouré, Mary di Michele, Susan Glickman, many poets were brought in. I remember Don Coles introducing Elizabeth Smart and observing her ravaged face and realizing I was encountering someone iconic. A woman who looked like hell the same way my mother looked like hell! Don was obviously deeply enamoured of her; which struck me as curious because generally he sided with a Philip Larkin poetry of restraint, a kind of unwriting of the heroic masculinist text, a vote for the humble, self-effacing vernacular consciousness. He was remarkably kind about my own orgiastic confessional style, and I appreciated that taste was a braver and more congenial critical faculty than it often is now. I'm not sure when I read *By Grand Central Station*, but of course I fell in love with it, and with the apostrophic style that permitted an interior ardency to sail, even if it was abject, or rather moved from the abjection of silence and abandonment to the agency of lucent capacious metaphor, a kind of tumbling, climbing, self-regenerative enunciative language cure! I think that book was a tremendously powerful influence for me, and in combination with the currency of the long poem in Canada, which was essentially the idea that you might have more to say than could fit on one page but that it wouldn't necessarily look then like a novel, and also the art-notion of the multiple and the serial as forms of revisitation to the text and perceptions of the self, and of the Question, in my case, the Question being generally interrelationships between women and sex and the repressions of the voice in the body, and the idea of contradictory repressed or minoritized voices gaining air. Perhaps Smart's early writing came out of an emotional longing to recapitulate the scene of loss. The writing in *By Grand Central Station* is a rapid retrieval gesture, repeated over and over (as on a train, with the rest of a static world flashing past) in the girl's psyche, a trying-to-get-there, "there" being the lover/mother/contact one could not have. When she begins to write again in the 70s she is trying to write from the hystereotypy of her own past, but she no longer feels the same lack; she has learned, by mothering her four children, to mother herself. Now she notices "such spritely beauty outside and all around" but feels this contentedness is not the grounds for good writing! Her angst to find her raw and daring new subject brings her to the question: "Shall I ever be able to write about my mother? The crunch. The painful ambiguities, dichotomies, would touch some terrible nerves—in her (after I've dared to touch mine)" (*On the Side of Angels* 87) and "So why do I still cry for my mother at 63? Mysterious and mysterious" (92). And then, as she wrestles with how to avoid writing what she needs to write, "No. The mother is messy, living, terrible, excruciating reality. Known or unknown. The idea. The one having been ONE, welded together. The revenge of the womb. That hopeless never-again-to-be state of well-being. Cast-out. Cast-out. Cast-out" (101) and then my favourite quote of all: "Have I loved enough? Never. But it's easy, alone and in their absence, to love people. It's their prickly presence that irritates and makes the love fly screaming" (105). (These are writings from the late 70s. In 1982, her younger daughter Rose dies.)

The generative charge of these four male profs, institutionally empowered at a particular cultural moment, to deliver to continued relevance the work of their female contemporaries as well as a previous generation of literary antecedents made my own green web of influence wide-eyed and daringly hip yet boundaried, well, by that Canadian literary moment's limits of race unconsciousness, the white blind spots to which were drawn attention and critical questioning by the major Canadian poets of colour whose writing came next from 1986 to 1992 and changed the way any of the previous testimonial of influence could be given.

$\mathcal{P}$ART FOUR

This allowance for revisitation, let's even call it that awful accurate thing, navel-gazing, for not letting one's attachment to mother go but returning to it/her/self with new gaze, fresh questioning, to the same bed or belly of material is, it seems to me, a deeply matrilineal approach. One does not move irrevocably on from it to attach to and challenge the difference of the other, one stays and examines and grapples with and revokes the differences of the it/her/self, the constant motion of identity and movement of time on perception, aware that the self is a motional construct interfacing with any other self. This is the tendency of any engaged relationship, not to let things go into silence but to return even annoyingly to the niggling charge to ask, to know to be in the same embrace, to see the same face making itself in relation to different circumstance. One in effect stays with the mother, or circles back to her, revokes, re-invokes, and is able upon repeated returns to find her. "She is not gone;" which one can observe coolly, with ambivalence and no excess libido of joy or despair.

Perhaps this can raise a crucial question for us as we examine the lineage of our feminist literary production. Have the writings of the most recent generation of women writers been in some sense abandoned by their academic, critical, writer-predecessors, one could say their "mothers," or "cool cousins"? Is it fair to observe that, in the academy of Women's Studies and Canlit and in the feminist-observant media, rarely are the works of my generation of writers examined, or revisited with the same earnest critical contextualizing gaze that was indeed visited upon their own work? Even as we discuss how it is that the contemporary ("new") generation of women writers have been influenced by several preceding generations, modernists and postmodernists, should we not equally ask what this gift of influence might crucially bring to younger writers, in order to continue the evolution of feminist literary inquiry? Should not the women writers who were described as being cutting-edge within Canlit in the seventies by their male contemporaries be generous enough to extend that gift of influence, to inform, excite, inspire, gossip, or gleam astonishment about the writing of this generation's poets? Or has anti-feminist backlash silenced the market for such cross-generational activity, as the outlets for review and criticism dry up by the month, leaving all of us scurrying for our own existence, far more at stake than any of us were fifteen years ago? Just how many of us are not sleeping, lying awake in the dark of one oppressively silent room, conjuring, daring our own revisitation, and to where, and in spite of whom?

Adoptive Mothering or the Art of Arching

Janice Williamson

for Bao

She cannot think alone. Words must be
Poised to the smaller scope, immediates ...

And when the active hours are gone, it's still
Her lot to busily bestir herself
With knots and nooses, all the slough and slips
Of day. When the evening's seal is set she must

Have chosen here to stay. To sit, to bear (Livesay, "The Mother" 39)

Bubble gum and penny candy after every restaurant meal. *Please mummy Can I have 2 and 5.* In the lobby of Noodle Noodle a glass globe of multi colours solves every problem.

Does the red one taste reddish? I ask.
The blue one tastes a bit blueberryish, Bao says.

(A chew out of shape mouth squirrel-rounded cheeky distended pleasure
tongue blued   pinked   orange)
——————————————————————— NO vegetables.

At home, the art of arching—swallowing artichoke leaves tip to choke. Spiked.
Home. This year nowhere to travel. Plagues and wars moor children. CNN stung parents.
Home. Mothering any armchair. Celadon greens *en route* up lattice fence. Backyard purpled table, garden world my world to explore.

Where is MY garden mommy? PEAS! Mommy, THAT'S A BATHROOM WORD! Don't say PIANIST Mommy.

Home. Unexploded munitions beyond the gate.

[Somewhere thirty three thousand. Or three thousand. Or one cluster bomb. Enough. Limbs stung off like leaves. How many appear in a poem?

And a steady diet of depleted uranium "DU" ingested, drunk, snorted. Is it safe?]

A minefield of words—*bomblettes*.

Home. Here battles begin with a squeal. Like blondes ...

I want yellow hair Mommy, not black like mine.

Are you listening Mommy? Look into my eyes Mommy. Are you there?

Home: Portuguese ships only sailed one way, never against the wind. Fado music, a yearning siren song grew out of the where in "Never to return."

Come here Mommy? I'm here Mommy.

What music will you sing of your birthplace? Orphaned girl ships set sail from China, rarely to return.

Are you there Mommy? Where Mommy?

&

She cannot think alone ... the art of arching between, the space not above or below, not greater than or less, but beside this and that. The child smaller than but no less. A space of time creaking not dead yet not fully myself either—wingeing again, belly bared. Any mother modeled on the magazine, spine cracking.

On Tuesday, the childcare centre plots to rent a limousine play Hollywood. Better Bollywood. Why not ravine play? Better birds: rabbit-sized Magpies Oscar nominees.

"Mudpie your spiked heels baby."

&

Thinking mothering fills me with worry about the five-year-old at fifty-two, a world besieged by what? More war and want? A planet depleted: the only advantage, the rich orbit in outer space.

Or fear

Words poised to the smaller scope, immediates ...   (Livesay, "The Mother" 39)

Immediate in its original feudal sense, a direct relation: "Who do you love more Mommy? You or me?"

Immediates: the way the moment crimps your while. As in this very instant, this here and now, this without intervention. Mothering as urgent, imperative. The critical burning issue. Mothering as directly affecting, unswerving, an undeviating expressway through your heart.

Adoptive mothering as "immediate knowledge" ... "intuitive knowledge, as distinguished from that arrived at by means of demonstration or proof." The kind of knowledge dogs possess, says the biologist, sheepishly inventing a theory of "zones of resonance" to explain canine intelligence and how dogs foretell the future and prepare for their owner's arrival home. Mothering as in "vital and precise" the critical minutiae, on the spot, in a blink, the dot in your eye ...

Or

im·me ·di·ate adj: *Right now. Do it please. My best friend. Prioritize.*

1.   happening without delay
2.   nearest in time, space, or relationship
3.   urgent or pressing
4.   affecting something directly
5.   relating to something known about from personal experience or intuition
6.   used to describe an inference derived from a single premise, without any middle term, and often by conversion of a categorial statement. (Encarta)

Mothering, that "conversion of a categorial statement," is what I intuit and know through my daughtering experience, past aunt lives, and the mothers of others.

Mothering immediates as in any "If this, then …" inference that simplifies what is complex in order to save the child from the burning house.

(For the moment, forget the complications of the single mother.)

Calculate the losses: the mother who can't save the children, who leaves long enough for—say—six children to burn. Before she drove away, he said, "Now you are alone." She heard four words forgetting their meaning until she reimagined their cries. A headline reads: Who set them aflame? She knows the story, the abject horror, regret and shame of "What if …" Imagine the jaws of her grief: no blame.

&

Make a list:
> *Housework.*
> *Housekeeping.*
> *Housewifery.*
> *Horsewifery.*

Now try dishes & game theory.

Think big. Iron ten pots ship shape or melt down for the good of your people.

See how they roam: clothes in the dishwasher, cups in the dryer. Of a morning, colour code your laundry or not. Everything is—as it should be, murky blue purpled—or beige. Colour it generic oneness: "Universe"©

Only imperatives work: *Keep it clean. Tidy down. Take charge. Organize. Sanitize. Prewash. Simonize. Unclutter. Cut it out. Deodorize.*

Stop the timewasters! (mail, email, newspapers, news)

Contract your world onto the head of a pin!

Hire a Sinker, a Sailor, a Floater, a Tailor, a Nanny, a Coach, a Cleaner, a Railer.

Dance while you can.

Artify domestic labour. You do?

Whip up Chinese baby food. Or phooey: meditate on minutiae. Cool out at home: be Buddhist or yoga spine arm through around hand extend into any warrior pose. Feet flexed, arch your candy floss.

On the other hand, kiss the cloth. Hire a priest to vacuum, pray in every dust bole. At midday, watch him chant around the toilet bowl. Wave as he levitates, casts off in your tub, renewed.

First: architecture matters—pillars sponged, floors touched up, walls marbled or itched. White on white the colour of paper or clouds, bleached linen or insulation, *knots and nooses.*

Baby teeth? Why hide them under her pillow? Throw mirrors on your Nairobi roof. Or bury them in Katmandu. Are your incisors straight?

Like her first tooth tenderly wrenched into fairy box or buried in the ground halfway around the world in the province where she was born. A bottom tooth thrown onto the roof in Guandong guarantees they grow straight and strong anywhere in Canada. Genealogy like horticulture, dentistry, magic or any epic novel demands no limit on the imagination. Look! Loonies under the pillow! Corn sprouts! Palmetto groves!

&

Listen: *Her lot to busily bestir herself,* she cleans her daughter's room, rearranges, pares down, cuts out, thins things, deadheads, plucks. Pink ceramic pony bought for pennies at Value Village disappears … she won't be missed.

Weeks later at bedtime *the day's confession eased from tired tongue* the almost six girl honeys: "I like my

88

room but not as much. The pink pony's not here ..." (The sudden going gone missing and She/I Regret The Tidy House.)

Sing: *Let it be.*

&

Beside herself, thinking:

   a. A dying woman charts her way by thinking: ***Beside*** *permits a spacious agnosticism about several of the linear logics that enforce dualistic thinking: cause versus effect, subject versus object, noncontradiction or the law of the excluded idle.*[1]

   b. **Beside** upends *cause versus effect,* makes room for maternal forgiveness & the art of error: my daughter is mine but not mine. Last night by ten, after stories and cuddles and a trip around all the beds in the house, this monstrous mah spits out words: "Sleep or I will smack you," a command that ensures tears, failure.

   c. **Beside** precludes *subject versus object,* makes us separate, not equal in power, authority or experience, rendered respectful and caring each to the other as best we can. No points for a smack. No smack.

Noncontradiction or the law of the excluded idle. (She slips & means *middle* but knows that idleness is what she craves, empty hours to feel lonely or misdirection, floundering in time, delicious unrest, pointless distraction. The small body urgent beside her wanting and then not, in her own time, not mine. The mind made over: her desire, her longing.

   Beside herself: she cannot think: Her/my tired tongue: the dance of can can't. Thinking tired thoughts missing any Other: Mommy or Daddy who might take her from me, shelter her in a separate story. (Just a while to catch her breath.) Aunties are good but nighttimes are lonely. *Waking in dark the presence of all the absences we have known* (Webb, "Non linear" 107).

&

*Gwendolyn was writing in the dream
I am in the heat of childbirth*

She at her standing-desk self-possessed (Webb, "Lines" 80)

&

"Mommy can you love me as much as a Mommy plus Daddy?"

To reassure she says, "Mommy loves you as much as Mommy and Daddy. But she doesn't have as much time as Mommy's and Daddy's together." Or does she? The woman who works from dawntime to bedtime. Tucks her into bed. The Daddies who make two jobs to make money quota work.

Say "Single Mother." Say it. You know the response: a certain hesitation, then withdrawal, or solutions, quick and easy.

"Hire a nanny," the couple beside me offer conspiratorially before disappearing out of earshot. Their wish is my command. No cash? Just do it!

What should she do with her daughter during the summer? I consult a mother of three who has given up her painting for maternal devotion, "For someone like you, Chinese all day summer school would be very good." "I don't know how you do it! What about All-Day-All-Summer school," says a helpful Stay-At-Home Mom. "Not for my children, but perfect-for-you-in-your-situation ..."

I should be grateful for the Chinese culture connection. Is it the all day summer school that irks me? What about play and exercise and fun outdoors? Should I expect otherwise? "For someone like you." Who is this *you*? Working mother? Single mother? Someone "like you" who writes and mothers?

89

&

Sniffing for poems, the forward memory
Of hand beyond the grasp.

And how mysterious the playing of children in the trees.   (Webb, "The Colour" 15)

&

Mothers can can't write, at least for a while. And if they write uninterrupted, sleeplessness becomes them: on holidays they climb Mount Kilimanjaro or Sherpa their way through life hiring "ethnic" help.

As though determined by regulation, on one side of the café, young to middle-aged white men bicycle show off their legs in khaki shorts, leg hairs bleached with miles left to go. On this side of the room, thin girls, some smoking, read manuscript pages and listen. Or refuse, arms holding tight to their conversation, biceps flexing opening paragraphs. Palms up shrugs perform interruptions chin ups.

Tied up in *all the slough and slips of day*, this mother writes about something that could be a calling, "At eight in the evening, I sit in the third row imagining myself the pianist Patricia Barber who sips something blue in her glass, slouching over a Steinway, bare arms crossed. Black and white keys sound plundered by forearm and even elbow. Lean forward, your hair touches the ivories, fingers move inside a maw of strings to pluck a rhythm or call. Talk to an upright bass. Inhabit the keys, make your home this mobile echo machine. A voice inside her sings, makes wry love to someone she doesn't want, then sends her or him away, comforting those of us who can't make it at the moment. Or think saxophone fingering, the wow sound the bald man makes. Full and waiting slips."

&

Thinking mothering at fifty-two renews me. Introduces different failures. Thinking mothering fills me with worry about the six-year-old who wants to be seven who comes to know me midlife stretching, running, breathing life into cells that want. Strings taut *to sing,* sag. A life lived unrecuperable: travels uninvited, lovers mysterious.

At the piano, the day begins or ends: the twist of perch, a twirl to meet her. The small child sits, one hand on lap, another poised for middle C. This large gap between her teeth, incisor twisted, invites a smile, turns to her mother waiting. Or resists to squirm, slouched down towards the pedals ...

...*Ready*... (the big voice angry: a small hand shifts) ... *Go,* the mother says, and a child taps C then G, A, G, F, E, D, C ... an alphabet twinkle twinkles (5X). Or rainbow fingers unfurl across the keys, the sail of light suspended, a note refracted left or right.

Time in your flight—O— a wristwatch strapped
To my heart, ticking erratically, winding down.

When the evening's seal is set she must

Have chosen here to stay.
To sit, to hear.   (Livesay, "The Mother" 39)

&

Saturday morning awakening. No dark winter light but the brutish radio counts corpses, charts kidnappings, lakeside body parts or an abused child on the loose.

The sound of footsteps padding down the hall, a creak at the turn of the door. And her small voice beside my bed. "Cuddles Mommy?"

90

How many kisses? Her soft skin, breastless body curved into mine.

"Mommy, when will I not have bad dreams? Mrs. Labbé took me and Katie-Marie and Maryam to a special place and bad people chased us around."

Later we visit the market bustling with a city searching for public space. First the vine tomatoes, peppers red orange and golden. Next stop: a magician in training, cards coming up wrong—Jack of spades gone missing. Unapologetic, she tries again. Her teacher instructs her how to float a match above an ace of spades, the tiny tell-tale wire dances invisible to my daughter entranced. After three shows, we leave under duress to look down the aisle for garden grasses and lunch. She walks beside me tugging at my arm wanting to return to the magic. We make our way through the shoppers towards the food.

"Would you like a hotdog," I ask. No one answers and I look around for a moment. When does a girl lost become girl prey?

I can't see her. Immediately, I scream and shout, "My daughter is missing. Where is she? Pink shirt. Six years old. Black hair, pigtails. Look for my daughter? Shut the doors. Stop what you are doing. Stop. My daughter is lost. Has someone taken my daughter? Pink shirt. Six years old. Black pigtails." And then a quick sense returns and I look at myself as I stand there weeping: "She is Chinese. Please find her. Baooooooooooooooooooo."

Bao tells a different tale: "After the magician we went to the gardening place and Mommy held my hand. Then she dropped it and I lost her and started crying and the magician heard me and came to find me and took me back to where they did the tricks. And then someone found me and brought me to Mommy."

> *Sometimes I hear you screaming between the paragraphs and poems. That doesn't really bother me. Screams should be heard and not seen.* (Webb, "Letter" 38)

As we make our way towards the food concession again, I weep with shock, relief, joy and embarrassment. A man in a cowboy hat and shirt comes to the table to tell me how glad he is to see me with my daughter. Others nod sympathetically. Over the next half hour, women come to tell me how they once upon a time lost their child, the terror shattering the instant they awaken to the loss, however temporary.

&

> *The Earth Mothers restrain themselves during full moon.*
> *They are now members of Zero Population Growth.* (Webb, "Letter" 37)

&

I try not to notice how relations between parents seem almost without exception imbalanced. One, usually female or the femme of the pair if lesbian, takes the place of primary caregiver leaving the other free for workaholism or not. On holiday visiting friends, the women, loving and dear, make a point of explaining why their partners con-tribute less homework or childcare. Some of the men are good cooks, all of them loveable though the lion's share escapes them.

Marguerite Duras writes a teaching story:

> *When both members of a couple are writers, the wife says: "My husband's a writer. The husband says: "My wife writes too." The children say: "My father writes books, and so does my mother, sometimes."* (Duras 68)

Fuck Duras, I think as I edit this story. Up two nights and three days with my daughter; her vomit and shit mark this aliveness. I am beside myself—what authors do according to Roland Barthes who tells me how our being

91

always runs alongside our writing whether autobiographical or not. At this moment I would like to tell him, my I sprints in the margins in poopy pyjamas.

During my daughter's illness, this mother mops the floor and occasionally weeps. I've made a will with multiple child guardians, but have none to cure me of this fear of my child dying. A friend recommends *Sex and the City,* a diversion I've missed. While the girl sleeps fitfully, I retreat into bits and pieces of *Sex and the City,* three seasons, as though girls' TV might cure me of pitiful maternal self-dramatizing. And for a while it does since I'm irritated by the voice of the writers and all the best New York babyless friends who condescend to pat the nursing woman's head or tell baby jokes and babysit as "fuckin' Mary Poppins." The virtue of this virtual marathon of golden spiked heels and my humourlessness is that it diverts me from the problem of hydration. My daughter has too many bodily sec/ex/cretions and won't drink to compensate. In the children's medical guide I've read about unbalanced electrolytes. In a perverse display of excess in the face of starvation, I pack a knapsack with enough toys and books for a week—just in case. At the hospital emergency parking lot, cars in a line at 30 below zero fog up like ominous ghosts. In the waiting room, the only Chinese I ever encounter outside of restaurant menus is the bright red SARS signs. We can pretend to avoid the sick people only by refusing translation. On the news, a local heroine and former colleague is appointed master of national security, a kind of Big Sister to keep us all in line. This news isn't entirely reassuring. As more ambulances arrive with accident victims, we wait several hours until we're ushered into a room where the doctor cajoles the girl into laughter and concludes she is in recovery and just fine, thank you.

Thank you. Thank you. Thank you.

&

This early morning in the bath, I read *The Globe & Mail.* On the front page Conrad Black is enthroned on his Palm Beach lawn. Lady-Black-Barbara-Amiel, collapses adoringly at his knee, her upturned bare feet slightly dirty. Peevish and naughty with giggles, my daughter pours water on the newspaper. Pity. The royal pair already drowning in scandal and debt now lie wet and wrinkled on the floor—no match for this child.

By afternoon my daughter not yet fully recovered and resentful of her confinement descends to the living room in tears, suitcase in hand filled with emergency supplies: purple pants, purple turtleneck and purple sweater, Sailor Moon pyjamas, and two stuffed puppies.

"Where are you going," I ask sympathetically.

"To a friend's for a few days," she says. "And then to another friend's. For a few more days."

"I'll be sad to see you go," I say. So the girl puts down her suitcase, blows her nose, drinks hot chocolate, plays Chinese checkers, loses, then wins and stays.

&

> *What are we whole or beautiful or good for*
> *But to be absolutely broken?* (Webb, "Breaking" 55)

Notes
1 Idle is middle in Sedgwick 2003: 8.

92

Wild Vein Through White Leaves' Ruff

Green, how much
I want you green

P.K. Page

Green, how much I want you green.
Great starts of white frost
Come with the fish of darkness
That opens the road of dawn.

Frederico Garcia Lorca

Landscape of crystals
rock salt and icebergs
white trees, white grasses,
hills forged from pale metals
padlock and lock me
in the Pleistocene.
See my skin wither
heart become brittle
cast as the Snow Queen.
Green, how much I want you, green.
Green oak, green ilex
green weeping willow
green grass and green clover
all my lost youth.
Come before springtime
before the brown locust
come like the rain
that blows in the night
and melts to fine dust
great stars of white frost.
Water, sweet water
chortling, running
the Chinooks of my childhood
warm wind, the ripple
of icicles dripping
from my frozen palace.
How sweet the water
moonstones and vodka
poured from a chalice
with the fish of darkness.
Come water, come springtime
come my green lover
with a whistle of grass
to call me to clover.
A key for my lock
small flowers for my crown.
The Ice Age is over,
green moss and green lichen
will paint a green lawn
that opens the road of dawn.

95

Ah, by the Golden Lilies

P.K. Page

. . . ah by the golden lilies,
the tepid, golden water,
the yellow butterflies
over the yellow roses . . .
                    Juan Ramón Jiménez

Jiménez, but for the roses
you paint a Rio garden
where every golden morning
the golden sunlight spills
on my Brazilian breakfast—
coffee like bitter aloes
strawberry-fleshed papayas
the sensuous persimmon . . .
My young head full of follies
ah, by the golden lilies.
Beneath the cassia boughs
where fallen yellow blossoms
reflect a mirror image
I barefoot in the petals
trample a yellow world
while small canaries flutter
over the lotus pond.
I trail my golden fingers—
for I am Midas' daughter—
in the tepid, golden water.
My blue and gold macaw
laughs his demented laughter
dilates his golden pupils—
a golden spider spins
a spangled golden web
for beauty-loving flies.
Above the cassia branches—
the cassia coloured sun.
Above the yellow lilies—
the yellow butterflies.
Jiménez, I am freed
by all this golden clangor.
Jiménez, your roses
denote a falling sound
a sound that will not rhyme
with sambas jocosas
macumba, feijoada
Bahian vatapá.
A different sun disposes
over the yellow roses.

God As Maker of the Alphabet

E. W. Brewster

Was the God who said
y'hy or (Become, light!)
only a voice, a moving wind?
a blind natural force?

Or was he *aleph* and *tau*
(*alpha* and *omega* if you like Greek)
the whole alphabet,
or all alphabets?
the words scrolled silently
from his invisible mouth?

Did he (she or it)
know all the languages
that would be born and die
with the nations that would make them?
yet to be and become extinct,
all numbers, musical notes,
the poems, plays, symphonies?
Was all the future
contained in his mind?

Later he named himself
at the Burning Bush
ehyeh asher ehyeh
I am what I am, was, will be

One Being
including all
at time's end
as at time's beginning.

"There is no other."

On P.K. Irwin's "Bright Centre"

E.W. Brewster

Small fish swim in the branches
of a Burning Bush.

Or is this the beginning
of the universe?
Bright light (*or*)
issuing from the mouth of God
with the silent letter
aleph

Beyond the light
is the deep (*tehom*)

home of Tiamut
the great sea-dragon
or maybe only a wide
emptiness, blue-grey.

So delicate
the blossoms of flame,
the darting minnows
with their large
upward-gazing eyes,
like stars suspended
in a seeming calm

but somewhere beyond the frame
a high wind is blowing,
life-giving
breath of Elohim.

the force of the untitled

Daphne Marlatt

for Marian Dale Scott
and her last "Untitled" (c. 1992)

i

leaving the Slade where
drawing grows in fascination
for the sake of Frank
("you won't need to live from your painting")

what is *live?*
what is painting?

forget the studio in New York
(what I want most is time
to work things out for myself)

forget paint in order to study
domestic science, get ready
for marriage—"give up
painting," your father advises

you know, Frank knows
you have this force a slender
crocus rising inside you
ferocious, trying to find
its spiral time

I shall not go to that
cocktail party

caught in the spin
between euphoria and gloom
criticism and paint, searching
for something more basically
universal, more symbolic,
more intellectual, more aware
of world evolution

than this inadequate self

knowing the crocus
could split rock

99

at the Contemporary Arts Society
working in talk
with Bethune and others,
revolution and art in equal
intensity, *helical,* he revises
Marxist dialectic,
ascending

crocus spiral

ii

lilac-heavy drowse of bruised
heads—tossed bottle, syringes, tinfoil
pain killers on the street mingle with clematis, sweet
azalea incense drug drop, smithrites' rank
shelter for sleep

> *Every week there are new targets*
> *and more families who feel the effects*

pushed to the margins, written off as
collateral damage, they make the rounds

Sisters of Atonement, Union Gospel Mission,
hospice and soup kitchens, Sally Anne clothing,
transition house, Downtown Mission,
Door Is Open, Mustard Seed

> *... the most*
> *vulnerable in our society*
> *are under attack*

late in 1935 you leave
ordinary kitchen clutter, sun
irradiating the wooden breadbox
socks yet undarned, the usual
list of to-do's erased by

an "inner necessity"
to stand

in the middle of Eaton's exactly
where you catch
the contrary movement of
escalators ascending, descending
faceless women queued on their way

down to the underworld of slashed
prices, or up to other beckoning
levels, always the weight of the next
storey pressing in on them, never
enough
                money, never enough
to go round (so the script says

privatize, cut welfare, cut programs
to generate more profit, cut care, slash
the unnecessary

                   —by whose definition?)

The inner necessity to paint was there,
in spite of the time, in spite of the misery,
the growing fear of fascism and war.

iii

in reaction to the mechanical
slaughter fields of war, you paint
Atom, Bone and Embryo, Cell and
Crystal

                  my way will become more
                  fluid, still delicately precise, less
                  geometric, less static

ever-disorder of dust on the mantel, coal-
dust, cosmic dust, all shifting flocculi and yet
the crystalline orders of mineral, thought,
regret

             the done and the becoming

in constant disintegrating balance, a marriage and
coming into your own (Peel St. *cloister*)
forms of interrelation—*in growing*
there is also dying

                Iconic, Totemic,
facade and depth turned expressionist
flare and splash

                              I like to paint
with as much of me as possible

leaving the terms of dialectic, leaving
the figure behind, *that my paintings*
speak for themselves

and the whole field opens up
its net of inter-relations
impasto with fluid edges
geometry's flat surface
grid-dance folding-
fan effect

          people separate
and yet belonging

luminosity as pulse, at home
in the net of retinal ground
iconic in your

eighties, *dancing*
with paint, thick and ethereal
rhythm, ribbons, this DNA
fraying edges

world gone
verb

its trace

Triple Takes on Carr, O'Keefe and Kahlo from Places of Their Own at the McMichael Canadian Art Collection, Kleinburg, ON Summer 2001

Penn Kemp

1 Massif

In Emily Carr's one self-portrait, broad brush strokes
obliterate boundary to fling her bosom across a can-
vas like horizontal wheat sheaves. Caring no fig for
convention, flesh streaks off edge outside all frame.

Wild woman of the woods, in a village of cat's eyes.
She nags snarling weather into domestic peace, pets
the wind, sweeps cloud down streaming cedar trunk.

In the paintings around her, implacable mountains rise
and sit arms folded, waiting their turn. Firm hands on
knees, another hill down the hall squares off discourse.

The mountain inside recognizes the other out there.

2 Canvassing Landscape

Taut skin stretched across cheeks, O'Keefe's old bones
talk louder than living animals, she remarks. She collects

hollows from the hills of oceanic desert to enter endless
cerulean sky through the certain two dimensions of paint.

3 Frida Kahlo, On Exhibit

*Watch me tear this painting, watch me rip it up and paint
another, better. Or worse, it matters, from my eye's eye.*

Body parts. Body parts to open the red sea of despond.
Circling upon her track, the hunted seeks the hunter out.

*My body is mine to display, mine to mind. Mine to cram
in open pits of roiling, wicked pigment. Watch me dye.*

Wracked without ruin, with no easy room to manoeuvre
on this thin bed rack, her mind stretches beyond skin to easel.

Palette splashed in fury, cast to contain a febrile agility,
might avoid the looming void beyond fervent defiance.

Moods thicken. Tint hardens to stone. Medusa glints,
solidified, just as snared as any light caught in her eye.

Sex springing from her head glitters seduction. Form-
al ribbons of snakes coil like a Spanish Infanta's dress

by Velasquez. Wild vein through white leaves' ruff.
A flat surface of sheer rock powdered to outlast flesh.

Frida draws her hair as whip lacerating her throat. Such
vegetation, grown long, twists to vengeance when shorn.

Linked chain around her neck, *cadena*. Monkey's paw
protective. Then jackal's inquisitively pointed ears, no,

just a black dog gone murky when eyes swim sea-green,
spark dashed with pain, or pills swallowed to kill pain.

*

Above her ear an amorphous, androgynous couple floats

turning in amniotic thought cloud. What nostrum must
be murmured over and over tumbling through such froth?

She-he-we. *El, ella, nosotros.* Confessions of mute rage
flickering phosphorescent over Sargasso's obsessed sea.

*

Her heart opens like a sacred heart of Jesus to reveal Diego,
Diego Rivera. Her third eye, a bronze medallion of Maria,

gleams so curiously blind to its own reflection before that
ongoing inquisition of other eyes, eyes she sought so long.

*Just try to forget me now. I dare you, double dare. Already
my art has outlived all you onlookers of this ostensible life.*

Coda

Medium is cool,
unmoved by pathetic
fallacy.

Unaffected by storm
or tantrum of syn-
aesthetic explosion.

Medium just sits here
typing while distinctly

three voices descend/
condescend to speak not
through medium exactly

but at me. Diem, carpe.
Pain chips lift and holler.

Stalwart, terse or fervent,
all three distinctly fierce
in their medium, paint.

Semantic Memory

Lola Lemire Tostevin

i

At the retirement home where I visit,
the lexical decision time test measures
the speed of word recognition.

Strings of five to seven letters flashed
onto a screen, each string representing
a familiar word or a nonsense combination,
such as memory and momery
                              (meme, a system of behaviour
passed from mother to daughter.)
Memory trace.

The test is repeated with twenty combinations,
the time it takes to recognize each word recorded.

Affection, attachment, love, care, sensibility,
are either too long or too short to qualify.

ii

The semantic decision time task judges
whether a sentence is plausible in the real world:
"The woman fell and broke her hip."

Unlike a line from a poem by Denise Levertov
"see me with embryo wings."

Little is understood of a mind
retracing steps, returning to origins.

iii

The incongruity. The cheerfulness
with which these tests are greeted.
Idle chatter.

Sounds pulled by their roots to bridge
unbridgeable distances, so any sound will do.

A sharing and a crossing-through
as mind and eyes try to adjust
to the sensuousness of *senescence*
and *forgetfulness*.

iv

The world lays down its new logic
as words spill out too fast or too late.

Meander invisible lobes, are carried along
currents slow as molten metal.
                    (Precious little sticks held
firmly between the fingers.)

In spite of sentences too garbled
to make sense, there is little doubt
you are in the presence of meaning
too absolute for words.

v

What is proper here is nothing more
than the impropriety of banality.

Hours staring at a screen.
                    (Firefly vigil
or interstellar dust?)

Enigmatic equations.
But also the satisfaction of knowing
that soon the mind will depend on nothing
outside itself. A place without beginning or end.

Time is older here.
And younger.

Only the pulse at the wrist
regulates the clock.

vi

What urge will save us now that sex won't?
                                        Jenny Holzer

When heart *is* site. Cabal pounding
at the chest as *love* lights up the circuits.

Less so for *eroticism*, the neural network
no longer as tightly strung.
                        (Poetically named, nevertheless,
for it is neither neural or network.)

The story shifts from its axis and slips
into waves. Stenosis. Software response
modelled on the brain's computing agility
masterminds the script, changes the beat.

Heart as site an image
                        (spurs mind and hand).

vii

The dogged suspicion that words
belong to some other place.
Some other time.

Alien to any country
To any class or genre.

Alien to this cerebral membrane
on which words suddenly appear.
And disappear.

Cut against the incorporeal hide.

Suite of Red

Betsy Warland

1

in the mail a red hat
just as her stubble hinted at flourishing, red
fell out of manilla envelope, out
of purple wrapping paper and the green-raw
silk on her head
yelped
wanted to bite, chase its tail

—enveloped by ancient red—

hiking down the Grand Canyon
skin softly greens

(complementary colours)
eyes prefer
to compensate

2

she had suspected
a delicately-thin layer of latex seduced
touch away from implication

three days after surgery
it is she who draws back the syringe

—gloves now on her hands—

the sensation of smooth remove hitting fast as
general anaesthetic

—the syringe, gloves—
she hadn't expected to find these
in the cartridge refill kit

beginning the procedure
she observes the opaque fog suddenly enveloping everything except

the site

and her body
chills with detachment

3

the pathology of plastics
(the Romans and their lead)
cultures of breast cancer cells
inadvertantly discovered to rapidly multiply
in plastic Petri dish

4

decision:
what is familiar
what is preferred
what is expected
what is calculated
what is efficient
what is gratifying

and what of the decision
no one wants to make?
—ruse of Pilate washing his hands—
protocol, statistics
herding our terror
evading contradiction

she asked for a dream
awoke on its smooth edge

—a knife hovered in luminescent space—

a kitchen knife, unremarkable
except for cedar-green handle

hours later
while waiting for the light to change she got
the yes of green

level with her breasts—the knife
hadn't been hovering but
calmly offered

in her red dictionary
months later
a word catches her eye
decide, de-, off + cadere, to cut

5

red continued to astonish her
—maple's red halo—

though each bud long-remained tight
lipped at their tip, red
filaments tentacled the sky

—tidal pool of red anemones—

maple's seven kinds of strength
one spoken:
"The red precedes the green."

how she knew to accept red
slowly syringed
into blue vein of her hand

6

the three white lab coat dreams
the fourth, a radiant bald woman
in three-quarter length red coat
striding out of the elevator

out her window
the green angle of hedge
barn-red house
crow

—the muscularity of green—

how blade & leaf assumes the spaces

at the cafe table
"You're lucky. By the time they found out
it was too late for my dad."
just then behind these words
red-buoyant tow truck pulling tilted
black hearse

7

two hundred and eleven feet
two hundred and eleven feet, two
hundred and eleven
feet, two hundred and eleven feet

—in the plunge—
the shape
the weight
water
makes
arrowing from
earth to
earth

migratory flight pattern
scales of fish
wake, wedge,
caveat, cleavage, pubis of

8

the water plummets behind her
not knowing, not knowing

she stands on the viewing platform
not knowing, not knowing

the camera expects a casual pose
she has been absent from most rolls of film
through the past three seasons

inside the viewfinder a green & a red light
informs the photographer if the subject
is in or out of focus
(the pose insists sameness into every situation)

she goes through the motions but is in the backdrop
body porous as water as air as leaf

Uncomforted
Margaret Christakos

Little Miss

Mother's not listening to vast thinking allowed so
flew over known hall sounds or faces most
chancing is our heart of failing who better
just right! Unflattened those voices had air filled
sides even which it flatters sadness to lucky!

Givingness

Since we are lucky! Moth's air the headlights!
Girls are luck to a mother not failing!
It is much sadness not with us though!
Seriously, if or how listening makes uncomforted where
or who you flatter to be true just
mistaken and why it must be so! Given
what she gestured! Which thinking about it did
confirm the probabilities even allowed good margin for
erring on both sides of those issues! (It
is great how we can talk about that
so openly!) It is so great! But your
hand-flicker up butterflied! Fled, flew, it hurt, not
mysterious, by yawning air or constellatory proof of
grief's silliness! We had our chances at her
bodies! Some young voices know better behave herselves!
Heel-click tonic-flutter on a hall or runway outside . . .
(How'd you make those sounds travel like that,
sitting here!) Regards unflattened faces or thinking or
not remembering it right! Not honest since girls
faking makes you just most gestured! That beyond,
far now, or better chances sear us proof,
how sitting or who is truer about reasoning
uncomfort! But let's fail us, each her burdens!
That you're not of her herselves! Outside that!

Deferred lament of the inadequately mothered women friends

The headlights not failing, us though uncomforted where true just so.

Given it did margin for issues.

(It about that but your hurt, not proof of, at her, behave herselves, runway outside . . .

Like that, thinking or since girls that beyond, us proof, about reasoning her burdens outside.

That.

M1. U.K. Breast Milk Toxic: 13 July 99
with each line prematurely weaned to escape charges of plagiarism

chemical cocktail	of pollutants
to higher	than of
toxic substances,	the babies
being exposed	limit daily
range of	from incinerators,
pesticides and	350 contaminants,
including some	and dioxin-like
tissue highly	lethal headlines
most recently	in animal
feed, introducing	food chain
including milk	was agent

Agent lethal recently was milk highly most including chain dioxin-like
introducing in food 350 limit and feed, daily exposed some
animal toxic being including headlines higher – and tissue chemical
– from contaminants, – – of pesticides – – the
incinerators, – – of range – – than babies –
– to substances, – – of pollutants – – –
cocktail

M2. Ada and Eva

So said the paper: Two sisters, identical twins. One with
thighs too skinny to harvest reconstructive fatty tissue for her

missing breast, gone to cancer, so the sister, true surrogate,
offers hers. No rejection issue and true love to graft

wholesale onto sibling flesh, her sister, herself. A breast in
waiting. Would that each of us could be so roundly

replaced, cells migrating back to home territory. Not said in
the paper: This donor sister, plumper and barren since age

nineteen from pelvic inflammatory disease wants children, and next year
the first sister will nurse a newborn with this thigh-breast,

perhaps her twin will run across fields, laughing, wet, loose

M3. Milk was recently lethal agent her twin will run across

Sisters, identical twins. One with higher – and tissue
Chemical reconstructive fatty tissue for her – to substances,

– – so the sister, true surrogate, introducing in

food 350 limit and true love to graft and
feed, daily exposed some sister, herself. A breast in

highly most including chain dioxin-like us could be so
roundly – from contaminants, – – home territory. Not

said in – – than babies – plumper and
barren since age of pesticides – – the wants

children, and next year animal toxic being including headlines
newborn with this thigh-breast, incinerators, – – of range

across fields, laughing, wet, loose of pollutants – –
– from pelvic inflammatory disease wants to higher first

sister will nurse a chemical cocktail cells migrating back
to home being exposed paper: This donor sister, plumper

toxic substances, onto sibling flesh, her sister, including some
Would that each of us pesticides and range of

breast, gone to cancer, so most recently hers. No
rejection issue and tissue highly said the paper: Two

sisters, including milk too skinny to harvest reconstructive feed,
introducing

Who will make the tears wet for the first time in English literature in a hundred years?

Susan Holbrook

YOUR TEARS will have to bubble out of faces, they'll have to shoot out like hard seeds, they'll have to fly up rather than fall, hit the ceiling but not ricochet down (they can't go down anymore). They'll bore right through the roof and hit geese in the stomach, squawnk. The tears themselves will have to squawnk or make the sound of a sleeping-bag zipper. They'll have to taste like rusty bolts or coconut pudding. They'll have to be double drops, Siamese twin drops, bobbly upside-down hearts that are indecisive about which way to stream, jig this way and that like little dancing bums. Then I'll feel sorry for you. Jessica watched her grandmother board the plane, and tears welled up in her navel. Walking back through the airport, people stared at the wet spot and she knew what it was to be a TeleTubby. He took my hand at the altar and his eyes shone and he puked. I started to spew too, and everyone around us said Aw, a few of them wiping drool away with tissues. She was self-conscious about her smelly tears but, dammit, sometimes you had to just let 'em rip. Cry me a liver, baby, raw, glistening clot or pan-fried with onion strips, either way I'll never lick your face again. At 9:02 on a Monday morning, Sarah's bundle of joy arrived, and everybody in the room squirted tears so enormous they had to dab at their faces with diapers. The doctor couldn't see through his own fluids and croaked simply, "it's a baby!" the nurses holding a bucket under his chin. The ranchhand was wracked with dry sobs, wept ribbons of sand onto the slick hide of the stillborn calf. Hold them back, brush them aside, it's the allergies, turn away, good idea.

Editing the Erotica Issue

Susan Holbrook

Crocuses glistened. Sparrows throbbed.

Would he approve
Of her nipples of mauve?

And that was what had first attracted him, her canvas flaps.

A father of four, he is nevertheless kittenish.

Her skirt had a stuffed look, which could only mean she was wearing ruffled panties.

Oh nutritious mound of sprouts.

Richard and Regina had been friends for a long time.

Dear editors: When I saw you were doing an erotica issue, I thought, Woody-licious!

And in the velour pantsuit of evening, even the sandflies laughed to see their joy.

Richard throbbed. Regina glistened.

In the land of Zamore, mailmen had a dual function.

"Oh, excuse me, I thought everyone was gone for the night," she says, foaming at the ears.

Her heart throbbed, and the surgeon saw that it was glistening in there. Quickly! More
crumpled wet sheets!

He carries me up the stairs under one arm, like a chicken.

Left a hickie as big as a toonie,
Monday acted like he never knew me.

Dear editors: I have been waiting years to share my expertise in this very special field
of writing.

Are you even glistening? I'm throbbing to you.

Oranges, all over.

Oatmeal Bath

Lisa Fiorindi

"Entre la peau et l'ongle d'un géant j'ai bâti ma maison"

Thérèse Renaud, *les sables du rêve,* 1946

Sitting in warm water, black shower curtain drawn, cream-coloured clumps of oatmeal collecting between my legs slightly spread yet pushing down, trying to keep my bleeding knees immersed in the water. My eczema has never been this bad. They say it's stress-related but I know it's also genetic and has to do with diet and the weather. Various factors come into play. Hard to pinpoint any one thing, identify any one cause. Accumulations, combinations, in what proportions it really doesn't matter. It's like the state of my marriage. Impossible to outline with complete certainty, complete preciseness, the cause of its decline. I coax a small clump bobbing softly, gently taking, breaking it between my fingers and spread it on my nipple. The bath is filled with the smell of grain, warm and moist, reminding me of bread and yeast. Breathing deep, finger circling.

Putting away the Christmas tree, wondering where I'll be doing this next year. Who will get the decorations I think. Surely we wouldn't divide them. Just what is the basis for dividing up Christmas? Would it be part of the settlement? How would you decide who gets what? Mitch picks an old candy-cane up off the wood floor. *'Me eat this Mommy? Me eat this please? Say yes, say yes!'* I open the wrapper for him and he happily pops the curved top into his mouth as he starts up the stairs, chasing after Grace, always trying to keep up with his older sister. Waddle, run, sway of diaper full and heavy the smell of feces almost sweet, I half get up off the couch to change him but he's too quick, standing there now at the top of the stairs, bare legs, feet firmly planted, hands waving. *Bye Mommy!* I won't leave him long I think and continue sorting, folding and tying tree branches together with kitchen string, depositing each colour-coded group in its own grocery bag, don't forget to tie a knot.

Grace puts a party hat over her nose and mouth pretending to peck at Mitch who is, for the moment, sitting quietly in the chair beside her trying to catch hold of the ice-cube in his glass. *'Look everybody! I'm a pecking-wood bird!'* she says. A few seconds of laughter, the wiping of mouths putting down utensils, people getting ready to correct her. 'A pecking-wood bird?' repeats my mother. 'No, honey, what you mean to say is a woodpecker. That bird you are thinking of is called a woodpecker.' Listening in from the kitchen, trying to spread the whipped cream stuck to the sides of the box back onto mine and my husband's birthday cake with my fingers. Searching for an appropriate spot to insert the two light green '3' 'O' candles while wondering why it is that people are always so eager to correct kids. Happy, pleased with themselves, believing as they look down arms crossed faces beaming, that they are finally in a position to set things straight.

Alone cleaning up their mess. Licking the ends of the candles then throwing them into the green garbage bag. Able to take some comfort, some consolation in the sounds coming from the bathroom. The tap tapping of toothbrushes against ceramic, glass, bright green and pink plastic held between teeth as Grace shows Mitch how a peck pecking wood bird needs to peck really hard before he can make a turd.

My mother wants to make me a patchwork quilt. Not because of my birthday, for that she's given me pearl-drop earrings with a European back so as not to be outdone by my inlaws who are actually Italian and live in Italy, nor because of Christmas or any other special occasion. She has simply decided that I need to be her next quilting class project. I don't object, not even when she tells the saleslady that it's *me* who's asked her to make this quilt. Somehow I feel sorry for her here under these lights, winter white skin, thick glasses looking intently at the material fingering this and that. Running her hand along bolts of fabric, flicking the tags, stooping down a bit to check prices. I linger in front of the new arrivals rubbing a pseudo-crushed velvet-velour with a wave-like pattern running across it between thumb and forefinger, envisioning a mini-skirt. Seventies I think. I hated the Seventies. Remembering trips to the mall with my mother, the feel of her warm summer bare legs thighs in my hands as I inspected, fondled the hem of her short skirt. Finding myself always caught between admiring it, thinking it pretty and hating it, wishing she'd take it off, throw it away so all those men's eyes wouldn't have to stop and look there, in that spot. 'Let's look at books,' she says, ordering one of the saleswomen over. 'Watercolour quilts, now those are nice. But you probably won't like them because I like them.' We stand side by side, flipping through pictures. I decide not to tell her that her scarf is slowly slipping, sliding out down the front of her coat, dangling loosely, right between her legs.

Earthbound, my new writing pad says. 100% de-inked recycled post-consumer fibre. Falling into its pages, soft and muted.

I climb out of the bath and my red patches of skin are still burning. I remember that as a kid I knew exactly how many patches of eczema I had—eleven. Two on the arms (one on each part of the upper arm facing outward), two on my legs (one on each part of the calf facing outward), two on my bum (one on each cheek), two on my ears (one long patch behind each of them), and lastly, I had it on my scalp in various places but it seemed logical at the time to count my head as one big patch. I didn't necessarily feel diseased as a kid, my eczema never got so bad that it bled, and having 'sets' of patches, one on each side of a body part made me feel almost balanced. But now, instead, twenty years later, I feel them to be signs that what I thought was safely inside, can no longer be contained.

They are painting the Ambassador Bridge blue. A next to impossible task it would seem, thousands of tonnes of steel, concrete, rising up and over the Detroit River. The workers move along at a steady, determined pace, carefully snapping up tarps around the scaffolding and make-shift stairs, ladders they have constructed. Orange hardhats atop navy hoods, wool ski-masks, an extra scarf wrapped around tight. Belts heavy with tools as they move up, down and around the girders. The slamming open and shut of the door on the portable john, the whistle of the metro truck announcing lunch as it tries to drive, move its way through the scattered canisters, tubes, barrels and other strewn machinery. And me sitting here alone in my car, watching.

We simultaneously push the two glass doors open out into the night. It's not snowing as hard as it was. 'Let's walk,' my mother says, pulling her hood up over her head, the black fringe of fake fur framing her tiny face. We get to the plaza but she's made a mistake, the quilting store is not there, it's in the next plaza up ahead. 'Should we turn back and take the car?' 'No use in that, we're almost there.' We keep walking and the wind and snow pick up. I have a hard time matching her pace. She speed-walks as a hobby.

'Cream,' my husband says. 'That's all you need. Go to the doctor and get him to give you some cream.' Is it really that easy I think? Could it really be as simple as that? Somehow I suspect, no, I know it isn't. But why? Why isn't it that simple? You've got a patch of eczema, an ailment, logically an ointment, some sort of treatment is what you need to clear it up right? But there are complications in going to the doctor's and getting cream. You wouldn't think so, but there are. First, I'm attracted to my doctor. I also think I've seen him look at me that way. He's married, but that fact of course is irrelevant when it comes to loneliness. And then again, maybe not. Maybe he wasn't looking at me that way at all. Maybe it was something I imagined that day sitting in the waiting room suddenly glancing through the small sliding frosted glass window where the secretary sits, quickly glancing to see him staring out for a moment, I thought staring at me, his expression deep in thought mixed with a sort of resignation and duty, clipboard and someone's chart in hand looking like he expected more out of life than this, being in this office with its four examining rooms from eight to six day after day. Not to say he isn't a good doctor. Quite the contrary. He's an excellent doctor. Kind, caring, and when the secretary takes her lunch from twelve to one, he answers phones. Actually, I think that's one of the reasons I'm attracted to him.

Grace's dance class every Tuesday and Thursday night. Sitting on a child's small wooden bench that extends all the way down the light green concrete wall, waiting with other parents in hallways. Losing myself in the conversations around me, the shuffle of children getting ready, changing shoes, skirts, fragments of instructions and music blending, wafting toward me through half-open doors *i love my scarf my pretty scarf its colour is ballet pink there are many things my scarf can do what are they let me think* step touch three and four

We stand side by side doing the dishes. He washes, I dry. I object to his using cold water not so much because I care about the dishes being disinfected as I claim, but because I just want to make conversation. He's just told me I can have a divorce if I want one, the house, money, he doesn't care teeth clenched kids with fingers in their ears, a long monotone rather loud *ahhhhhhh* sound interspersed with giggles—they don't know what else to do. Mommy why are you crying? Did something happen? Did you hurt yourself? Bang your head? Finger? Arm? Stub your toe? Bite your tongue? Tell me where it hurts.

Parking my car, deciding to walk along the water, the men and the sounds of their machines behind me. The day is sunny sharp and clear. My memories, my thoughts like this river and its pieces frozen broken and flowing, coming up going down, resurfacing somewhere else. The sounds of things vying for place as I look out onto the water, stopping, noticing the chunks of ice on chains once used to dock boats that made their way back and forth with ease from this side to the other, their trips between Windsor and Detroit continuous, non-stop so that there was no longer a sense of arrival or departure. Feeling the railing shake hum beneath hands, black wool mittens my grandmother made, holding one up to shade my eyes. Focussing on the centre of the flow where thin layers of ice, crystalline shingles, made, swept up by the wind, collapse into music soft and delicate clear and lucid, crumbling, shattering into water.

arms down ballet ready   lift your arms and make an O fingers do not touch you know bring your arms down let them flow into fifth position you go   step and point   let me see how beautiful you look and *s p i i n n n!* patta-cake polka is a treat patta-cake polka can't be beat step and point and step and point now stop where you started and stay in line or you don't get any scarf gallop to the right jetté jetté arabesque side together side together point and dig   *olé!*

Sunday morning soccer. The announcer's voice irritating me this morning. The Italian too turbulent and excitable for me today. Deep voices of men singing stadium songs in unison just beneath the play-by-play words and rhythms. I'll never understand him, unable to eat or drink while watching the game. 'Sono troppo nervoso' he used to say in those days before we were married and still living in Italy. Trying to explain to me his connection, his feeling for his team, a need to share in their anxiety, pit of stomach nervousness and desire to win. Taking my writing pad out from atop the hamper under the small pile of dirty clothes sounds of men chanting seeping in under the bathroom door.

llll is for lion *mmmm* is for meadow Grace snuggles in happy warm hugging my arm enjoying the feel of her tongue and lips and the vibrations they produce *whyyyy* is for window and *llllluna* is for *lll shhhhh!* now go to sleep you know mommy loves her babies

This time he sits in the bath. He looks as if he's lost weight. I sit on the lid of the toilet seat not saying anything, he doesn't tell me to leave. His body is slight, graceful, almost feminine. I remember this was one of the things I was attracted to, attracted to and at times repulsed by as the conditioning for the masculine type muscles jocks that I went out with in high school kicked in. He'd always wear silky shirts, thin lady-like sheen socks tiny brief underwear also a thin sheen cotton that his mother bought him. But then that was the style in Italy when we lived there. I was attracted to that feminine quality in him, always wondering about his stories nights out with the gay guy of the village, late nights spent in Florence, the young boys who couldn't yet drive offered rides, sitting in the backseat with transvestites. The strangest thing he'd tell me, to see a body with breasts and a penis. Farsi una pipa it's an easy twenty, thirty thousand lire laughing smoking popping Esctasy. There's a picture of him one year at Carnevale, this gay guy's arm around him both dressed as pirates, make-up on. The year before I dressed as a woman he said, and *I was beautiful too.*

Anthony, although at the time I still called him Professor Martins, once told me over drinks at his house that marriage was impossible. Well, he didn't use those exact words but something about the necessity of arrangements. I didn't believe him. I was eighteen he was fifty-four. That's a pretty heavy thing to lay on an eighteen-year old who still believes that one day, if you try hard enough and find the right person, you might be able to live happily ever after. The thing was though, that my therapist at the time, also a man in his fifties, a psychologist who I was supposed to be seeing for an eating disorder, anorexia-bulimia to be exact, kept telling me the same thing. No, marriage is simply not possible. And if two people do happen to stay together for the rest of their lives it is not because they have a healthy relationship, quite the contrary, it is because their relationship has become perverted, twisted, something like a brother and sister who occasionally share the same bed. That's what he said. It wasn't that, though that frightened me, made me think he was making a pass. It was the fact that he kept asking to see my writing. Would I write something for him? Even if I dropped it off sometime say during the week no need to wait till our next appointment just stick it in a brown envelope he stands in front of me making the motions with his hands, one holding the envelope, the other dropping something in. I'd love to read something you've written. Well I wouldn't love it I think although this is not what I say, in fact I'm nodding? Nodding my head yes, I could bring you something.

Is the paint pumped up? Because if it is I want to know. I want to know what's going on behind those flaps, tarps so neatly snapped together around scaffolds of wood and steel. Snapped so tight they barely flutter the wind and trucks passing overhead. It's a sort of urgency I feel as if something is going to happen a panic something impending what I can't say some catastrophe measured by the inches of paint on that bridge.

Driving alongside an eighteen-wheeler gliding Daimler Chrysler, I want to flag him down. 'Hey, you've left your boot brush,' I want to say, 'there on the step.' Left it sitting on the stainless steel runner as he hopped up into the cab. I attempt getting closer, trying to pull up so I can see him and then deem it too dangerous. It'll just have to sit there I think, sit there until he stops. And then, wait, hey yeah, it is sitting there, not moving an inch while the truck pulls itself forward at eighty kilometres an hour. How can that be? Magnetized, I think. A magnetized bootbrush. Very clever, now noticing a plethora of boot-brushes, almost one for every truck I see. Thinking that perhaps it means something, whether you have one or not, whether you place it to the left or to the right of the door, or whether it sits right in the middle. Stepping on the gas, moving into the *Local Traffic* lane, wishing that I could somehow know more about the secret language of truckers.

There's a picture of us, me nine months pregnant, my husband's hand pressed firmly on my belly, trying to define it, show the shape of it through my maternity blouse. Always tying my laces and clipping my toenails. Family members amazed at his kindness, smiling, me agreeing with them while secretly suspecting that he was doing it more for the baby than for me.

I'm writing in the pose he always makes fun of. Hunched over, head down, hand clasped around the base of a pencil, sometimes pen, come on, get a life. I'm sure! Day after day attached to that pen, contorts his hand sticks his tongue out the side of his mouth, exaggerating the effort to write. What kinda life is that? Come outside, play with your kids, can't you see they want you? Sometimes I think he's right, even laugh along with him as I put the pen down but today for some reason, I decide it better to ignore him.

Fantasizing about one of the fathers at my daughter's dance class. I find myself doing this a lot lately, young, old, men sitting beside me, driving in cars behind me, type irrelevant. Categories boundaries disintegrating breaking. Unable to keep everything in check.

I'm breathless as we push our way in through the single door. The sound of wind-chimes as we stamp our feet on the small rectangular mat shaking off snow. Looking down she notices her scarf. 'I thought I felt something,' she says. We pretend that she doesn't want to ask why in the hell I didn't tell her she had a scarf dangling between her legs and that *I didn't want to tell her* because I was enjoying watching her look ridiculous.

'Now see, this is what you do.' She nods toward the far wall where a series of shelves holds five or six small bolts of fabric grouped together according to colour. 'If you're going to do blue, you stick with the blues. Red, you stick with the reds. You have to stay within these five or six variations of colour and pattern, with the odd colour of a different group thrown in for contrast.'

'So, I don't get to pick my own fabric?'

'Yes, you do. I'm just telling you how to do it.'

'But I want blacks and blues together.'

She stops for a moment in the middle of the room, quilt-covered walls looming.

'It figures.'

When we first met, I didn't speak Italian and he didn't speak any English. We would spend silent hours looking at one another thinking we understood one another perfectly. I wonder how often silence is mistaken for understanding.

I feel for him as he sits there night after night alone watching TV. I feel for him and I want to join him as he walks slowly up the stairs to sleep by himself. I want to join him, take him by the hand, tell him it's OK, I still love him, but I can't and continue to lie completely still, perfectly immobile in between my two children, the room heavy with the warm breath of sleep.

Another oatmeal bath.

From *Imaginary Person*

Natalee Caple

*I*MAGINARY PERSON is a suite of poems written largely in the voice of a woman playwright living as a man and bearing a strong resemblance to August Strindberg. Some poems are written in the voice of the playwright's wife, Siri.

Franz says that every man carries a room about inside him.
If you listen in the night the rattling of a mirror betrays the secret walls.

Franz hates the winter, hates the coal buckets, hates the bloody whiteness of the frozen plains of ice.

I am far down in the silence.
Dismounted, following the tracks of dogs. There is no room inside me.

I would like to wear a Chinese dress and read my work in public. I would like to lie beside the masters without shame.

Discarded

To give up your card
Pluck all the leaves
Drain the wine and throw away the glass bottle
Hesitate—a human moment

Sweep the rain from the stoop
Strangle the bird that does not sing
Devour the liver of an animal
Respect the devil in the Devil

If I shall exist forever how will I know when forever begins?

Become a man. They have all the answers

Siri

She was running along the high road
I noticed how her feet lifted
I was sitting at the edge of a little stream
Thinking of drowning myself

She was running along the high road
I noticed her legs were bare
I was wearing a pair of suspenders
Thinking of following her

She was running along the high road
I noticed her arms pumping the air
I was like her under my suspenders
Thinking of grabbing her waist

She was running along the high road
I noticed her cheeks and lips bright red
Touching myself harshly by the little stream

My mother was a maidservant do you understand?
My mother went cold and rotten inside
Not able to say, "I need a rest."
All she saw was space wanting the space to tighten
She never lifted her eyes
One day Hemingway
Will bend a girl over a chair
Remember how sweet the boys can be
Lie down like some, some crushed pigeon
And say it again, my mother was a maidservant she never went to Spain
She drank she split the blue vein
Bathing only in the poem
Half-human in the stone café
Action always action
Stars spin in the new universe
The absolute moon is terrestrial

Are there other eyes out there? Does another mouth tongue alien words?
Take the rainwater. Take the microscope
Seamonsters thrash in miniscule oceans

When the universe is mute the imagination sings

As soon as the idea subsides
Flower bells tip out the rain
Smoke rises from the corner café
Children relish playing, Papa
Whipping each other with sticks
Madame fingers the ivory keyboard
Thinking of Bluebeard, dreaming his brain

Siri begs me to stop thinking. Come on—I say—come on!

Crying makes the hours pass
The evening hours already swollen
But her little nipples make me laugh
I kiss her musical mouth as if she is a hundred nameless girls
Desire flush to the furthermost terrain

Modern Sins

The sin of electricity will be the failure of the night to resist the day
Your activity all sinister in the mud-smeared hut

Shattered myths of matrimony a sound like footsteps round the bed
The words that lie dreamless on your flat warm stomach
Irreverently read by every new master

A new master a new slave a new mouth a new hole a new day a new thought a new shape
a new bruise a new taste a new sheet a new word meaning something new anew

Leap into Nothing, Joyful

"Leap into nothing, joyful," or, Dancing with the Dead

Di Brandt, Rebecca Campbell, and Carol Ann Weaver

COLLABORATING WITH the dead is something we all do, all the time; dialogue with ancestral presences is not a choice so much as an existential circumstance, bio-cultural obligation. *Awakenings* was the first time I did it deliberately, consciously, choosing to collaborate with another writer, a literary mother/grandmother, who a mere decade ago—it seems like yesterday—sat across the table from me in the Green Room coffee shop at the University of Manitoba, inscribing a copy of her newly released limited edition chapbook, *Awakening,* to me, while complaining in her cheerful, robust, clear-sighted way about the too self-reflexive and therefore not politically oriented enough developments in poststructuralist theory and cultural practice in the North American academy and beyond.

Dorothy Livesay and I met in 1985 when I was joining the newly formed feminist editorial collective of *Contemporary Verse 2,* a magazine she founded while Writer-in-Residence at the University of Manitoba in the late '70s. Dorothy was, in her typical way, both delighted and annoyed at the way we younger women (Jane Casey, Jan Horner, Pamela Banting and I) were taking up her proudly woman-centered vision for cultural production in general and the magazine in particular. She was delighted we wanted to give the magazine new energy, a new look: she was annoyed we wanted to revise its mandate to fit with our own poststructuralist/feminist graduate educations, as if her own heroic pioneering example and direction hadn't been enough.

A few years later I forgot I was a little afraid of her at a reading she gave at the Planetarium Auditorium in Winnipeg, her simultaneous fierce sense of independence and aggrieved air of woundedness at having been repeatedly underrecognized in her long life, so dramatically studded with important, pioneering literary achievements. " O, I wish I'd had a grandmother like you," I gushed after her energetic reading, "like the old ladies in your fabulously funny poem, 'Salute to Monty Python,' facing down the motorcycle gang with their handbags, not to mention giving the finger to a skeptical youth-oriented readership, at the same time. My own grandmother was a very tough strong Mennonite woman," I added, not really thinking, "but she practiced such strict obedience to her patriarchal upbringing I'm finding her a really problematic role model as I'm trying to figure out how to become a writer myself: I wish she'd been more like you."

"Who are you?" she said, staring a little. So that's how our friendship began. She told me her own daughter had married an Old Mennonite farmer in southern Ontario, practicing strict obedience to traditionalist Mennonite ways: "I wish she'd been more like you." Well, and then I found out we'd both lived on Lipton Street, in the same neighbourhood, though decades apart, and in many ways, shared literary/cultural interests and affinities despite our generational differences: our love of plain speech, orality, social justice for minority groups, praise for the erotic, a frank approach to cultural politics, adventuresome spirit despite social obstacles, spiritual connection to landscape, affection for Winnipeg and the prairies, and of course our ambivalent Mennonite relations.

I wanted to write a tribute to Dorothy Livesay, my alter-grandmother, my other, literary mother, by way of saying thank you for her formidable example to women (and everyone) in Canadian letters and culture generally, and for her valuable personal friendship and mentorship during the difficult years I was carving out my own access to a literary career, at the huge expense of most of my family and heritage and friendship ties, badly in need of literary mothering. Rereading her inscription to me on the front page of *Awakening,* I remembered with a start that she'd given me the most valuable and personalized copy of the 300 copy print run (published by the Hawthorne Society, Vancouver): the first ten copies were lettered, and my copy was lettered "D."

Rereading the poems more than a decade later, I found them less enigmatic than I had originally: frank, bold yet understated, the clear-sighted words of an old woman peering over the nearing cliff-edge of her life, into impending death. As I get older and begin to approach that cliff-edge myself—certain friends my age having already leaped over, and I myself having felt twinges of its nearing—these poems with their matter-of-fact cheerfulness and even humour about the most dire, alarming aspects of aging begin to make sense.

In every decade of her adult life, Livesay pioneered literary topics pertinent to the time and coinciding with her own life experiences, from youthful romance in the '20s to supporting the breadlines and commenting on the dehumanization of factory life in the '30s and '40s, to criticizing Japanese internment and exploring the entrapment of marriage for women in the '50s and '60s, to exploring environmental degradation and questioning the efficacy of war in the '70s, to celebrating female sexuality and grandmotherhood in the '80s. She published her famous "foreplay" poem, "Let Your Hand Play First," in her seventies, my students exclaim! Her *oeuvre* reads like a veritable catalogue of the twentieth century, except that she was not its typical poetic voice, she was often its first, its leading, its front line's most visionary inventive one. Why should that not be true also going into old age?

Collaborating with dead grandmothers is an interesting experience: I decided I didn't want to respond to her poems, nor interpret them, so much as just "be with her" in them. So I followed her intuitively around on the page, sometimes poem by poem, sometimes stanza by stanza, sometimes line by line, writing whatever they suggested to my poised hand. I felt a bit like a little duckling, imprinted come hell or high water on this particular mother figure, waddling after her across terrifying open spaces, whoops, here we are wafting across white space to the other side of the page, here we go over the cliff edge, whoops, here we are back on dry land, just barely.

I also made an intuitive choice about sequencing whose ramifications I didn't understand until later. I began with the last poem in her *Awakening* sequence, not really knowing why, looking for a place to begin, I suppose, a point of access, and worked my way back from there to the first poem. Long after I'd completed the dialogue, which became the long poem *Awakenings: In Two Voices,* published in full for the first time here, I realized it was Livesay who had written the sequence backwards, from the point of take-off, death, retrospectively to the many varied moments leading up to it. So in fact I had righted the chronology, from the point of view of a witness trying to accompany an elderly person in the journey toward death, though it seemed fitting and right, and characteristically bold, of Dorothy to have begun with the end-point, the finishing line, the topic at hand, let's not beat around the bush, we know what this is about, and reflect on the process involved, from there.

Looking back at my companion poems now, I would say their basic tenor is consolatory, but not in the usual way we think of that gesture, not by way of direct address, gestures of comfort, or other kinds of personal engagement, but rather, more obliquely—though perhaps not less deeply—through echo, identification (I see what you mean!), through imitation and resonance. And by holding up the natural world, the large regenerative beauty of earth and sky and grass and trees, so beloved by Dorothy Livesay and not as directly accessible to her in old age as previously, to her bright spirit, caged now in the strictures of elder disabilities and a narrow apartment, getting ready to fly.

Was it consolatory for me to be able to be with her spiritually in this way, when I wasn't able to be with her in real life during her last years, nor able to accompany my own mother's aging and journey toward dying, having been shunned for several years from my own family, my Mennonite mother and cultural heritage generally, because of my iconoclastic writing? Yes and yes. There was also that other uncannily beautiful thing happening during this dialogue, this dance with Dorothy, among the living, among the dead, the kind of reversal of roles that happens at the end of parents' lives, when the children become the parents and parents the children. I felt, profoundly, not only that I had become Dorothy Livesay's heir, her alter-daughter/granddaughter, but in so doing also her keeper, caretaker, interpreter—one of many, a lovely company—across various complex distances.

And then there was further trust involved, a further leap over another kind of cliff-edge, in handing the completed poems to composers/musicians Carol Ann Weaver and Rebecca Campbell, not knowing what they'd do with them. At the première at the Wider Boundaries of Daring festival in Windsor, I chewed my nails nervously, not knowing what to expect. Would they have had the courage to hear all the dark edges in our poems, excavated from tough middle and old age experience? Would they have had the nerve to leap over the cliff edge, to dance in thin air, to "leap into nothing, joyful," with us?

Dorothy Livesay repeatedly claimed that music and dance were the sources of poetry, the sources of her own poetry, though I had always found her poems more imagist than musical. She was clearly oriented to a frank oral speaking voice, but her poems are more often declamatory than incantatory. Even her chants take their energy more from agit prop political action lines, it seems to me, than from song. My Mennonite upbringing was pastoral and thoroughly musical, but strictly limited to classical piano and traditionalist Mennonite singing styles. Had Dorothy's profoundly modernist/contemporary and my hybrid medieval/eighteenth century/postmodernist sensibilities meshed sufficiently in this ghostly transgenerational dialogue to enable coherent collaboration with yet another two distinct contemporary voices and sensibilities?

The song cycle Carol Ann and Rebecca created and performed was exquisite, profound, powerful, a melding of four distinct voices in an experimental poetry-and-music song cycle, in a genre I'd never encountered before. And then a spooky thing happened. Suddenly she was there, Dorothy Livesay was there, her spirit hovering just above the singers as they performed, in that shimmery space we had discovered to dance in, where there is no distinction between the living and the dead. "O I'm so pleased," she said." I'm delighted," she said. "Thank you," she said. "Here we all are, we did it," she said. (D.B.)

* * *

I had known and admired the work of Di Brandt for some time, and had worked with her previously in the composition of a four-song song cycle, *Out of the Quiet,* which became part of a longer, multimedia dramatic work, *Quietly Landed?* and was recorded in my first CD, *Daughter of Olapa.* I have felt that Di Brandt's voice speaks extremely clearly and lyrically beautifully about parts of life which are, to me, essential but difficult to name, and sometimes deeply hidden. Working into her poetry is like working into my own soul, finding streams which I wouldn't have known were there, yet which become familiar when I encounter them in her poetry.

Similarly, I had been acquainted with the musical work of Rebecca Campbell for many years, and most recently had been particularly stirred by her hauntingly innovative poetic/musical CD, *Tug.* Rebecca's ways and concepts of working, artistically and poetically, run a close parallel to those of Di Brandt, and feel intuitively, instinctively, linked to my own way of thinking. She had previously participated in my *Dancing River* CD project, as vocalist. To be able to work collaboratively with these two artists, and to have the privilege of working with the powerful words of Dorothy Livesay in addition, felt like a reinvention of myself, a profound relocation in the artistic world I so cherish.

While working on settings of both Brandt's and Livesay's poetry, I found my musical voice gravitated toward a minimalist sound which pares away the excesses, and comes to bare bones and open structures. Instead of 'developing' the ideas, I found myself listening to them and letting them whisper and frolic in an almost African, circular, organic manner. In recent years I have been working intimately with music from Africa and African musicians. At the same time I find it necessary to work with people of my own artistic and cultural background so as to continue to discover artistic universals—those streams which run deep within both an African culture and a Canadian culture. Otherwise, I would fear remaining a mere tourist in both contexts.

During the improvisational process which became the compositional method for *Awakenings,* it became

131

sheer coincidence and a very natural, effective structural device that Rebecca worked mostly with the Livesay poetry and I worked mostly with Brandt, thus complementing Rebecca's and my contrasting but compatible musical styles. While I had anticipated our respective styles of music to energize the whole sense of the collaborative process, I was more than rewarded by the very nature of the cross-exchange of our artistic ideas.

While Rebecca tended to work with more vernacular, folk-like songs, and I with more avant garde music, after sharing our initial sketches with each other we began to exchange ideas, creating further methods of composition. Also, in rehearsal, certain compositional shapes emerged, not possible without workshopping these pieces together. To enhance her sound she created soundscapes from found sounds which she placed on a mini disc, and then debated using them. I encouraged her to incorporate them, and even jokingly offered to use them if she didn't! In turn, I was very influenced by her way of reworking the poetic text in order to shape lyrics for her folk-like songs. In my settings I attempted to do the same, shaping the original text in ways that allowed for the music to be as fluid as possible.

While I had imagined folk versus avant garde/contemporary song writing as our working continuum, I was amazed that some of my songs became more vernacular as well, ranging from bluegrass to gospel to jazz to funk as well as my more 'trademark' style of contemporary song-writing, while Rebecca represented country, folk, and avant garde, within the particular style of her personal soundscape. Both of us effected minimalist music throughout, which had been one of our original concepts. As well, we sang and played each other's music, furthering our combined stylistic exchanges.

Neither Rebecca nor I were prepared for the incredible impact this poetry was to have on us as we worked on our songs. Both of us found ourselves frequently writing highly personal, essential 'life-songs' based entirely on Brandt's and Livesay's poetry, yet expressing intimately our own secret journeys. My two most personal interactions happened during settings of Brandt/Livesay's "Solstice," and while merging a previously written gospel-flavoured song of mine with Brandt/Livesay's "The Solitudes," further shaped in turn by Rebecca's extensive vocal improvisations, which became then "Nestle Me Down," a song subsequently commissioned as a choral arrangement.

Nor could Rebecca and I have anticipated that our mutual love of Bach's *Goldberg Variations* would lead us to recapture his reprise concept, ending and beginning with the same song, in our case with Rebecca's setting of Livesay/Brandt's "Leap Joyful" sung *a cappella,* in the same spirit as Bach's reprised "Aria." (C.A.W.)

* * *

Awakenings feels like a truly Canadian collection of songs, whatever that means. Perhaps it's the sound of the mosaic in the music, with its lending and borrowing and alluding; perhaps it's the strong evocation of place in the words, our shared love for an impossible landscape. Di Brandt's poetry, written in 2001, interacts with, and responds to a work of Dorothy Livesay's, written ten years prior. Carol Ann and I composed, alternately and independently, musical settings for this poetic duet. In essence, I think we composers simply tried to stay out of the way. That, perhaps, reveals the most Canadian quality of this piece: the unabashed but ultimately utterly unself-conscious pairing of the humble and the bold.

The collaboration between Carol and me is an unlikely coming together of two disparate voices, but to my ear, Carol's and my contrasting aesthetics create a certain aural tension that is befitting the piece. My background is as an interpreter; composing is relatively new to me. More often than not, I've been the poet whose words are set to music. Carol is first and foremost a composer. So we came at this material and this process from different stylistic and methodological starting points. But the essential threads are audible. They are: my voice, the piano, the themes explored, and the sound of the words themselves. Hopefully, the musical settings we've created for this collection of poetry steer clear of the wholly esoteric realm, and breathe life into the words.

Setting these poems to music was a largely intuitive process. I read the piece in full many times; I pulled the pages that spoke to and/or sounded like me and I invited them to define my living/working environment. And so I lived and worked amongst them—a row of poems along a wall—until songs were conjured. Carol and I worked separately and with little regard for one another's progress, trusting in the innate geometry of the poems, and allowing for the process by which we came to call them songs to be a transparent and audible aspect of the piece as a whole. For example, the fact that some lines and stanzas show up in both of our compositions is simply a reflection of their particular and essential role within the piece as a whole, be it poetic, narrative or simply evocative. This is also reflected in the choice, upon which I insisted, to print the source material and not our interpretive variations, with the *Awakenings* CD (released Toronto 2003, music composed and performed by Rebecca Campbell and Carol Ann Weaver, recorded by David Travers-Smith).

Beyond the challenges and rewards that this project has presented to me as a composer, it has also pushed me as a singer. Over the course of *Awakenings'* evolution, I've dug deep into the material, finding beauty and wisdom therein. Hopefully, Carol and I succeed in evoking the spirit and depth of those words. To interpret them has meant finding my own story within the songs, which is always instructive, invariably rewarding, and the only way to really communicate truthfully and effectively through song. (R.C.)

Awakenings: In Two Voices
Dorothy Livesay and Di Brandt

(Words in italics by Brandt)

After all
It was a house
of cards ONLY
one breath
blew it
down
I kissed
earth

Tangle of wild tansy
in every crack

old rag and bone shop
left open
to rain

Into my thought
music intrudes
cleansing the air

Clear high notes
piercing the sky
Music as a garden
    grows dandelions
      and daisies
      indifferently

Like weeds, grandma said

Through the window
tall cedars toss
blitzed by wind
helpless
forced to dance

The knife edge of pleasure

forced to dance
blitzed by love, oh

But the roots are there
mothering:
seeds of fire

Underground rivers
diamonds
leaf mould

*

The Impossible Poem

Impossibly,

and yet

I built my house

this hundred year old wood

in the dark

held

Watch out

through stormy weathah

potholes

surround it

enough room for ghosts

ancestral promises

Smother love

breaking open

Stones

heap of wooden boards

in a field

*

What should we do

And why why why

I asked my old Philosophy

After so much light

what could we do

through rainstreakedclouds

to banish   this dark

this,   black, this

depression?

                              otherworldly   glimmering?

All she found answer for

        The old heart speaks:

was Fan the spark   fan

        live embers in the belly

the spark

        throat a fountain

That must be

                moon rocks   in our eyes

our vision

*

We speak

        We were speaking

of the woman

upstairs

        of our mothers

nothing left

in her fridge

        giving themselves

        so strangely

                away

Shouldn't we

take her

        imprudent

    something?

an altercation

    argument of sisters

arises

    let her go

Do not interfere

    yes no yes no

with another person's

life

    her empty fridge

    her long life

*

The apartment

    Wild scented meadow

door

    grasshopper sung

is not locked

    sun drenched

we can come

holding us

in

you are still

earthbound

in bed

in love with grass

asleep

rub eyes

and wonder

everybody   rub

eyes

*

Conversations

The dream

These uninvited

re-dream

insistent

the dream

haunting us

on the bathroom

floor

        to the grave

  and again

        if necessary

on the bed

        to be notice

*

Motifs

As though
And when

   you could overturn
   you dug up

   my turnings
   all my tender shoots

      fine tunings
      sprouting

   the space around
   so close

      my cup
      to you

   and *finalmente*
   and Voila!

      eat me up
      gobbled them up

   You greed is
   Your heart was

      never enough

walled against

the time it takes
tenderness

to bat an eye
halls of receding mirrors

splinters eternity
multiplying

*

The Left Overs
The Others

These are the men

These sisters and cousins

who never made it

who will not escape

who clung to mother

the leaking boat

careening crazily

looked askance at father

toward rock and quicksand

fell for you

as the last gasp

will not remember

the killing games

from hospital

in grandpa's yard

These are the men

These sisters and cousins

140

your mother loved

        who played along

          carefully

who never

        watching their backs

    grew up

        turning as the wind turns

who stare through you

at a non-world

        remember   *precisely*

of memory

        nothing

and there's no way

        And there's no way to love

you can shake him

OFF

        or leave them!

before the gates

        here at this braking

        shore

    slam

    shut

*

Of Slogans
    Too soon old

It is folly

    she said,

to be wise

           too late schmart

Even when you have stopped

killing

              After the killings

We will kill

you

              judgement

Two wrongs

do not make

                  and then more killings

a rite

   *

Witchcraft

Burned

              Dismembered

     and burned again

                in courtyards

     thinking this man

                  country houses

       at least

                  barley fields

       at last

              Coming back

moves with my moving

              can they

   Encompasses my hand with his

              living

Holds it in public

                                sustain their gaze

    holds it

        on and on

Light begins creeping into doorways

and always he is holding
                                leap   through
        onto my hand

            branch into trunk
                                    dragon flames

High towards the sun
                                    hah! unscathed

    *

        Waking Early

            Transparencies,

                pink dawn

Do not hurry
                                above the trees
into the turmoil
                    Poetry of birds
of day
                        symphonic,

                            country matters ....

dally
                    yawn
    dally

        daily
                    slow   pleasuring

143

the day

*

The Solitudes

Face nestled

Lying down

in goose down

facing the day

not yet   not yet

alone

is harder now

Across the continent

must learn

old veins sigh

to bend

without

enough

enough

breaking

*

Good Questions

The spun world

The molten core

is unravelling

heaves

put your teeth

                    burning rocks

into that cloth

                        in the air

and pull-l-l

                Jester,

                fire eater

be a part

                    dance   dance

                    juggle

                        on your pyramid

of change

                                    of sticks

*

If the notes are here

                And here   and here   and here

on the page

                    these animal calligraphies

the schoolboy said

                  every child can read

how do they get up there

             into sky?

                    every moth   every bee

How does Sunday (I ask)

                    The fallen tree

become Monday?
                              leaf covered

                    sinks gratefully

Catch as catch can

                                   tender   red earth

*

Solstice

The long distance
                         Trailing meteor dust

    keeps getting

                         we come
              shorter and

                                   falling
              shorter

The long distance
                                   Down
         To death

*

Here
              Toes nudging

146

on the edge

of life
                        the cliff edge

I peer
                                scan
over the ledge

into a vast

darkness
                        the great   dark

the killing place
                        crossing

                                diamond laced
emergent

                        that roiling

sea

*

The way out
                                Ether
is the same

as the way

in
                                        swirling

A choking
                                Every molecule

daylight

                                vibration

for both

is blinding

                                shattering into   *Space*

an onrush

                         Handful of asteroid dust

of bleeding

DON'T

                                left behind

Don't look

before you

LEAP

                      Leap   *into Nothing*

                           Joyful,

                      let them weep

Estirando los limités. Translating P. K. Page in Mexico

Claudia Lucotti

𝒥N THIS ESSAY, I want to comment on the work of two women poets of the Americas of the twentieth century, Rosario Castellanos and P. K. Page, and discuss how translations of Page's work which manage to retain those characteristics that make it so markedly different from our Hispanic poetic tradition—instead of just putting her central ideas and images into Spanish while using our traditional style and tone to do so—would undoubtedly enrich our panorama of modern poetry, particularly that written by women.

Towards the end of the last century, Latin American *modernismo,* headed by writers like Rubén Darío and Manuel Gutiérrez Nájera, came to life and flourished spectacularly. Their work still contained certain remnants of Hispanic Romanticism, but was basically concerned with modernizing poetry in Spanish by doing away with many of the older romantic preconceptions and introducing, by means of references to the exotic or the cosmopolitan, great changes in artistic sensibility and expression. The result was an elegant, highly lyrical, and suggestive type of poetry, considerably influenced by French Symbolism and Parnassianism, but not identical to either. According to Noé Jitrik, the difference lies in the fact that, though Latin American *modernismo* paid a lot of attention to fluid and harmonious metrical patterns and strange unusual imagery, this was fundamentally due to a search, on the part of the writers, for a new type of continental poetry divorced from bourgeois western capitalism, that would express their particular experience and spirit in a more authentic way. This meant distancing themselves from the positive "dictatorship of form" so as to concentrate on sounds and accents, which in turn resulted in connecting with hitherto unexplored forces of the language, often present in words and phrases that had still not exhausted their potential sonority. All this provided them with a more intangible, less productive type of poetic language and invested the poet with a religious aura (Jitrik 110-20).

One could very well sum up this *modernismo* by quoting the following lines from Rubén Darío's *Cantos de vida y esperanza:*

> Y muy siglo dieciocho y muy antiguo
> Y muy moderno; audaz, cosmopolita,
> Con Hugo fuerte y con Verlaine ambiguo
> Y una sed de ilusiones infinitas.

(Very eighteenth century and very antique
And very modern, audacious, cosmopolitan,
With Hugo strong and Verlaine ambiguous
And a thirst of infinite illusions.)

Nevertheless, this search for a poetry that privileged suggestive accents and rhythms to the extent *modernismo* did was an extremely problematic one, since it often ended up obsessed with sounds and melodies *per se;* also, these sounds and melodies were usually to be found in neologisms or archaic words that contributed to the construction of lines full of unusual images sung or chanted by an extremely individualistic and intuitive male artist. And a particular strain of this new type of poetry which centred around some of the more obvious and superficial characteristics of *modernismo* together with the undying presence of nineteenth-century romantic love topics was slowly to acquire a central and long-standing position, perhaps not so much in the minds but most definitely in the hearts of the middle classes and the less educated—read also women—where, among other things, it soon took on the role of a sentimental adviser of sorts.

With the 1910 revolution in Mexico, many things changed radically, poetry included. The new intellectuals and writers distanced themselves from this *modernismo* movement and became even more modern and critical, though they continued, basically, to belong to the more educated, upper classes. The new poets, best represented by the Contemporáneos, were also involved in fighting the easy and problematic nationalism which plagued Mexican culture after the revolution and which tended to produce rather sentimental art forms. This struggle on the part of the Contemporáneos led to a highly influential school of poetry in Mexico, which became increasingly intellectual, high brow, and academic, but not artificially solemn. Perhaps Octavio Paz is its best known representative, together with Jaime García Terrés, Tomás Segovia and Rubén Bonifaz Nuño. Many unsophisticated readers, though, felt unease and displeasure towards these changes and stuck to the older forms (Blanco 130).

And yet this is a brief summary of a literary history in which once again men figure and women do not. The revolution did not do much to change their lives, education or possibilities. Basically the only woman poet to be really taken into consideration by male critics and intellectuals was, up until very recently—if not up until today—sor Juana, the seventeenth-century nun (Valdés vii).

In the 1940s, things apparently started to get better. A number of women poets appeared on the scene: Guadalupe Amor, Rosario Castellanos, Dolores Castro, Emma Godoy, Margarita Michelena, and Margarita Paz Paredes. Critics began to talk about this type of poetry and a literary publication called *Rueca* (*Spinning Wheel*) was founded and run by women. But all was not well. Most of this writing by women was intensely lyrical, closer to verse than to poetry, and centered around traditional feminine issues, in which women still functioned, even in their own works, as objects.

Many critics have come to the conclusion that these limitations were basically the result of women poets trying to imitate poetry written by men, which is problematic enough (Flores 25), but in this case what made it worse was the fact that they were following the steps of the *modernistas* mentioned above, those who were themselves copying the earlier more revolutionary and creative ones, in texts that took delight in language almost exclusively at musical and ornamental surface level, and which were quickly becoming the official models to be emulated at all costs.

Rosario Castellanos (1925-1974), born in Chiapas and the daughter of a wealthy landowner, stands out among them all as the most promising, creative and daring poet, especially as she gradually became involved in writing about experience from a woman's perspective. But this was not enough; due to a number of unhelpful factors such as a highly conventional education, the lack of a more plural and diverse literary tradition—particularly as far as female models went—and the absence of a supportive environment, she was not quite able to free herself from the claws of the stereotyped remains of this type of sonorous, solipsistic poetry.

Consequently, she was unable, as Virginia Woolf mentions in "Women and Fiction," to leave off being vague and fluctuating and pass on to new stages marked either by a more political and social stance—that of the gadfly—or else by looking beyond this for an even deeper meaning to life—the stage of the butterfly (Woolf 50-52). Castellanos was trapped within the boundaries of a mediocre poetic tradition, which is sometimes much more dangerous than none at all, and with all the resulting consequences for this type of tradition, though apparently innocuous and naïve, was not innocent at all, since it contained very definite ideas as to what women, poets, and poetry should be. Also, the rhetorical and linguistic devices she was familiar with, basically those which a poetess was expected to use in Mexico in the 1940s and 50s, limited her work to such an extent that her experiments when trying to write about the experience of women, in her last books of poetry, never managed to succeed completely. In her final poems, a change seems to be starting to take place, but she died before really finding a voice that could have contributed to establish a new trend in Mexican poetry written by women.

Specifically, during the 1940s and 1950s, style is characterized by the presence of beautiful sounds, stately rhythms, and a passive, distant, and solemn tone which is the result of her using the official poetic diction and devices. All this produces a work divorced from the world in which it originates, and which establishes itself in the process as an intricately wrought construct. Castellanos also tends to use vocatives, exclamation marks, interrogative or conditional forms, and the formal *"vosotros"* (the second person plural personal or objective pronoun, no longer used in Latin America), all of which contributes even more towards an artificial, declamatory effect of tremendous isolation. Her poetic persona is so locked up in her own words and worlds that not only is external reality absent but also—and this is what is most noticeable—a basic interest and capacity on the part of this persona to connect and establish some sort of communication with what is not her own self.

The titles of some of her books serve as good examples of her poetic language: *Trayectoria del polvo (Trajectory of dust), De la vigilia estéril (Of the sterile dust), Lívida luz (Livid light),* and the following lines from one of her early poems, "Apuntes para una declaración de fe" ("Notes for a declaration of faith") (1948) also illustrate her style:

> Aquí parece que empezara el tiempo
> en sólo un remolino de animales y nubes,
> de gigantescas hojas y relámpagos,
> de bilingües entrañas desangradas.
>
> Corren ríos de sangre sobre la tierra ávida,
> corren vivificando las más altas orquídeas,
> las más esclarecidas amapolas.
> Se evaporan, rugientes en los templos
> ante la impenetrable pupila de obsidiana.
> Brotan como una fuente repentina
> al chasquido de un látigo.
> Crecen en el abrazo enorme y doloroso
> del cántaro de barro con el licor latino.
>
> Río de sangre eterno y derramado
> que deposita limos fecundos en la tierra.
> Su caudal se nos pierde a veces en el mapa
> y luego lo encontramos
> —ocre y azul—rigiendo nuestro pulso.
> Río de sangre, cinturón de fuego.
> En las tierras que tiñe, en la selva multípara,
> en el litoral bravo de mestiza
> mellado de ciclones y tormentas,
> en este continente que agoniza

bien podemos plantar una esperanza.

This state of affairs, that is to say a poetry that never transcended the more obvious characteristics of *modernismo*, that never went on to something else, worries me as it not only affected Rosario Castellanos and her generation but a great amount of poetry written in Mexico by women right up to the present.

It is within this context that I think of P. K. Page (1916-), whose first poems were influenced by the *avant-garde* artistic atmosphere of Montreal in the 1930s. Moreover, though she never reached the extremes of those who joined the Communist Party, her work was tinged with a critical concern for social issues. I feel that translating and circulating Page's work in Mexico, particularly her 1940 and 1950s poems, could contribute to open up new horizons and serve as a possible model, thus helping to break the impasse our poetry has been caught in. I stress the fact that what we need is not just other types of poetry written by women, which of course we do, but particularly the type of poetry which came immediately after the Romantic moment, as it is exactly there where our tradition got bogged down. Also, a large amount of more recent poetry written in English by women would undoubtedly be read with greater insight and appreciation, if this previous moment were better known.

P. K. Page's poetry of the 1940s and 1950s presents an interesting combination of formal and thematic elements, though this is not an unusual situation within the English Canadian literary tradition. On the one hand, she is obviously aware of the changes poets like Yeats and Eliot had introduced in the poetry of the period and which had been termed Modernist poetry by English literary criticism. On the other, she shows an interest in the social and the political, which is also a characteristic of English poetry with Auden, who in the 1930s already sought to write in ways that would register an explicit engagement and responsibility with the place and time he belonged to. For a number of reasons, the fusion of these two aspects, which did not really occur simultaneously, is very much present in English Canadian poetry, particularly in the works of the members of the *Preview* and *First Statement* groups. The members of the first group, to which Page belonged, even issued a declaration in which they stated that they were socialist and antifascist writers who wished, in their work, to combine the lyrical ingredient of the new poetry with a clear didactic spirit, by means of powerful images that would allow them to sing but about social issues.

The poems of P. K. Page are a good example of all this. From the very start, what we find is a very special voice that combines the use of traditional modernist poetic devices, such as the presence of powerful imagery and the careful handling of free verse, with the more practical and conversational diction and intonation of modern poetry, closely linked with a specific reality. The final effect is a poetry that breaks with the formal and aesthetic discourse of a solipsistic persona and provides us instead with one that fosters critical thought and is able to establish some sort of exchange of ideas regarding an other. In this sense, her poem "The Stenographers" quoted below, which traces the movements within a critical mind that observes twentieth century office life, is probably one of the most representative:

The Stenographers

After the brief bivouac of Sunday,
their eyes, in the forced march of Monday to Saturday,
hoist the white flag, flutter in the snow-storm of paper,
haul it down and crack in the mid-sun of temper.

In the pause between the first draft and the carbon
they glimpse the smooth hours when they were children—
the ride in the ice-cart, the ice-man's name,
the end of the route and the long walk home;

Remember the sea where floats at high tide
were sea marrows growing on the scatter-green vine
or spools of grey toffee, or wasps' nests on water;
remember the sand and the leaves of the country.

Bell rings and they go and the voice draws their pencil
like a sled across snow; when its runners are frozen
rope snaps and the voice then is pulling no burden
but runs like a dog on the winter of paper.

Their climates are winter and summer—no wind
for the kites of their heart—no wind for a flight;
a breeze at the most, to tumble them over
and leave them like rubbish—the boy-friends of blood.

In the inch of the noon as they move they are stagnant.
The terrible calm of the noon is their anguish;
the lip of the counter, the shapes of the straws
like icicles breaking their tongues are invaders.

Their beds are their oceans—salt water of weeping
the waves that they know—the tide before sleep;
and fighting to drown they assemble their sheep
in columns and watch them leap desks for their fences
and stare at them with their own mirror-worn faces.

In the felt of the morning the calico-minded,
sufficiently starched, insert papers, hit keys,
efficient and sure as their adding machines;
yet they weep in the vault, they are taut as net curtains
stretched upon frames. In their eyes I have seen
the pin men of madness in marathon trim
race round the track of the stadium pupil.

This poem clearly combines a careful use of language with an explicit concern for a social issue, thus including a more public dimension. Yet the formal aspects of the poem are not simply vehicles chosen to talk about the social; the language itself creates its own instances through which the work-conditions of secretaries are realized. The poem registers the movements of a thoughtful, restless mind dedicated to observing office life by means of images constructed with everyday language and producing unusual contrasts and comparisons, some of which are not particularly pleasant. At times, these images take on a symbolic quality, but the fact that they are grounded in the everyday ensures that our reading always keeps a particular, and in this case not ideal, situation in mind. The poem also possesses a complex rhythm in which the monotony of this sort of life is counterpointed with an increasing intensity that relates first to anguish and then to madness, all of which is perceived and registered by the speaker and also by the readers, who find themselves functioning as unwilling witnesses of a rather miserable state of affairs.

In fact, according to Gary Geddes, Page's poem "strikes one as a kind of tapestry of metaphor, on which the routines and nitty-gritty of office life are described in terms that draw attention to their tedium, mechanization, and mind-deadening qualities . . . Such detail and stylization give imaginative expression to the problem of workers alienated from the product of their labours as no Marxist treatise could do" (Geddes 553).

Nevertheless, having decided to translate Page, it is necessary to pay particular attention to the specific characteristics this translation should possess, since the great challenge is to transfer the poem into Spanish but without our traditional rhythms and tones taking over. Therefore, what is needed here is to produce a translation that can break with all this and come up with a poem that is able to register the workings of a complex eye and mind, by paying equal attention to the rich texture of the imagery, the different rhythms and tones which go from the monotonous to the frenzied, and the overall observant and pensive attitude of a speaking voice that is not positioned elsewhere.

Here one should bear in mind a number of the ideas Lawrence Venuti puts forward in his book *Rethinking Translation;* for him a truly successful translation is not the one that possesses such degrees of fluidity, harmony and familiarity that it does not even sound like a translation. Doing something like this would in fact erase all traces of otherness, both at the linguistic and the cultural level, giving us more of the same, more of what we already have, and so the translated text, instead of opening up new worlds for us, leaves one as isolated as before, convinced that all poetry or literature works in the same way.

Bearing this new concept in mind when we translate, what we search for is to produce a text that will maintain those very differences we found in the original that made it so new, interesting, and attractive that we decided to translate it, so that it would provide us with something different to what we know and are. Here we should also remember that Venuti insists that a true translator's job does not only consist in how she chooses to translate a text but also in what she translates. This choice, according to him, can even have ideological consequences, in the widest meaning of the term (Venuti 1-13).

To return to Page, the specific task was to achieve a translation that would maintain in Spanish a more colloquial and less obviously poetic tone. For this, whenever possible, I avoided the more pleasant tones and tempos, the devices too closely associated with previous types of poetry, and particularly a use of language that instead of relating to present day life produces a final effect of abstraction and atemporality. This last point relates to a very particular characteristic of the Spanish language: the fact that the most "ideal" translation of an English text into Spanish, i.e. one that apparently respects all the grammatical and poetic features, is many times not quite right at all, since the tone of the original normally becomes more abstract and elevated when translated, and to modify this implies a far deeper process of rewriting as one has to strive to reconstruct the whole text at a lower pitch. In fact, poet and critic Michael Hamburger has said that in Spanish, words have a tendency to remain abstract, related to an essential meaning and therefore untouched by what we make of the things themselves, which in turn produces the impression of a lack of interest in what goes on in the world around us (Hamburger 206).

A more textured, socially engaged, and richly imaged modern voice, then, is what I basically strove to achieve in my version, which I include:

Las taquígrafas

Después del breve vivac del domingo,
sus ojos, en la marcha forzada de lunes a sábado,
suben la bandera blanca, parpadean en la nieve de papel,
la bajan y se quiebran al sol del enojo.

En la pausa entre el primer borrador y el papel carbón
espían las horas serenas de su infancia:
el paseo en el carro del hielo, el nombre del repartidor,
el fin del recorrido y la larga caminata de regreso;

recuerdan el mar donde los hielos en la marea alta
eran calabazas que crecían sobre la verde viña dispersa
o algodones de azúcar gris, o nidos de avispas sobre el agua;
recuerdan la arena y las hojas del campo.

Suena el timbre y acuden y la voz arrastra sus lápices
como un trineo por la nieve; cuando las cuchillas se hielan
la cuerda se rompe y entonces la voz ya no jala la carga
sino que corre como un perro sobre el invierno de papel.

Sus estaciones son invierno y verano—sin viento
para los papalotes de sus corazones, sin viento para volar;
cuando mucho una brisa para revolcarlas
y dejarlas botadas por ahí—los novios de la sangre.

Aunque se muevan, se estancan en el milímetro del mediodía.
Esa terrible calma es su angustia;
las invaden el labio del mostrador, la forma de los popotes
como hielos filosos que rompen sus lenguas.

Sus camas son sus mares: agua salada del llanto
las olas que conocen, la marea antes de dormir;
luchando por ahogarse reúnen sus ovejas
en columnas, las ven saltar escritorios en lugar de cercas
y las miran con sus propias caras gastadas por espejos.

En el tejido gris de la mañana las de mente de percal,
bien almidonadas, insertan el papel, golpetean las teclas,
eficientes y seguras como sus máquinas de sumar;
pero lloran en la bóveda, tiesas como mosquiteros
estirados sobre un marco. He visto en sus ojos
a los monitos de la locura vestidos para un maratón
correr por la pista del estadio de la pupila.

In order to preserve historical specificity, I chose everyday local vocabulary and slightly worn out words so that the tone of my translation would not be overbearingly poetic and therefore very different from the original. This is why I talk about *"subir"* and *"bajar"* instead of *"izar"* and *"arriar"* for raising and lowering the flag, for though the latter are probably more correct, they have a more formal ring to them. I also include a number of terms that belong to everyday speech in Mexico such as *"repartidor"* for "ice-man," *"papalotes"* for "kites," *"dejar botados"* for "leave them like rubbish" and *"monitos"* for "pin men."

Also, I kept the images which relate, at least at one level, specifically to the cold winter, as real and as possible, otherwise this new text could easily end up referring to a more general, unsubstantial realm instead of being anchored in a specific local reality. For this, words and images that relate concretely to the Canadian winter were preserved with care, which implied finding out about "sleds" (*trineos*) and "runners" (*cuchillas*), and not including some culturally closer reference instead, and all vocabulary connected with snow and ice were integrally respected.

What I have knowingly sacrificed in my version, so as to be able to retain a less artificial, declamatory tone, are the rhymes and half-rhymes. But I felt that this was finally an acceptable decision, for to have attempted to preserve them in the translation would have meant making a number of changes in diction and syntax which would, in turn, have made the poem sound more obviously contrived. Also, eliminating these aspects contributes towards bringing down the tone a little in Spanish.

Regarding the careful prosody of the original, this translation tried to retain the different tempos of the poem: the briefer, slightly *staccato* tone, reminiscent of short-hand, of the more secretarial moments, the gentler sounds and rhythms of the lines that introduce memories, and the longer, more breathless sections in the second half that connect with anguish and madness. Consequently, I searched for short, hard sounding words for the office moments and attempted to produce a structure that would not allow the words to fuse together; for softer, more pleasant sounding words that flow together and produce a feeling of mental associations for the childhood memories; and for a strange syntax to hold the poem together in an unstable fashion for the second half. All of this was to provide variety and to contribute towards the feeling of thoughtful complexity which gives life and meaning to the original, and to protect the translation from being read in a more homogeneous, declamatory fashion typical of many poems in Spanish, constructed around remote personae totally divorced from their worlds.

P. K. Page, together with a number of other modernist women writers, clearly contributed towards creating the basis for the rich development of poetry in English written by women in Canada, a poetry that recreates the intelligent and complex workings that go on in the mind of a person firmly embedded in her time and place, and that is open and aware of the presence of others. Here, it is important to stress that this trend has continued to flourish and in recent years has resulted in a way of writing poems that puts aside a vision of poetry and poets as essentially solipsistic and in its place creates texts anchored in the concrete experiences of different women. And this produces poems that, while always engaging the imagination in powerful ways, also introduce a colloquial, many times humorous, voice which is critical and dialogic.

Not all literatures work in the same way. Nevertheless, the fact that other types of boundaries are also shifting, has resulted in more contact between our countries and cultures, which in turn has meant that previously unthinkable models, influences, and ideas—particularly regarding women—can now be taken into account. In relation to poetry written by women, the possibility of introducing the work of P. K. Page in Mexico, along with that of a number of other poets, will provide women poets there with new horizons. This, of course, does not mean that a process of imitation should take place. Each poet and community of poets will have to work out their own solutions. But this does not lessen the value that this possibility of listening to a new voice has for us.

The Pictures Sing, A Composer's Musings

Jana Skarecky

$\mathcal{J}$ HAVE SUNG all my life. Loving the voice as well as poetry, I have often been drawn to writing vocal music, both solo and choral. I have set to music texts by poets such as Hildegard von Bingen, John Donne, Gerard Manley Hopkins, Margaret Avison, Viggo Mortensen. For me the music always flows out of the text, adding my layer of expression to words which I find inspiring. I have very much enjoyed working with the poems of P.K. Page.

When I discovered her work, I marvelled at Page's vivid imagery and sensitivity to language. The title for my song cycle, "Green and Gold," was suggested by the vivid colours woven through the three poems which became its lyrics. "Summer" almost swims in greens, while "Grey Flies" is etched in golds.

P.K. Page is not only a poet, but also an accomplished painter. Many of her poems are brimming with colour; their words paint pictures in vibrant hues. I found this also true of "Planet Earth" which I set to music a year later. In fact, while composing "Planet Earth," I first did coloured drawings for each verse—watery blues tinged with greens for verse 2, the more sombre "wine-dark," grey, and green of the sea for verse 3, and shining gold for verse 4. Having recently become much more active as a painter myself, I feel the importance of the different artistic media flowing into each other, touching and enriching each other. I often find that painting what I am composing is a wonderfully enlivening experience which can bring fresh insights into the creative process.

I had a special experience at the Wider Boundaries of Daring conference with regard to "Green and Gold." The piece was sung beautifully by Melinda Enns, and I spent the weekend steeped in poetry. As I was about to leave Windsor to go home, I stopped at the Art Gallery of Windsor to see the exhibit of P. K. Page's paintings curated by Barbara Godard. I slowly walked around the room where her exquisite pictures were hung. Finally I came to the last one, entitled "The colour of the flower is yellow": a radiant golden flower surrounded by a wilderness of green. It was the title of my song cycle. I knew then that "Green and Gold" was absolutely right.

"Sisters" and "Summer" form the outer, faster movements, while "The Evening Dance of the Grey Flies" is the slower, more reflective central one. I find all three to be powerful poems with rich imagery that is delicate yet crystal-clear, and with a fine sense of flexible rhythm. I always strive to have the music flow out of the text. Having the wonderful high soprano voice of Melinda Enns to write for, with her great clarity of diction and tone and fine musicality, I wrote the vocal lines to be very lyrical and expressive. The accompaniment flows from the dramatic to the peaceful, through various layers of dissonance and consonance. I was pleased to hear Melinda say later that she found herself singing these pieces at unexpected times, that they "lived" in her subconscious in this way, and that she found them satisfying to sing.

The poem "Sisters" was the last one I found for the cycle, or rather a friend found it for me. I have two daughters, who at the time I wrote the piece were eleven and seven years old. Suffice it to say that the poem expresses some potent sibling dynamics with which I was quite familiar! The fluctuation between aggressive and gentle approaches is expressed in the music as it moves between the rhythmic and often polytonal sections and the more lyrical, flowing material. The "gentle" music is in fact made by combining in counterpoint the two lullabies I had written for my daughters when they were born, and had sung to them nearly every night for years—Renata's "Sleep My Darling, Sleep" and Juliana's "Sleep, Sleep My Precious One."

"The Evening Dance of the Grey Flies" was the first song to be written, and I had Melinda's voice very much in mind as I wrote it. The song is full of delicate textures, mirroring the "fragile, slender-winged" images of the poem. Intervals of fourths and fifths play an important role, leading into the fanfare-like accompaniment in the section that "conjures Charlemagne." In contrast, the next image of "your face, grey with illness and with age" has very subdued and stark accompaniment. There is a moment of light at "shone suddenly like the sun," just before the very still ending.

"Summer" is exuberantly green and flourishes with evocative images of life, fertility, celebration. I composed this piece in the summer, much of it during my travels in Northern Ontario in August 2001. I was struck by the strong energy of the VERBS in this poem: "grazed," "fell," "flowed," "gonged," "struck," "spun," "sprung," "chorused," "foamed," "lustered." The form is more strophic here, the "darker" and more mysterious music of "from the damp wood" contrasting with the brighter and more active "flowers foamed at my knees." The piano interludes between sections flow easily between triplet and duplet rhythms, reflecting the variety of plant life in the summer.

Soon after the Windsor performance of "Green and Gold," the organizers of the "Extraordinary Presence" conference focusing on the creative work of P.K. Page, to be held the following year at Trent University in Peterborough, Ontario, approached me about having it sung there as well. Feeling deeply moved by P.K.'s poem, "Planet Earth," I began setting it to music for this occasion. The performers in Peterborough were to be soprano Mary McLoughlin and pianist Donald Anderson. Time went on and the piece still wasn't finished—but with a great burst of energy towards the end I did complete it in time. It IS true that I was sending it to Mary in installments as I finished inputting each page into my then new Sibelius music program. (It is also true that this was the first time I had used the software, and I had to learn fast!) I was very pleased with Mary's positive response and her commitment to learning a challenging new work in such a short time. The piece was written with love, and she performed it with love—which of course made me very happy—as did P.K. Page's appreciative comments when she heard it.

Meeting P.K. at the conference was a wonderful experience for me—hearing her speak, seeing a large collection of her visual art, seeing her surrounded by university students who were hanging on her every word as she discussed current literature with them at a party at midnight—she hardly seemed like someone who could be 86 years old. She is gracious, elegant, very "present in the moment," has a lively sense of humour, and altogether is one of those people who seems forever young at heart. Her book of new and selected poetry entitled *Planet Earth* was being launched that weekend, and as part of the event it was a thrill for me to hear her read the poem I had been living with for such a long time, every nuance of which I had been exploring musically, and which I had come to love. It was especially gratifying to hear the inflections in her voice express the words in such a similar manner to the way I had set them to music.

Since then I have had the privilege of corresponding with P.K. as well as visiting her in Victoria, B.C. She did say to me that she felt her "voice" as a poet was more of an alto voice than a soprano—so the next P.K. Page poem I set to music will be for alto! (I've already started ...)

The poem "Planet Earth" is written in the glosa form—beginning with four lines of a poem by another poet, each of these lines then appearing at the end of one of the four ten-line stanzas. I set each of the opening four lines (from "In Praise of Ironing" by Pablo Neruda) to the same melody at the ends of the stanzas as they had at the start of the piece. There are meditative piano interludes between the stanzas, which (as reviewer Barb Scott of the *Peterborough Examiner* put it) "allow the listener to absorb the changing atmospheres and pictures of the poems." She went on to write, "Music adds greatly to the understanding of poetry, adding a new depth of feeling, and projecting moods and emotions portrayed by the words. Both singer and pianist showed remarkable abilities in understanding and interpreting the composer's score and the poet's words. The musical score was full of contrasting colours—light, dark, blazing—and there was magic and mysticism in the words."

I had already been working on setting "Planet Earth" for some time, having chosen it from P.K. Page's book *Hologram,* a collection of glosas, when I heard the announcement. P.K. Page's poem "Planet Earth" had been chosen by the United Nations as the centrepiece of a year-long Dialogue among Civilizations through Poetry, to be read aloud at several sites that are considered "international ground," owned jointly by the people of the world. I could only agree that they had made an excellent choice! I have felt blessed by the richness of P.K. Page's poetry, and being able to steep myself in it while experiencing the music that flowed out of it has been a real joy. The words take flight. The images dance. The pictures sing. The art forms intermingle and transform each other ...

> "It has to be made bright, the skin of this planet
> till it shines in the sun like gold leaf ...
>   ... and, newly in love,
> we must draw it and paint it our pencils and brushes and loving caresses smoothing
> the holy surfaces." (Page, *Hologram* 43)

II.

Evening Dance of the Grey Flies

P. K. Page

Jana Skarecky

slen-der-winged ___ and slen ___ -der-legged ___

scrib ___ -ble a pen-cilled script ___ a-cross the

sun ___ -lit lawn.

As grass and leaves grow

black _____ the grey flies gleam ___ their

cur ___ -sive flight a gold _____ cal-

-lig-ra-phy. _____

It is the

light that gilds their frail bod-ies, _____ makes them fat and bright as bees — re- flect-ed or re-fract-ed light — as once my fist burn-ished by some beam I could not

see_____ glowed like gold

mail and con-jured char-le-magne

shone _____ sud-den-ly   like the sun

be-fore you   died.

Satya-gra-ha-ha-ha

Phyllis Webb and The Spirit of Inquiry

Betsy Warland

$\mathcal{I}$N 1993, after four professional decades as a nationally known and regarded poet, Phyllis Webb made an unusual shift away from poetry to collage and painting. Since I myself trained as a painter while I was developing as a writer, I'm curious about Webb's shift, for I made the opposite choice: I abandoned my visual art practice to become a professional writer. At that time I was frustrated by the one-dimensionality of painting and by its elitism—how many people own a "good" original painting? This was during the late 1960s in the United States when anti-Viet Nam, Civil Rights, Student Rights, and Feminist Movements were powerfully articulated and advanced through the evolution of their own vibrant literature. Poems reached a wide, populist readership. Poems changed people's lives. Poems were accessible and affordable: they were everywhere playing an intoxicating role in new ideological and artistic developments. For ten years, I had worked in both painting and poetry. It became evident to me during this time that there was more opportunity for me as a writer than as a painter.

Throughout the subsequent years, however, I missed the physicality and sensate qualities of painting. I missed the porousness of painters being able to walk into one another's studios and respond to one another's paintings *throughout* their making. I missed the ease and eagerness with which visual artists talk about their work as I still find writers shy away from these exchanges, and even have superstitious fears regarding the notion of discussing what they are working on.

Happily, in the last number of years I have become involved with the visual arts once again through writing critical essays for art catalogues and reviews of shows. In the intervening decades, linguistic and literary theory has profoundly influenced visual art production. Alongside this, the incorporation of text with visual artwork, the accompaniment of text within visual artwork, and the use of text as art have become pronounced. The interfacing of visual art and literary art has become so extensive as to create a kind of fraternal twin relationship.

This is the "climate" in which Phyllis Webb migrated into her visual art practice. Although she has inevitably been influenced by this climate, her transition into a visual art practice has been shaped by her own necessities, her own instincts. This is what interests me. Consequently, I am not so interested in making critical judgements about Webb's evolution into visual art, in terms of, say, its formal sophistication, as I am in exploring what it might reveal about her as an artist. I believe that Webb's shift may well confirm a very important aspect in the creative process, which is the spirit of inquiry. This spirit of inquiry may well be more important than the form or even the content of the artwork. What is of greatest import is that this spirit continues to thrive and push forward. That's what intrigues me about Phyllis Webb taking "the path less travelled" at the peak of her literary life.

In one of the essays in her collection of essays, *Nothing But Brushstrokes* (1995), Webb gives her own account about the beginning of this shift away from writing to making visual art:

> In the spring of '93 I bought a new camera, an inexpensive, fully automatic Minolta Riva 35, and began to see in a subtly different way. Or had I begun to see in a different way and then bought the camera? I rushed around taking photographs, getting excited about my new view of things. At this time I also saw paintings, wild sprays of colour in my head, fantastic patterns. Do I have a brain tumour or should I take up painting?"
>
> I mentioned all this to my friend Sally Hulcoop, who then gave me a belated birthday present on July 4: watercolour paints, brushes, paper. An inspired gift. I tested out the colours on tiny sheets of a note-pad, doodles really, but the "ideas" came with ease. I moved on to the nicely textured paper of Sally's gift. I couldn't draw—never could—but some compulsion took over and I painted for three days. And stopped.
>
> One night later in July, after midnight, I got out of bed like a sleepwalker, steered myself to some photographs, and began to cut them up. At the kitchen counter I made my first collage. Where did this impulse come from? I don't know.

It's worth mentioning here that getting up out of a dream state, or a sleep state, and composing a collage is not atypical of how Phyllis has written many of her poems.

> I do know I'd become short-sighted in the last couple of years, as often happens when cataracts are forming (this degenerative disease our lives). I like the symbolic significance of the long view, so often desperate, being eclipsed by the phenomenal close-up.
>
> And now I was juggling the two activities: obsessively teaching myself how to paint, reading instructional art books, experimenting with tools papers, paint, textures, techniques. For the quieter more meditative times, and with a certain mind-set, I sat in a chair with a tray by my side cutting up bits of photos, fussing with a composition until something clicked, like a jig-saw puzzle.
>
> In the middle of August you might find me up at three in the morning trying out a new tube of violet or purple lake, attempting to capture the comet showers of the night sky. I'd probably been painting all day too, though painting is too fine a word to apply to an activity I'd never tried before; but I was learning. As the months passed so did my almost chronic depression. Painting my Prozac. Collage my keeper. Colour my chemical. I was possessed. (Webb, "Might-have-been" 84-85)

I wanted to have a conversation with Phyllis Webb about her shift from poetry to painting so I arranged to visit with her in the summer of 2001. Phyllis talked about the fact that while she gradually stopped writing there had been a transitional image in her mind of herself playing the violin. She recognized that she had a great desire to learn how to play the violin and play in a string quartet. But this wasn't very realistic, for among other considerations she has a bad elbow.

There is a parallel process between music and making visual art. Creative modalities for composing music and visual art are similarly porous. A listener's and viewer's reception is also porous. It is quite possible to be deeply affected by music and visual artwork of another country whereas we stand helpless before rows and rows of books in this same country's bookstores, completely unable to decipher its narratives, unless we've become literate in this "foreign" language or unless these narratives have been unlocked through translation into our own language. This raises the question: might the literary arts be more dependent upon igniting the specificities of identity than other art forms?

In 1993, then in her mid-sixties, Webb felt drawn to explore a central Buddhist question about the nature of identity: she found herself asking, "Do I exist if I am not a poet?" It's not just an intellectual question. This questioning of the signature of our identity is a profound, frightening question for any one of us. It's a question that requires considerable courage to explore.

In 1991, Phyllis' mother died at 102 years of age. That's a long relationship! During our conversation, she talked about how her mother was very proud of her as a poet. Her mother was not highly educated, but had an intense interest and investment in grammar and in language. At this point in our conversation, Phyllis commented, "Secretly, one writes for one person, as I think Stephen Spender said." Phyllis acknowledged that for her, that one person was her mother. To what extent Webb wrote for her mother; to what extent her mother was her first reader; and to what extent the death of her mother deflated her desire to continue writing poetry, is unclear. It stands to reason that her mother's death did contribute to her move away from writing, yet to attempt to quantify this, on my part, seems intrusive and irrelevant.

To Phyllis's question "Do I exist if I am not a poet?" I would like to add a second question, "Do I exist if I am not a daughter?" I add this question in recognition of her long relationship with her mother, and the significance of that relationship to Phyllis and her writing. I'll illuminate my sense of this question with a passage from my prose book *Bloodroot: Tracing the Untelling of Motherloss*. The use of the term "blood bank" in this piece is multi-referential including the ochre-red soil of the terrain I was staying in while writing in the Santa de Christo foothills of the Santa de Christo Mountains in New Mexico.

> Standing on the blood bank I wonder—when does the
> bloodstream stop? Is this what death is for?
>
> When parents die—abandon blood vessel— they still
> circulate within our thousands of miles of arteries and
> veins.
>
> We believe they die but perhaps it is we who finally die
> to them.
>
> Blood type: blood never forgets, knows its script inside-
> out.
>
> Blood pressure: to be free of its red-red weight. (169)

When the original maternal cord of language and narrative has been severed by the death of one's mother, one sometimes can reassume that early state of fertile formation more on one's own terms. There are indications of this when Webb assesses her nascent experience in a new medium in the same essay after working in collage and paint for about a year.

> It's been an incredibly productive year in which I've acquired a little skill in painting, polish in the col-
> lages, and tennis elbow. Whether it's art as therapy or art as spiritual quest, the pursuit has given me
> back something like the pure vision I had as a child. (Webb, "Might-have-been" 86)

This concept of 'pure vision,' I think, is quite central to how I reread Phyllis Webb's books and looked at her visual art. I am reminded of South African visual artist, William Kentridge, who speaks of it in this way: "There is a sense of the clarity of impulse we get as a child, seeing something new. The clarity of sensation" (Cameron 71).

Webb talks about painting as being more mindless than writing poetry. I translate that into child-mind; it is not mindless at all, but freer from the dominant written language-bound habits of our adult ways of thinking: "what we call perception is mostly habit" (Warland, *Colour Quartet* np). This is partly why Phyllis Webb may be so invigorated and intrigued by moving into visual arts.

The book of Phyllis Webb's which most enabled me to understand this major transition in her art practice and production is *Hanging Fire,* her most recent collection of poems published in 1990. Let's look first at three short paragraphs excerpted from a lyric prose piece entitled "Performance," evidencing a desire to extricate oneself from the restrictions of persona.

> Who is this 'I' infesting my poems? Is it I hiding behind the Trump type on the page of the book you are reading? Is it a photograph of me on the cover of Wilson's Bowl? Is it I? I said I say, I am saying ...

And ...

> I am performing this poem thinking of bill bissett at whose last performance he did not perform. He put on a record and left the room. 'Wow,' as bill would say. But the whales have made it through Active Pass. They pass on the message: Put on the record. Sonar pulses ring for miles. Paul Horn is in the Temple of Heaven playing flute ... Put on the record.

> I devise. You devise. We devise. To be together briefly with the page, the fallen timber. Or with me here standing before you wondering if the mike is on, if my mask is on, persona, wondering what to read next, or whether you'll turn the page. (67-68)

This, for me as a reader and a writer, points to a recognition of the limits of written language. One line I have written in relation to this is "all language is longing." If we were to agree for a moment, that all language is longing, then I would say it's possible that Phyllis has reached an abeyance of longing, that she has re-entered that pure vision I mentioned earlier. Perhaps it is a nascent polymorphous language, longing to be totally present and relatively free from expectation, that was most enabled by a shift in medium and the learning of its "new" language. I now read the four concrete poems in *Hanging Fire* as gestures toward her move into a visual art practice.

I found two of these poems to be almost shockingly prophetic when rereading them only a few weeks after September 11th. They are remarkable, implosive wordplays on "hanging fire" and "hanging fear."

<pre>
    hangingf   hangingf   hangingf   hangingf
         ire   ire   ire   ire
</pre>

And the second:

<pre>
                    hanging f
                        ear
                    hanging f
                        ear
                    hanging f
                        ear
                    hanging f
                        ear
</pre>

(Webb, *Hanging Fire* 39, 40)

These poems enter us with the immediacy and totality of a painting. Yet like a painting, we can spend time with them and discover their extensive subtleties of meaning. These poems also possess the kind of porousness of reception we experience with visual art and music, though they are ultimately confined within the specificity of the English language.

I'd like to look at one more poem from *Hanging Fire,* however, I must comment first on *Naked Poems.* For me as for so many other writers, they were a tremendous influence; I can't imagine being a poet without having had *Naked Poems.* They're that important. As elegantly erotic suites, they not only embodied my first Canadian female sense of minimalist poetry (for which I had been searching as a young poet), they were also the first poems to authentically convey the tender yet charged subtle gestures between two women lovers.

Rereading *Hanging Fire,* I recognize it to be one of the most astonishing collections of poems published in Canada. More than a decade after its publication, I feel very excited by seeing anew how disparate and exploratory the forms in *Hanging Fire* are compared with most Canadian poetry and with Webb's other books. There's a rawness, a visceralness, a free-wheeling, defiant, intractable, colourful disruptiveness in this book. As a collection of poems it is among the most visionary, both formally and perceptually, of any book of poems to date in our country.

In the following poem, "The Salt Tax," Webb deftly interweaves India's poverty and spiritual knowledge with historical British colonization and American self-obsessed confessional TV. It is a hologram of the economic globalization that has since been realized; a foreshadowing of the new global feudalism fuelling, in part, a new global terrorism.

"The Salt Tax"

SATYA-GRA-HA. SATYA-GRA-HA. I never saw the MOOVEE-VEE-VEE-VEE or the OP-OP-OP-RAH (by Philip Glass) and at the age of three I could not, in 1930, have grasped the meaning of the salt tax-ax-ax-ax, but might have seen a pho-oh-toe of Gandhi in the newspaper (and the power of TROOTH, as children do), of the skinny old ma-ahn and his 78 followers trickling down 200 miles to the edge of the Arabian Sea at Dandi on the entrance to the Gulf of Cambay.

Today and yesterday and the day before, the sliding doors opened to let me (age 61) see him (age 61) again as a vision of sparse white cloth, and hear-ear-ear again 'child's play,' which is what he said walking 10 or 12 miles a day had been all the way from Ahmedabad.

Satya-gra-ha-ha-ha, he had written before the trek, seriously to Lord Irwin, 'Take your own salary. It is over 21,000 ru-ooh-pees per month…you are getting over 700 ru-ooh-ooh-pees a day, against India's average income of less than 7 annas [4 cents] per day (eh-eh-eh?). Thus you are getting over 5,000 times India's average in-come-come-come! On bended knee, I ask you to ponder over this phe-nome-non-non …'

On bended knee? And they walked on over the strewn petals, the strewn leaves, cheered by many villagers, the salt of the earth-earth-earth, on-onto the Arabian ocean's taste of tears, sah-ah-tya-yah-yah-gra-ha-ha-ah ah, beautiful grace as they bent down to steal a handful of free-ee-dom. (Webb, *Hanging Fire* 30)

These poems are less self-conscious and at the same time they're more intensely curious. They're very present. More discursive and insightfully political, the ironic outrage in Webb's use of exaggerated vowels can be intensely felt when reading "The Salt Tax" aloud. Less solitary. More spatial. Again, more porous and public. Like paintings that unapologetically occupy public space, even in our domestic homes. Assert their presence steadily—they're always on the walls, right? They're always there. Contrasted to books, which we have to decide to select, pull off the shelf and open up.

Visiting Phyllis' home is a very different experience than it was before she became a painter. Her working life and her work are now more transparent. Her art is tactile, sensory: her home throbs with it. Not only are her paintings on the walls, but they're stacked here and there throughout her small house.

Looking at five examples of Phyllis Webb's visual work, I will begin with two of her collages. The majority of Webb's collages were made between '93 and '96, and to me, they are the closest to her poetry in terms of their strategies, particularly prior to *Hanging Fire*. I asked Phyllis to write a descriptive note, including dimensions, materials, title, dates, context, on each of these. In order to embrace the spirit of this "Conversations Across Generations," I wanted Phyllis' visual artist's voice to be part of this commentary.

"Moonwalker" and "Torso" are a pair. They are 8" x 11" and were assembled in '96. Phyllis was "interested in their sculptural quality. The snow-covered grasses produced a northern flavour, and there are influences of Inuit art." They are meditative and considered like much of her poetry and give one the sense of calm and balance which one immediately recognizes yet remains outside.

"Veiled Woman: Afghanistan" is acrylic on canvas, 18"x 24". It was done in 1997. Phyllis wrote about it as follows:

I tried one or two or three portraits before this one. Teaching myself how to do the eyes, nose, mouth, ears, hair, etc. This one came out of my subconscious. I thought I had almost finished it and was quite pleased with the mouth and hair, particularly. I went on a trip to France for about three weeks and when I returned I disliked the painting. The hair seemed very stiff and I thought I'd just black it all over and use that as the base for another painting. But when I made a slash down the central axis, the eyes virtually spoke to me and said: "Stop!" Then I changed the hair and loosened the overall effect, a strange mix of abstraction and realism. I felt kind of strangled when I looked at it, but I felt it was more than a personal thing going on here, hence the title.

"Oops, Pops, USA," delightful on the surface but politically sobering underneath, was painted in 2000. Acrylic and collage on canvas, it's 36" x 48". It's the largest painting Webb has done. She speaks of the painting this way:

I want to paint on a large scale but I work in my kitchen for the most part and this limits the freedom of motion. If I had a big studio and large canvasses I'd probably be much wilder in gesture and handling of paint. I felt a bit scared to confront this, my largest painting, so far. Rather like risking long lines in poetry.

I think the satiric quality, the writingness of this piece derives from this anxiety of how to fill up the space, which is not big at all, when you compare it to most contemporary canvasses. It's a commentary on pop- and op-art movements in the 50s and 60s. The main references are to Jasper Johns and his use of the American flag. That text beside the old flag says: "It's seen war, it's seen the passage of 185 years, it's seen hopes and dreams and it's about to see better days." The clocks refer to Robert Rauschenberg who used such found images in a collage-like way. Number 5 echoes Robert Indiana's use of numbers and before him, in the 20s, Charles Demuth's: "I dreamt I saw the number 5 painting." And then Marilyn brings Andy Warhol on the scene, and the little blue target: Kenneth Noland.

Phyllis thinks the hat in the painting reminds her of Joseph Beuys or Edward Hopper. A painter friend, upon seeing the painting and all its intertextuality concluded, "So you're still writing!"

The final painting is "Cross Word." This one is arresting, visceral. Its crossword grid of black and white is stained with angry red and yellow washes. The crossword tilted square is marked off by uneven, aggressive black strokes that create a rough line somewhat reminiscent of the nineteenth-century practice of inking a black border around an envelope alerting its recipient that its contents announced the death of someone they knew. Referenced as well is the blackbox containing the aviation records of a crashed airplane.

Surrounding this 'cross word' box is a field of broken colour. Between this field and the box fulcrum point (the box becoming a diamond shape becoming a roadway warning sign) are two strips of red text ("cross" and "words") that futilely attempt to bandaid the scene. At the centre of the grid one then notices that Webb has outlined two adjacent squares in a variant red. Gradually an awareness of an aerial view of the World Trade Towers becomes apparent. Another association is that of two people rigidly "squared-off" in angry opposition to one another. Acrylic and collage on canvas, 24" x 24", "Cross Word" was painted in 2001.

Reflecting on "Cross Word," Webb queries:

> Are the words emerging? I wanted to start a series of mixed media paintings using pieces of crossword puzzles and imagined that they would be a very pure image. I found the puzzle in this instance produced optical effects that actually brought on a panic attack. The puzzle therefore got messed up and less vivid. I used the square canvas to echo the grid patterns of the puzzle and textural effects.

In this painting everything comes together: specificity and porosity, a "renewed" written language, and surprising visual evocation. Czeslaw Milosz suggests that when "events burdening a whole community are perceived by a poet as touching him in a most personal manner ... poetry is no longer alienated" (94-95). Everything is related—we clearly see the circuitry between the global and the personal.

There's the obvious play on crossword puzzles and angry, cross words (these two words emerge in the painting) but also the power of words when we arrive at intersections of profound difference (crossings)—individually and collectively—and possibly a Christian referencing of The Cross and Italian fifteenth-century paintings with blood projectiles gushing from Christ's crucified body: the crossing (betrayal) of one another. The crossfire. Crossbones.

Phyllis Webb's last book of poems, *Hanging Fire,* and the past ten years of her work as a visual artist (sketchily represented by the collages and paintings described above) provoke valuable and refreshing questions for any "established" artist working in this intensely uncertain period. The integrity and imagination that propel Webb's spirit of inquiry are rare, inspiring. This reminds me of Shunryn Suzuki's saying, "In the beginner's mind there are many possibilities; in the expert's mind there are few" (21).

Although my reflections on the last twelve years of Webb's literary and visual work may resist conclusion (as do Webb and her work), I would suggest that *Hanging Fire*'s compellingness as a work of art becomes even more apparent when read in the context of Webb's most arresting visual art work, and when reread in the context of our time. It is the alignment of these two bodies of work, literary and visual, that confirms for me Webb's visionary reach. And it is the insistence and inventiveness of her artistic reach that inspires me.

Deeply compelling art such as Webb's is art that is hauntingly timeless while curiously retaining its original specificity, including temporality. This is the art that continues to meet the major events of different generations, eras, centuries. It is the art that unflinchingly confronts, sensorally evokes, and compassionately assists us in generating the necessary insights for the particular time in which we live and create.

Phyllis Webb, "Veiled Woman, Afghanistan," 1997. Acrylic on canvas, 46 x 61 cm. Artist's collection.

"I am only a partial fiction": Phyllis Webb's Hanging Prose

Nicole Markotic

$\mathcal{J}$N THE PREFACE notes to *Hanging Fire*, Phyllis Webb announces
a dialogue with Daphne Marlatt's essay "musing with mothertongue" (1984). She cites Marlatt's words that

> in poetry ... sound will initiate thought by a process of association. words call each other up, evoke
> each other, provoke each other, nudge each other into utterance ... a form of thought that is not
> rational but erotic because it works by attraction. a drawing, a pulling toward, a 'liking.' (qtd. in
> *Hanging Fire* np)

Webb places herself in dialogue with Marlatt's supposition that words "attract" each other, call up other words, sometimes simply by "liking" each other. In an interview with Smaro Kamboureli, Webb discusses how this quotation from Marlatt intrigues her because of the "magnetic attraction almost, that draws the words and hence the ideas toward each other in this erotic fashion" (*Dream* 193). On a page facing Marlatt's epigraph, Webb inserts a short epigraph of her own, saying that she has been "tracking" words that arrive "unbidden" in her head, "to see if there are hidden themes, connections, a sub-rational rationale. It seems there are" (*Hanging Fire* np).

Webb allows for the possibility that words "call up other words," that her dialogue with the world is one based in the very language she moves through and within. In *Hanging Fire,* that world is Europe: in part because Webb travels through several east European countries, but in part because that "Eastern Block" represents a politics (perhaps not realized in the Stalinist agenda, but one that gestures towards a socialist possibility) within which Webb has always firmly placed herself. As she herself says in the Kamboureli interview, "the middle section [in *Hanging Fire*] is the one that gathers the political material together. Once I got into the Lenin poems, the others seem to drape themselves around" (*Dream* 203). Rather than simply list Webb's political affiliations and argue how her politics influenced and inflected her prose poetry, I decided to write toward and against her text, to create a new story as a way of reading her disjunctive narratives.

I am interested in a dialogue about how prose and poetry fit into each other's belongings, each other's countries. For me, the prose poem is a writing strategy, one that pushes known forms up against each other, bumps and grinds into new writing. Prose can re-arrange the expected boundaries of poetry, can disrupt the narrative line, can usurp the primacy of critical discourse. Using this strategy, I try to live as a dual citizen in language, a thief who steals nothing but colour from a map, commas from a sentence, nationality from nations. I turn to Phyllis Webb for what she calls, in her essay "On the Line," her "shorelines," her "sure lines" that make up the physics and geography of the page. In *Hanging Fire*, Webb writes into and against notions of nation and belonging. I read her words as advice column, as train schedule, as blithe determination to see the hidden and to take her reader along for the ride.

The impetus for this essay derives from Webb's prose poem, "The Salt Tax." In the middle of a poem that pays tribute to both Philip Glass and Ghandi arises a disjunctive language that both creates and interrupts narrative. In the second stanza she says, "the sliding doors opened to let me (age 61) see him (age 61)" (*Hanging Fire* 30). That coincidence of word play and age-recognition spoke to me. I dove back into *Hanging Fire* using my father's background as word coincidence, as a "drawing, a pulling toward" to read Webb's writing. These "fictions" surrounding my father offer fictitious companionship to the critical text.

When my uncle died recently, it hit me how irrevocably I'd lost my father's country (Croatia, reconfigured as Yugoslavia). My uncle, long estranged from his past, still spoke the language, still knew the stories. But, unlike my father, my uncle had retreated into a translated self. Like many Europeans, his English-speaking memory could touch only as far back as 1946. Phyllis Webb, in one of her many serial prose pieces in *Hanging Fire*, says that "Long suffering is active, alive with plenipotentiaries of the dead and gone, the lingering on of the living" (47). When my father died several years ago, the dying was fast, the death a surprise despite his illness, despite the doctors' words, despite his own body. My father's archaic heart pace-maker, his circulatory problems, his constant overeating and dieting, his propensity to diabetes, his cancer, these all seemed mere obstacles on route to his living forever. My uncle's lingering was instead his process towards death, not a denial but a reaffirming of his childhood spent escaping the inevitable.

Lennard Davis, in an essay arguing that literary cultural productions are "virtually the only permanent records of a society's ideological structure," adds that "texts are not simple affairs; they are complex productions" (248). And they have to be complex because "they do double and triple duty as entertainment, enforcing normalizing mechanisms, and finally—and importantly—as sites of transgression and resistance" (250). It seems to me that prose poets try to escape the ideologies of the line break not so much by retreating into the sentence as by re-imagining the line as containing the entire page; the line-break constantly pushed forward until it hits the end of the page, the turn of the story from poetic line into prose cauldron, the written word thumbing its nose at one traditional form and thereby transgressing, resisting, and recontextualizing another.

In their "Introduction" to *The Line in Postmodern Poetry*, editors Robert Frank and Henry Sayre ask if "the character of the poetic line [is] 'natural' ... or [if] it is somehow determined by historical and cultural forces from outside itself?" (x). Part of the naturalization of a form involves its definition, in this case verse as distinguished from prose. But I am suspect of any search for the "natural" in writing (and elsewhere), especially in prose writing, which hides inside sentences that seemingly imitate "natural" speech. The "natural" is as much a construct as any artifice, and deeming one particular style of writing as "naturally" more like speech than another unfairly privileges what is a learned preference, what Frank and Sayre call a "historical and cultural force." Phyllis Webb's "natural" is that disjunctive hesitation between the purity of poetry and the murky quagmire that appears to be prose.

What makes a sentence a line of poetry rather than an excerpt from an essay or a novel? When I visit Paris for the first time, my main tourist objective is not the Louvre but the Père Lachaise cemetery—rows and rows of granite and marble marking who the names engraved onto these stones have been: Baudelaire and Zola and Colette and Oscar Wilde, whose grave slab is covered with a thousand lipstick kisses and has a large sphinx (with its genitals half knocked off!) perching on top. I leave a stone on Gertrude Stein's grave. I intended to leave my bra, but don't think I could top Wilde's gaudy display. Stein, who made the sentence so unnatural as to slip it inside the poetic line, there for the reader to slip on, invites more messiness, demands the ugly. Stein lets us slip—slip on, slip into, slip up, slip-slide. This is her gift to the Twentieth Century. Webb, writing into that muck, slips and slides poetry into prose and sentences into a book of poems. In the poem "Sliding Doors," her persona rambles ecstatically about the shift from one continent to the next, from home's persona to the wandering "I" the book shall undertake. "[T]he flight's on time," she proclaims, at the beginning of the book. Her adventure's beginning, her "daily grind" coming to a temporary halt, she has one foot "through a place called EXIT" (18), and she's sky-surfing the edge of edges.

Prose, according to Godzich and Kittay, in their remarkable book, *The Emergence of Prose,* appears to have no edge, but rather continues seamlessly from page to page to page. "Without edges or margins, what does prose look like?" they ask (171). Readers don't pause at the line breaks, don't read meaning into the format. Prose—in this way—is invisible, its edges so sharp readers don't feel the slice and dice of words, toppling over into poetic limbo. Jonathan Culler argues that the "most obvious" topography for poetry's formal organization "is the division into lines and stanzas" (183), while Marjorie Perloff laments simplified readings that would designate any texts as "poetry" that merely display a justified left margin and ragged line breaks ("Linear Fallacy" 861). Between these two designations, what, then to make of the prose poem? By expropriating two distinct genres, prose poetry presents itself as a form of writing that embraces both. I explore this hybrid writing as one that crosses between the desire to exceed formal considerations, and the narrational insistence surrounding such considerations. In Webb's poems, I shall look at the problematic of poetry that embraces the form of prose narrative, yet invites poetic readings that disrupt conventional conceptions of narrative.

Webb's short narrative, "To the Finland Station," describes travelling away from and towards literary events—into Russia and back out again (*Hanging Fire* 43). Abandoning her rhythm of line breaks, she proposes the personal journal to reveal herself missing friends, meeting a family, trying to see the countryside through Lenin's blinking eyes. The poem's sentences, its narrative content, shifts my reading back to my father's Europe.

Growing up, I told friends my father was from Yugoslavia because, inside the ignorant and lucky 1970s, no one knew what or where Croatia was.

"Vladimir?" my friends asked, when I spoke my father's name, "like Lenin?"

"Yes," I said. "No," I said. "Well, once."

The narrative Webb tells to herself is the story of escaping stories and travelling in trains through a landscape that represents a particular history. A young man's parody of Lenin's statue causes his arrest but, no matter how silent his commentary, his living body imitating the statue invokes Lenin's famous speech. The poet tells herself stories of herself. She loses herself in art galleries, rides tourist buses, walks past poets' graves (with real and plastic flowers), and renames her new friend as only an initial. She plays with the language on the page as well as the languages that surround and caress her. She toys with words, smells them, picks them up, puts them down again, gives in to their tricks, and their cat and mouse games that cross the "rules" between "he, she, it" (66).

Susan Stewart, in her book about the ways in which people preserve memory through the narration of everyday objects, *On Longing,* says that the toy is "the physical embodiment" of fiction: "it is a device for fantasy, a point of beginning for narrative ... [t]o toy with something is to manipulate it, to try it out within sets of contexts" (56). Webb treats each word as a toy, each poem as the embodiment of serious play, treats narrative as tricks and games. In "Cat and Mouse Game," mouse thinks the poet is a sunny day; poet thinks so too. She exits the scene, leaves behind the "fun & names / disrupting the bloody text" she carefully steps away from (66). "The inanimate toy," says Stewart, repeats the still life's theme of arrested life ... But once the toy becomes animated, it initiates another world, the world of the daydream" (57). Webb does more than merely invoke a sunny-day daydream, she reveals the corporeal flesh beneath playful animals in a field. By suggesting their animation, Webb suggests that the "natural" in this poem are toys *and* beasts. They are more than mere toys she manipulates for the reader's pleasure, they are the fully animated field she has dreamed. "Cat & mouse" begin as fun and games, and end as fun and names. The poet ponders "law and order" in this text as the cat and mouse play beside and around her passive self. They embody her desire to sink into the pastoral world with known rules and evenly-spaced three-line stanzas, but they also disrupt her measured landscape, and the persona leaves her reader with a "bloody" ending, a text with consequences. She leaves the lyric known, and moves towards fragmented, disruptive narratives, stories she only half-knows, plays cat-and-mouse with the reader until we exit our familiar landscape.

Croatia is where my father always said to say he was born. Croatia has become a name that Canadians now understand. We still don't know exactly where or what it is, but a few years ago it came to mean the site of the fallout of the fall of communism.

The raggedness of right line endings reminds me that, like my father and my uncle, I have an immigrant tongue, a tongue ragged and loose at one end, locked and hinged at the other. A tongue that will not behave, will not pronounce the words the way they lie on the page. English is my second language; this is true of many Canadians. In the country we like to call multicultural, English comes second (or third, or fourth) to many of its inhabitants. But, I don't mean that I have come to English after first learning another language. Like many kids of immigrants, the lack of English—that gap—is my true first language.

Webb understands gaps, indeed, she writes multiple gaps onto the page, into her line-breaks, threads gaps throughout her seemingly solid sentences: "we need all the light we can get," says Webb, in "Ignis Fautas" (*Hanging Fire* 36), and the sense of the word light here is not explanation, but illumination—bright from within, a sound howling and roaring, dark and burning, intelligent and alive.

I grew up saying "Croatia" first, and then "Yugoslavia" as explanation. David Albahari, a writer who has now chosen Calgary as his home, always answers, "Yugoslavian," when people ask, "Are you Croatian or Serbian?" The question has become inverted, but my father would recognize it as having the same semantic twist.

Webb's prose gives instructions such as "Turn the turtle over," "Find the treasure," "Call the hot-line":

> Memorize the Plan. Do not try to understand it.
> Make a new plan. Make a list. A longer list.
> Forget it. (*Hanging Fire* 31)

The ancient Greeks hid inside the belly of a horse in order to successfully invade and conquer Troy. Webb's prose rumbles inside the belly of her poetry, or her poetry shifts awkwardly within the abdomen of prose, not in order to conquer the reader, but to trespass the rules and transgress predictable genre categories. Sometimes trickery is about invasion, and sometimes it is about letting the Others know that you are already inside their fortress, their homes, their language. "Know the code. / Translate it into a foreign language. Any foreign language" (31). The reader, seduced by an expected narrative, rereads the violent Trojan response into one of poetic exercise, rewrites history as a series of cryptic invasions, exaggerated hide-n-seek, and language play undulating beneath our skin.

My father, mostly Croatian, part Hungarian, part Jewish, a little bit Gypsy, moved to Germany to hide out from World War II. My grandfather dispatched my father *in* rather than *out*. I'm convinced my grandfather was either brilliantly clever or criminally negligent. My grandfather, the liberal, had to hide my father, the communist, from incoming fascists. One by one my father's friends were arrested, convicted, executed, or transformed into generals. The wind blew fiercely at right angles during the war, and my father's one-time peers swung from the role of rebels to the responsibility of leaders to the loop-end of ropes.

Feminist poets must resist and reinvent patriarchal language. In order to take away its history; in order to reveal its history. We cross a border every time we pick up a pen or turn on the computer or hum into a tape deck. For many women, this is not simply a gendered border, but an ethnic one, a racial one, a religious one, a sexual one—a border so criss-crossed by social lines that stating identity needs multiple passports. In "Self City," Webb declares that "words / jump the gun," and my eyes read the line-break as literal leap—from a notion of self to one of getting ahead of that self, jumping forward too soon, jumping into violent words, finding oneself attracted to a patriarchal poetics that silences women at the same time as it has gifted us words.

In her poem, "Thinking Cap," Webb nudges the "attraction" she feels towards (mostly male) modernist poets, specifically invoking William Carlos Williams's "The Red Wheelbarrow" in her opening lines: "the red hat / sails" (*Hanging Fire* 64). In this poem, her memory drifts in and out of the prominent poet's words to end at the silent plums that "couldn't // speak." Along the way, the poem offers ironic advice to a nameless (and voiceless) woman: "fasten your seatbelt / lady and don't smoke." As Pauline Butling says in her important book on Webb's poetry and poetics, *Seeing in the Dark*, "Webb's paraphrase [of Williams's "This Is Just to Say" poem] highlights the connection between plums and women as objects of desire … and thus reminds the reader of the long tradition of woman as art object silenced by male desire" (102). Women remain absent from many "male" narratives, even when those narratives encompass us so completely we disappear.

After the war, young men still alive, those young men who'd been communists—but only the right kind of communists— reconstructed themselves into the leaders of the new government. They imprisoned and then put to death my grandfather; they let my father and my uncle leave the country. My grandmother, her sisters, her own mother, lie hidden beneath this war-time story of men. They remain trapped in the story, these women, their words devoured by the raging fires, or hanging on burnt clotheslines, waiting for readers to snatch them up like coals.

I snatch at Webb's poems. Her language enters my body, her sentences struggle to be more than what I know are "just" sentences. She's telling me stories, important stories, she's hanging fire by a thread, and it's licking itself clean. I know so few stories of my father during what has become "his" war. Except for getting out, he told me nothing of the *during*. Webb, who can only write about eastern Europe as a visitor, reminds me that language needs to enter and enter and enter. I plot her sentences as subterfuge, dream of line-breaks as mutation, prose sentences as eternally punctuated by my desire to hear her tell me that the fiction of writing is in the words, in their arrangement, in their disruptions. Says Webb of her poems in *Hanging Fire*, "When I write prose, I usually try to write logically and proceed in an understandable fashion; whereas in the prose poem I'm deliberately upsetting logical expectations" (*Dream* 204).

Becoming an archaeologist, working on digs in the desert, and tying bits of string around sticks to protect what appeared as bare patches of land, my father learned to dig through layers of dirt and bones to uncover earlier cultures, pre-existing languages, domestic objects either lost or discarded. He was good at his job, he was patient with the transition, knew that staring at dirt long enough could bring out a bent fork, or a page from the Bible, or a thimble. He was a communist, and then he was against communism—no inbetween, no transition period. All my thinking life I have resisted notions of the one and the other—either/or binary oppositions claiming that as soon as I label a thing, I then also earmark its opposite. Webb constructs prose poetry that challenges the narrative, that lets each line drift towards its opposite at the same time as the lines tell us the inbetween, the betwixt and the among: the stories that live inside and alongside the very junctures that dispute endings that stop:

> the Cretaceous period slotted between Jurassic and
> Cenozoic. See chart under GEOLOGY. See geology under
> the chart. (*Hanging Fire* 21)

My father told stories of playing soccer with old shirts tied into knots, of sneaking into early-day movie theatres every Saturday, of paying the town doctor with a chicken. But he didn't like to tell me about meeting with his angry adolescent friends in their fathers' cellars, or writing revolutionary pamphlets, or hiding inside dressers before the sun came up. For these stories, I need to seek the words in another language, inside the shape of other people's stories.

In Webb's "Seeking Shape, Seeking Meaning," the line breaks suggest a pause or break in the poem's narrative momentum:

> Cadence in scene, in the seen, seeking out pattern,
> finding where the eye catches, heart hooks, tangible
> order, a cadence. Tantrums of tears at such pure
> spirit, radiant things, on which the eyes close. (*Hanging Fire* 21)

The line breaks surprise the reader by contradicting the predominantly prose form. The punctuation and the end breaks force the reader to reconsider the pause imposed by a comma or end emphasis; the reader must reread previous lines as well as reading forward to the measure and beat that both drive this stanza forward, and reign it in with enjambments that belie linear termination.

Certain memories of my father coincide with my reading Webb's *Hanging Fire,* hanging on every memory-evoking word. The notion of memory that invades these poems is generated from Webb's idea of writing the "concretized" membrane (*Dream* 211): what we know about a person or object, projected out of the body's internal monologue into the specific outer world. As Webb says about her writing process for this book, "the strategies of the unconscious are very subtle and certainly not random if you watch the test patterns long enough. Countering the passive mood of some of the poems are those dealing with the Marxian class struggle, animal rights, violent revolution, if only by means of glancing blows" (*Language* 296). The poet's memory emerges not through what Webb dismisses as "dogma" poetry (*Dream* 197), but rather, through the accidents of the persona's agenda bumping up against the concrete details she experiences in the world.

How and why does memory operate? I do not mean to examine her words scientifically, but invoke here a personal narrative to question my own assumptions and presumptions about a text that also makes use of memory and its pitfalls as the entry into a world sprung from words. The details that leak into and out of these poems come from my own interest in the membrane of language that forms thinking. Memory—that dishonest mechanism—mediates the authentic from the fictitious, occupying one and then the other. Memory invades both the "real" and the "fictional," never choosing just one, never abandoning either. The poems in *Hanging Fire* challenge readers to differentiate between the "authentic" and the "fictitious," but also to confuse them, to recognize that "authentic memory" is as much a construct as fictional narrative. In the penultimate prose piece in *Hanging Fire,* "Performance," Webb interrogates the authority of the poetic "I." "Who is this *I* infesting my poems" (67), her self-reflexive persona asks. "I devise. You devise. We devise" (68). The poet shifts from one subject position to its opposite, to the all-encompassing "we" that an "I" implies, yet also denies. "I am only a partial fiction," she says in the final stanza/paragraph—partially true, partially fictional—authoritative, yet also partly absent, memory mixed with longing mixed with a persona who questions her own role in the poem at the same time as she embodies that role. She moves toward the mike, she reminds readers to turn the page, she focused the poem's end with a tangible and tangential "outgoing breath of the whales." Stewart says that "[a]s experience is increasingly mediated and abstracted," the authentic memory is "placed beyond the horizon" of lived experience, and is instead articulated as distance. "In this process of distancing," says Stewart, "the memory of the body is replaced by the memory of the object," since memory relies less on itself (on the experience of the body) and more on the experience of the object (133).

Webb invokes the reader's experience of objects in order to re-invent the mythological story, in order to *convert* the fictitious into the authentic. In "Paradise Island," Webb's persona follows a woman, who shoplifts toothbrush, tampax, an alarm clock, vaginal spray (70):

> The woman from the mainland, of no fixed address, is removed to Victoria, a little bit of Olde England. And then it's Monday. She's 39 and she's suicidal. They'll keep her in jail until a doctor comes—perhaps on Wednesday. (69)

Does it signify much that I am thirty-nine right now? That my father was thirty-nine when he and my mother finally and completely settled into North America? Webb's persona knows all about the shoplifting woman, a displaced Eve, but drops the story as soon as it threatens to become a story. My father had many stories about growing up Croatian, but not a single story that took place between 1939 and 1945—time has a way of stopping for poets who come to know too much about other people.

My father's poets spoke into and through the 1940s, convinced themselves that fascism was cruel, was defunct, was the enemy soldier, was ultimate truth. I read Americans rewriting Europe and try to discern the poet's voice, distant and pleading, breaking up into two-inch lines. Breaking my breath, my heart break.

Webb's gesture towards prose is not so much subsumed by her poetry as it is enticed and toyed with by the line-breaks. She insists on writing both prose and poetry onto the same page. Her poems' transgressions both imitate and are absorbed by each other, which ensures their enduring advantage of hybrid limits, cross-boundary boundaries, endless turns and returns. Crossing borders offers writers and readers a chance to peek into poetic openings, and to transmutate lines and words and language itself. I read Webb's poetry and imagine myself inside my father's words. Her multilayered offerings become poetic openings and possibilities, transmutations of lines and words and language itself. She ends her essay, "On the Line," with the tongue-in-mouth reassurance: "I talk like this only to myself with my mouth shut. Laying it on the line" (*On the Line* 71). Lucky for us, she lets us eavesdrop on this self-perpetuated behind-the-lips conversation. I see her words on the page—laid onto the line—and I also listen to the stories hidden inside my father's language.

In *Hanging Fire* Webb says, "The work is kin" (38); for me, reading these texts, *her* work evokes *my* kin. I read her prose poetry with an accent—hers and mine—and hear in the English a tinge of the Croatian tongue I do not speak.

"There's no reason for letting my mind lose its colour": Sheila Watson's a/chronological montage of unruly elements

Aritha Van Herk

SHEILA WATSON'S modernist performance is of a particular colour and streak. Her work incorporates the textual ambiguities of Wyndham Lewis and Marshall McLuhan, but transcends their dissociative sensibility. Instead, using the eye of a coyote/artist, she proposes in the clefts of fiction a poetic intensity that blurs the boundaries between all possible genres, asking generic questions which modernism glanced toward but could not foresee. Watson's work is designated as occupying a modernist moment, but the texture of her *oeuvre* defies any pedigree of cultural determinism and articulates a distinctively Watsonian fracture and laceration. Her writing defies that aspect of the modernist project dependent upon "a tensed relationship between the metropolitan and the national, between the universal and the local, between heterogeneity and specific national (and personal) identity" (Deane 358), even while it inhabits these tensions. The questioning and questing that shape Watson's fascinating divergences occupy an urgency utterly distinct from voices sharing Watson's Canadian time and milieu. "He's a unique," Paddy says of the parrot in the bar in the town below the folds of the hills where *The Double Hook* fishes for glory (*The Double Hook* 97). Watson too is "a unique," articulating a set of breakages that employs damage as generative gesture. Her work engages in a struggle between silence and speaking, but a struggle that takes place beyond a readily circumscribed plane. Within a bricolage of landscape (the bare, enigmatic hills), textual disruption (the smoky but clipped and elliptical syntax), and a tilted defiance that refuses to amplify and develop any "plot," Watson's work wrestles with and escapes both the lyric tension of poetry and the tedious determinations of prose. Coyote's cry, his lament's external analepsis declaring a cosmology of uncertainty, is not a reference to indigenous mythology, but a citation of the echoed howl of a coyote's coyote, a recitation of the assertion that few are unique in "this whole bloody universe of men" (The *Double Hook* 97).

The Vision, or Coyote's defiance

The escaping post-Victorian writer, on her way to Banff, sees a coyote trotting unconcernedly across the Trans-Canada highway. They are both, plot-driven writer and footloose, tongue-lolling coyote, tempted by fate, by elsewhere, by new beginnings, by a rogue mythology that refuses all the tricks of assumed tricksterhood, the too easy assignations of wiliness. The road is merely a ribbon of asphalt and, for the coyote, not to be followed but evaded. For the writer, the deliberately paved and tractible course is a curse, and the coyote a laughing escapee from the deliberations of periodicity.

Modernism in Canada: a beginning. Kill poetry so that it cannot fish. Kill narrative so that it cannot tempt. Do not assign to either a matriarchal designation; the old woman (old and woman, but powerfully present) is conjured by her community, the hills, and coyote himself, not literal, but a ghost-figure, both conscience and scapegoat. Begin to write a transfusion of poetic prose that dares to cross a highway and run toward the back country, the margin. A writing on its way to Kamloops, the high dry table of the Cariboo. Death, declares Watson's narrator in *Deep Hollow Creek,* presumes life; "and the flame, however thin, must be lit before it can be blown out by the thousand unsuspected gusts noted by the compilers and annotaters, and amassers of vital statistics within the universal bills of mortality" (*Deep Hollow Creek* 8). Death becomes a happy ending, a locution devoutly embraced. Contemplate then modernity's resistance to realism, its tango with fragmentation and anxiety. Is all coherence lost, merely a coyote shadow crossing at an oblique angle? Can modernity's continuing atomization sustain the curious coherence of the fragment, its jagged edges proud of their cubist inclinations?

And as for piety, contemplate Felix with a fish spine, contemplating the divine, "Saint Felix with a death's head meditating" (*The Double Hook* 18). Watson's elusive narrators wear all manner of disguises, the better to evade any gestural coherence, either gender or genre. Community's internal disenchantments provoke the conflicted atomization of a world in fragments, the ground shifting underfoot, the future corrosive and secular.

Watson's own modernist poetics is comprised of tone, pitch, muscle, a faint ripple in the cleft of the hills where snow drifts and the coyote watches and watches, occasionally laughing, carrying away souls "like a rabbit in his mouth" (*The Double Hook* 51). Coyote has come down from his observation post in the hills, now lives among the mongrel scrub. Sometimes he speaks an echolalic and invisible chorus of yips and howls, sometimes he lopes across an open space, confident, ears aperk. Catch me if you can. *Canis latrans.* Habitat a variety of wooden and open areas. Dog-like, but undog-like, a rogue, a conniver, a textual metaphor. Unremarkable in his gray-yellow coat, but his large ears, pointed nose, and bushy, black-tipped tail, which he holds down while running, remark a sly intelligence. A matinal sleuth as well as a nocturnal hunter, haunting fields and back yards, the late-night deserted parking lots of universities, the low bushes of concealment and its muffled scuffles. Living on mice and berries. Unafraid, laughing at the world, cross-genre. The contingent authority of the one who does not need to examine his own freedoms.

Witness Watson's textation of Dog Creek, just across the Fraser from the Gang Ranch. A place to be reckoned with, the modernist spread, horses and dogs and herds and the metronome passage of seasons unruly as the weather. Stoves cooling in the night, the hills hunched like porcupines, and spring signalled by rhubarb poking a thick pink tongue out of the snow-bound earth.

The modernist moment of invention becomes Watson's cross-country trek. *The Double Hook,* written in Calgary Alberta, although the idea came to her "right in the middle of Bloor Street" (Bowering 1198), myth "amplified from the word" ("Myth and Counter-Myth," *Sheila Watson: A Collection* 123) which uncovered a plethora of mythologies doubling back and forth in their tracks. The best weapon against myth, says Watson, is myth itself, never reconstituted, dried and preserved in order to uncover its essence, but fluid and active, ineffable. And what modernism that? Migratory, ambivalent, quixotic. The restlessness of passage, destination nowhere.

What kind of writing is Watson's genre? Novella, fable, prose poem? Meditation, sacred text, last will and testament? Predicament, evocation, hymn? Theology, metamorphosis, fracture? A vatic language refusing punctuation or quotation marks, the comfort of any textual rumble seat? Or simply writing, a process engaged with its own desire and dyslexia.

Modo, or "just now"

Immediate, this *modus vivendi,* such a shock of cold water bubbling under the ice in the folds of the hills and in the cabin where the spring breakup refuses to break. The "animate dust" (*Deep Hollow Creek* 106) of a hill of ants. The impatience of a horse mounted bareback, the fugitive grace of lengthening shadows. "Impossible to spy into the works of nature" (*Deep Hollow Creek* 122), that changeling force. Threading a needle with red thread held close to the eye, a piercing coordination.

And even more immediate, the public nuisance of death, a body that cannot be buried. In summer the ground is hard as nails and in winter the ground is frozen. Only a brief moment of softening, a sudden relaxation waiting for surprise will enable dust to meet earth. Or a burning, the house where James pushed his fishing mother down the stairs burnt to the ground, "blank smouldering space" (*The Double Hook* 125). The fall and the crime paradoxically erased, the momentary made history, cruelly metaphorical.

Just now. The match flare of a moment. Stella, at the end of *Deep Hollow Creek,* lighting a cigarette. "When the match burned her finger she became a spectator of the scene—Juno by the chair—herself—Browne open at her elbow—the match extended—the twinge of seared flesh" (*Deep Hollow Creek* 141). Here, now, she begins again, Stella the star, the stone, the silent, ready to set out. But for now, that *modo,* she hesitates.

The Labyrinth

Regulation first. New criticism's tautology and *quidditas.* How Canadian modernism measures its own sphere, evaluates, aprises. Raised eyebrows and unintentional authority. Riding the rails, building the Banff/Jasper highway as a cure for unemployment and disaffection.

High modern or low? Watson's work inspired Robert Kroetsch's comment that Canadians went "from agrarian to post-industrial in a leap that excluded high modern from our experience" leading to what he declares is a "necessary act of decreation" ("Death is a Happy Ending" 206-207). But did Canadian experience take that pole vault over the ice floe of modernity? Fragmention and anxiety, the inchoate and the sensory boiling through the veins of time. Decreation neglected in our reading of the times, launch pad pure Victoriana? No chance to revel in a doubtful agonistes. The moral storyteller seeking to avoid the embarrassment of the story? The ideologies of difference centrifuge to a prolegomenon to chaos? In the writerly world of Sheila Watson, every god-given law is challenged. Providence rides shotgun on the world. The pure oxygen of discontinuity reads her poetic lines.

The Double Hook, Four Stories, and *Deep Hollow Creek* are zigzag poetic narratives, coyote trails that lurk from house to house, that slide under fences and that cast lines to fish in creeks that refuse to thaw and run. Even the woven cloth of family invites its own murder and frayed dissolution, its own flight and return and theft. Nature, the church, the community, family, in flight. Man, this bare forked creature, in flight, "the price of his escape" (Watson, *The Double Hook* 103), inevitable return.

James murders his mother and runs away, only to be robbed of his own bid for freedom and compelled to return, his journey the long line in a poetic quest narrative. The widow Wagner sings chorus lines, and Lenchen bears the brunt of singled-out mother and orphan arias. Kip eyes the world and Felix Prosper (consider the lilies) plays his fiddle and contemplates the skeleton of a fish as the frame of a poem, the delicate tracery of spine, the intricate construction of biology.

Watson's lines zigzag from one house to the next, from one yard to the next, from one woodbox to the next, without logic, only pontilistic connection. She fishes a poetic line that follows its own invention—narrative itself a mere visitation in the stream of dissociative consciousness that marks the hook's doubleness, itself the oxymoron of doppelgänger and double entendre that persists in trailing the irrational sequence.

In "Brother Oedipus" the roots of the willow have grown into the plumbing, and "disturbed the whole system" (*Four Stories* 13), until finally in the church all the gathered contradictions of "new aesthetic tastes, new intellectual perspectives, new occupational interests, new moral conceptions" ("The Rumble Seat," *Four Stories* 57) dissolve into disobedience, the church pew (that seat of diatribe and determination) become a rumble seat in the story by the same name.

In *Deep Hollow Creek,* Stella, who has taken a job teaching (that dissemination of information's cultural aesthetic) in the remote Cariboo, zigzags from the Flower house (where she initially boards) to the schoolhouse, from the general store to the schoolhouse, from her cabin to the brow above the valley and back to the schoolhouse, where the cursive reader is witness to not one pedagogical scene. What exactly does Stella teach? The three Rs, we expect, but in truth, Stella teaches multiple Ss, and S stands for escape. Stella in *Deep Hollow Creek* descends to the town in the valley, the same town where James in *The Double Hook* seeks escape from his bed and board and crime. She tries to teach what she thinks she knows, struggling to understand the Shuswap who live beside the community and who watch her but who refuse to walk the parallel line of her pedagogical strategies, instead appropriating only the most unexpected material for their use. Stella occupies the sonnet of schoolteacher as mere visitation, low modernist, the pointer at the front of the school, water dipper and firewood more important than the rote of words for the ten children sent to occupy the one room's itinerant wisdom and surely crumbling free verse.

Oracular

Indiscriminate and generous, persona for the long poem, the parrot in *The Double Hook* repeatedly orders drinks all around, his "voice raised on a note of authority" (*The Double Hook* 97). This parrot, having learned by rote the most popular if not most frequent phrase of his milieu, parrots an incipient language of marketing, sales and civilization. Once James has been cured of flight, about to circle and return, he imagines the parrot, that modernist voice, who "lived between two worlds . . . probably asleep now, stupid with beer and age" (*The Double Hook* 103). The desire the parrot articulates is programmatic, the orthodoxy of forgetting. He is the last gasp of the old world, brought to this remote community as both exotic and unique, clamorous but watchful. This parrot is not caged, but interruptive, sidling along the bar and rattling its tin cup like a Wyndham Lewis metaphor hanging over *The Double Hook,* speech a terrible revelation. Vincent Penhale of Lewis' *The Vulgar Streak* presages the parrot's metaphor: "He felt uneasy in his exposed position—like a parrot up in a cage, making loud remarks he did not understand, but *knowing* he did not understand them. A most luckless sort of parrot" (Lewis 217). James' kinship with the speaking animal frames his frustration and his own sense of lucklessness. "Buy the parrot some beer, he said. It's little enough he must have to live for. One parrot in this whole bloody universe of men." To which Paddy replies, "Men don't often have their own way. It's not many have the rights of a dumb beast and a speaking man at the same time" (*The Double Hook* 97). Modernity has altered the double-text of beast and man, dumbness and speech reversed. The only escape is to merge those voices, human tongue disencumbered by coyote's cry and parrot's rote.

Stella in *Deep Hollow Creek* takes the schoolteacher's job but refuses to teach, inverts the imperative of knowledge. She teaches but will not play the teacher for the community, to live as they expect/wish her to. Instead, she takes the abandoned cabin and lives alone, a solitary line, despite resistance. "Women don't do it in this country, [Mockett] said. There's only one kind of woman lives alone and it's not for quiet's sake she does it" (*Deep Hollow Creek* 72). Stella then becomes a troubling intrusion in the community's narrative, not boarder, not visitor, on no side but her own and the side of her dog and horse. Discontinuous, she breaks the thread of expectation, becomes coyote/outlaw.

And old Gabrielle, the Shuswap oracle, when Stella is set to leave the valley of Deep Hollow Creek, visits her, asks for a teapot and a sweater. When Stella brings out a good sweater, mended but whole, as a gift, Gabrielle fingers it, then puts it aside and refuses, saying that she has better sweaters herself. Stella, who cannot interrogate her own willingness to take and give, almost realizes how close she has come to the disruptive line of coyote. "Perhaps it is as well she didn't take it, she said to Juno. I might have seen her in it and by some strange delusion fancied her as myself" (*Deep Hollow Creek* 141). Stella seeing Gabrielle in Stella's hand-down sweater and fancying her (Gabrielle) to be herself is as close as the educated and teacherly might come to the more elemental occupation of creek and hills. Stella herself not herself. Seeing herself when she was not that her. And not that self.

Shape-shifter

There is scant time for reading as process in *The Double Hook*. The lamp is lit for looking more than for "enlightenment," an aid to those who see and hear too much, reading the world rather than any textation of that world. Instead of reading, the lines and their personae play with fire in a distemper replete with waiting. Instead of reading, the reader, "the old lady, mother of William of James and of Greta" (*The Double Hook* 13), fishes, and by fishing refuses, despite being killed, to die. She is a modernist poetics, casting its shadow over the cast line, made to bear the brunt of patriarchal designation. And so, while she, that old lady, has been read as maternal, she is in fact a figure dressed in the paternal sweater of discipline and punish, finally punished.

In *Deep Hollow Creek* Stella reads in order to endure her own pedagogical isolation. Stella takes on reading as an escape act, minimalist, reductive, a way to evade her own plot, character, setting, and especially theme. When Miriam (her visiting friend) asks why she doesn't just relax after school, Stella responds, "It's part of my life. . . . Just because I'm here there's no reason for letting my mind lose its colour like one of the cabbages in Mockett's root cellar" (*Deep Hollow Creek* 95) and returns to her poetry. She engages with a poetics of evasion to slip between the literacy of the past and the literacy of the present, to bulwark her participatory separateness.

Even riding her horse, a horse she cannot shoe, trying to imagine the imprisonment of winter, Stella remembers poetry. "Poetry could rise to eloquence. One could fob off a fact with a line. The right eye scanned the testimony of the left and in the margin, the hand wrote lyrical self-pity. The hand wrote *To be considered: Thoreau on the shore of his lake—Steffanson in the Arctic*" (*Deep Hollow Creek* 66). Stella cannot survive without the pragmatic community around her, and yet, she abjures its sound and fury, reacts more passionately to the line that transcends the fact.

Most important of all, Stella learns to doubt her own rote-learned discourse, realizes that "If I hadn't come here, she said [she is talking to her dog, Juno] I doubt whether I should ever have seen through the shroud of printers' ink, through to the embalmed essence. The word is a flame burning in a dark glass" (*Deep Hollow Creek* 112), the word and not genre the transcendent site of language. Yes, Stella has come to that moment of seeing through a glass darkly, and yet utterly changed from all previous seeing.

Geometries: line breaks

Fences mark the geometries of *The Double Hook*. Graves and their burials mark the geometries of *Four Stories*. Confined cabins geometry the long winter hours of *Deep Hollow Creek*. Stella begins in a square room, a square room with a wooden table and a square window without a view which hooks up to the ceiling. This room, which the Flower children have been evicted from, enacts a perfect symmetry, despoiled by Stella's unwelcome presence. There's a teacher in town. There's a teacher in them there hills. Teacher/coyote/poetry reader. Come out with your hands up. The roads in each text pretend to occupy a geometric grid of survey lines, but instead become traps, gumbo sinks, inevitably impassible, temptations for departures but ultimately re-routes, doubling back on their own escape and flight. Every road returns to the creek and stops, no end-stop but a line pulled toward the edge of the page, flooding across the margins.

Water is modernism's geometry. The snakey temptation of river. Water, old ladies fishing for glory and catching death; magic lakes that appear and disappear at will; the liquid of possibility finding its own outlet and enjambment. This is the light at the end of modernism, Watson's coyote a slippery river that turns and turns again. Water, water rights. To whom belongs that poetic elixir, water? The coming of the water is the coming of spring. "In the springtime when the water broke on the hill and the feed lots turned liquid and spilled the winter corruption into the creek, the water was useless for anything but stock. In the summer it was an endless source of argument and in winter, when the frost came, holes had to be cut in the creek with an axe. Water slopping from the buckets froze on the feet as it fell, froze the pail to the trouser leg and the bail to the gloved hand. Even in the house the water froze when the fire burnt out" (*Deep Hollow Creek* 42-43). This evasive element, fluid and uncontainable, shaped only by container, that genre-binding receptacle, and those who fish in troubled waters will earn their own watermark or their own delineation.

Up behind the flats, Stella is told, there is a magic lake, a great black lake that appears and disappears, only revealing itself to those who have the vision to know that water is intrinsic to a flat, dry poem or narrative which would fight and argue over fish and fury. That lake, lacustrine infusion, is the home of the coyote. Water will not be shunted into lines.

Bread: the possibility of lyric

The spare novel, flatbread that refuses to rise. A slender text living in a one-room cabin in the Cariboo, its lines fractured and yet assonant. The invention of the world out there, criss-crossed by the trails of the fishing writer, Sheila/Stella who doesn't teach much, just rides and takes care of her dog and reads.

Rose Flower's bread sours before it is baked, the yeast gone high and rancid, a failure to rise and sweeten in the baking. Rose is Stella's first landlady, with whom she boards when she arrives. Rose displaces her own children for Stella, and Stella, mourning her privacy, moves alone into the cabin. She refuses to stop or stay put in that country, although she knows that stopping houses work their own black magic. The daunting jangle of an out-of-key piano. The tangle of weeds beside wooden steps that dismiss verandas. Men willing to drink deep and long of draught beer. Coulees and clefts for coyotes to lurk around, to howl from.

And the lyrical intensity of stealing, theft repeated like a vanishing world, the terrible distemper of loss made into gain. Gossip and phones and debt. The coyotes circle the bone-thin cattle. The coyotes wait for the thaw, wait to send their song out through the softening air. The coyotes show their teeth in parodic smiles.

Quiet becomes sub-text to colour; the quiet that surrounds the words a riotous dis-quiet of interruption. The reader looks for events. The lines move. Nothing happens. The dog has puppies. Nothing happens. Winter comes. Nothing happens. Stella goes away for Christmas and comes back with Miriam Fairclough, who is a textual distraction. Nothing happens. Spring comes. Nothing happens. "Everywhere the thing which wasn't, became, and the thing which was, altered" (*Deep Hollow Creek* 139). The lyric of winter. Nothing happens. But everything as well.

Watson refuses to light the lamp, to provide "illumination," the pirouette at the end of every bad lyric poem. Stella lights a match to her cigarette and bends down so that Juno (the dog) can blow out the flame. The dog refuses, not being the human equivalent of a denouement, and the small flare singes Stella's fingers. Juno is merely dog (cousin to coyote), refusing to be metaphor, protectress of marriage or women, although she is Stella's constant companion, duplicitous as a plotless novel, as eager to roll in the rough dry grass of the Cariboo as the language of the novel rolls in an antithetical syntactical sparseness.

Avoiding Origins: Breaking Continuity

The final story in *Four Stories,* "The Rumble Seat," shatters and then brings together the mythic and the quotidian. Pierre the ambiguous (Pierre Trudeau, I want to ask?) searches like a modernist for post-modern associations. Pierre the discomfitting, the man who rants and rails, proceeds to characterize Canadian modernism. "The ecclesiastical establishment from the centre to the circumference of its pedestrian certitude, unaware of the origins and significance of the sexual revolution, insensitive to ubiquitous erotic stimuli, blind to the taboo-activity already permitted by fraternity-pin relationships, deaf to the voice of sexual starvation, untouched by the anguish of induced or illusory guilt, convinced, despite undisputed genetic truth, that an acquired characteristic, called original sin by that pseudo-modernist T.E. Hulme. . ." ("The Rumble Seat," *Four Stories* 53). No room here for new criticism, no hesitation about anxiety and its clenched desires. Surfeit, excess, blind gluttony over the arcane and esoteric.

The hair line between the metropolis and the nation etches division, the local enjoying its own upstartedness, its own regionalism, tongue-in-cheek. Pierre says, "This is Toronto . . . Riddles are beside the point. Here we have obstruction, obscurantism, and worse" ("The Rumble Seat, *Four Stories* 53). Modernity to the hilt, and delighting in the armour but still mirroring bonhomie, clamour, mourning. Refusing the play of play, the perforation of riddlement.

The reader, eager for poetic origins, hunts in vain for Antigone's debut, for Europa's line of clean laundry, the salesmanship of Daedalus thumped down to earth and selling machinery to dusted out farmers in the west. It's all gathered into Sheila Watson's poetics, the entire modernist debate and its debacle swept out the door, the looming quarter-section and its subdivision masquerading as a symbol, entire and yet fragmented. Breakage without compensation.

True black, the absence of all colour. The thematic thrust of "The Black Farm" Pluto's engine and its universe. The colour which can't be rubbed on or off but is the essence of all colour and its colourlessness. The message that Daedalus sends to Oedipus: *"All black is white. There are no eternal verities"* (*Four Stories* 36). So much for origins or models too. A modernist crisis of faith, demonstrated by how the lyric collects the world to rob it of its colour, the narrative resists the world to rob it of its implacable temporality. So far ahead of ahead was Watson, showing the cracked consolations of myth and plot, "drunk with the wonder of the commonplace" (*Four Stories* 28), and awestruck by the quotidian and its eloquence. Watson's characters reside in silence, talk to their animals, refute the narrative purchase and trade of the world. Watson's characters speak lines of disconnected poetry, shut their eyes on the turning world and think words without connection. They circle the fire of meaning and watch it burn meaning to the ground. The binaries of maternal/paternal interspersed, the binaries of poetry/prose erased. Only bricolage and its inherent dissent fractures cracks delicious as stained glass.

Watson proposes as a solution for poetry a trickster line, nature itself in cahoots with the absurd, like the man who crosses the uncrossable river in winter, escaping incarceration by "taking advantage of nature," a liquid solid, a fluid articulate. Watson proposes as a solution for prose a trickster image, fleeting and ineluctable, a latch that "needs oil" (*The Double Hook* 124) more than a plot that needs an outcome and a resolution.

Silence and speaking

The world is flat but love is round.

"It is her great poetic gift to make words vibrate" (Godard 157), says Barbara Godard of Watson in her groundbreaking and eloquent essay on *The Double Hook*. "In the very act of making the medium of her art her subject" (Godard 165), Watson kills both matriarch and patriarch, dislocating the syntax and hierarchy of genealogy. Her lines occupy an ellipsis that has always denoted woman as absent, silent, disposable, men as active and questing. The old forms shudder and crack open.

Our fathers' kingdoms are graveyards of desolation, jails, screened verandas, fenced acres, broken brush, brick walls, terrible ploughings, fierce orphanages, deaf debates, funeral parlours, unfaithful lovers, book thieves, soggy sandwiches, sneering metaphors, lost causes, bristling bayonets. Our mothers' kingdoms are steamy with blood, unrisen bread, bitter loneliness and widowhood, porcupine quills in a dog's nose.

Our fathers' kingdoms, contends Sheila Watson, haunt our ink bottles ("Unaccommodated Man," *Sheila Watson: A Collection* 111), but are not inescapable; our mothers' kingdoms too resound with doubt and grief but still can light a stove and oil a hinge. But there is a slender crack, a very small crack where the light gets in (now there's a modernism) and where the thawing water wells up from its winter of confinement, and where the spirit of language can thread its own needle, evade plot, spit on cheap metaphor, unlearn history, resist the encrustations of nouveau Victoriana and every simplistic duality.

Reduce, abbreviate, condense. Become enigmatic, elliptical. Spare down the bed. Refuse long-winded sacrifice, the awful reach of the awful fulsome. Double everything, even rebuke, even sensation and its excess. Kill your liturgy, fly in the face of both fatherhood and its enforced motherhood, run away to buy a parrot drinks and return because there is no away, only the denouement of return and its arrested development, its slow headlong rush, its respectful disrespect.

Nobody goes fishing. It's all catch and release now, the toy-gestures of human and piscatore, hook and mouth, latin and absolution. But Watson's women fish for words instead of glory, escape verisimilitude, resist the very plot that they have been trapped into, and in the end, trick even the trickster.

Watson writes the colour of words against an ashen sky and a white ground. This is my day. What does she want? It's easier to remember than to forget. I knew it was the old lady. There's things people want to see, things people want to read. They need all the water they can get. Make yourself at home. She must be sleeping. There's been more than I can stand. I want this house to myself. Come for the teapot. There's no way of telling what will walk into a woman's hand.

What then, might proclaim such a creator's creed?

"A surgeon," said Oedipus, "interferes with the natural cycle of growth and decay." He is a thing monstrous in nature and tolerable only because of the perverted philosophy which we inherit from that barbarous age, the age of reason. That age set loose a whole pack of surgeons—the economist, the social reformer, the town planner, the street cleaner, the organizer of departments of public works and the curriculum reformer. Behind it all I see the bland-faced Locke with theories of equal rights and baths for everybody.

"You have been drinking," said our mother. ("Brother Oedipus," *Four Stories* 14)

The voice of reason and imagination. The voice of feelings, although "no woman's got a right to have feelings" (*Deep Hollow Creek* 34), the disputacious contention. Both reason and imagination contribute to the temptation to romance Sheila Watson. Her many mythologies interrupt their own ghosts. The skeletons in the closets. The stranger who enters the community, and pokes her nose into the closet. A woman waiting to drink thin coffee from an enamel pot, already the repository of gossip and confession. The kitchen stove still the centre of the universe, the coffee pot still its grail. So much for houses and their propriety. So much for fishing and its lines. So much for bridges and their crossings. So much for graves and their confinement.

Baths for everybody. Drinks all around. Church at the end of the road. School for the restless. "She lifted her eyes to the hills, which were brown and naked in the morning light" (*Deep Hollow Creek* 113). Brown and naked, this bare bricoleur Watson, artist of "depouillement" (Godard 158). Region and reason washed clean, stripped down to their essentials. "Something else," even more shapely, the incipient possibility of "this part of the country," that country of a mind's colour ("What I'm Going to Do," *Sheila Watson: A Collection* 182).

Contributors

Di Brandt's award winning poetry titles include *questions I asked my mother* (1987) and *Jerusalem, beloved* (1995). Her most recent collection is *Now You Care* (2003). She has been a poetry editor for *Contemporary Verse 2* and *Prairie Fire*. Her nonfiction titles include *Dancing Naked: Narrative Strategies for Writing Across Centuries* (1996), a collection of essays on cross-cultural poetics. She is Canada Research Chair in Creative Writing at Brandon University and adjunct professor in English at the University of Windsor, where she co-hosted the conference/festival, Wider Boundaries of Daring: The Modernist Impulse in Canadian Women's Poetry with Barbara Godard.

Elizabeth Brewster, one of Canada's most respected poets, published *East Coast* in 1951 and has followed it with five books of fiction, two volumes of autobiography and twenty collections of poetry, most recently *Collected Poems I* (2003). An earlier collection, *Footnotes to the Book of Job* (1995) was shortlisted for the Governor General's Award. Her many other awards include an honorary doctorate from the University of New Brunswick, the E.J. Pratt Award, the President's Medal, the Saskatchewan Lifetime Achievement Award and the Order of Canada. Born in New Brunswick, she has long resided in Saskatoon where she is Professor Emerita at the University of Saskatchewan.

Rebecca Campbell is a singer/songwriter/musician/photographer/arts administrator who has performed and recorded extensively throughout North America and Europe with many luminaries, especially as Jane Siberry's right hand woman; with Justin Haynes (*Tug*); the pop collective Fat Man Waving, for which she was lead singer and percussionist (*Parade*); and with Three Sheets to the Wind, her a capella group (*Grace Under Pressure*). She performed in Meredith Monk's Atlas in New York in 2004-2005 and in the spring of 2005 did a music camp in Rankin Inlet, Nunavut. In 2004 she was nominated by an Ontario Arts Council jury for the K. M. Hunter Artist Award.

Natalee Caple is the author of *A More Tender Ocean*, a book of poetry which was nominated for a Gerald Lampert award and three books of fiction including the recent novel *Mackerel Sky* (2004). She was the 2004 Markin-Flanagan Writer in Residence at the University of Calgary.

Margaret Christakos, a poet and fiction writer, was born and raised in Sudbury and has been based in Toronto since 1987. Her five collections of poetry include *Excessive Love Prostheses* (2002), winner of the ReLit Award. Her novel, *Charisma* (2000), was shortlisted for the Trillium Award. In 2004-2005 she was Writer in Residence at the University of Windsor.

Lisa Fiorindi grew up in Windsor, Ontario and completed her M.A. in English and Creative Writing at the University of Windsor. Currently, she is pursuing a Ph.D. in Comparative Literature and Women's Studies at the University of Toronto.

Barbara Godard is Avie Bennett Historica Chair in Canadian Literature at York University. Since the Dialogue conference she organized in 1981, she has fostered conversations and collaborations across linguistic, cultural and generic boundaries through the feminist literary periodical, *Tessera,* she co-founded; her books, including *Gynocritics/Gynocritiques: Feminist Approaches to Canadian Women's Writing* (1987) and *Intersexions: Issues of Race and Gender in Canadian Women's Writing* (1996); and translations, recently Nicole Brossard's *Intimate Journal* (2004). In collaboration with Di Brandt, she organized the Wider Boundaries of Daring conference/festival in 2001.

Susan Holbrook teaches North American literatures and creative writing at the University of Windsor. Her primary research explores feminist experimental writing by authors such as Gertrude Stein and Nicole Brossard. She has published two books of poetry, *misled* (1999) and *Good Egg Bad Seed* (2004).

Cornelia Hoogland, poet, playwright and scholar (University of Western Ontario), recently launched her fourth book *Cuba Journal: Writing and Language* (2003) selections from which—as well as from *You Are Home* (2001)—were short-listed for a CBC radio literary award. Hoogland has performed and lectured internationally (Cuba, Brazil, Philippines, U.S. and England) in the areas of poetry and drama.

Jan Horner, who lives and works in Winnipeg, is a poet whose publications include *Elizabeth Went West* (1998). Her first collection, *Recent Mistakes* (1986) won the inaugural McNally Robinson Manitoba Book of the Year Award. She was a member of the editorial collective of *Contemporary Verse 2,* founded by Dorothy Livesay. In 2001-2002 she was Writer in Residence at the University of Western Ontario.

Penn Kemp, a prolific artist, who has performed internationally, has published twenty books of poetry and had six plays and eight CDs produced as well as Canada's first poetry CD-ROM, *On Our Own Spoke*. Since her first sound/concrete book was published in 1972, Penn has been pushing textual and aural boundaries, often with actors, poets and jazz musicians. Her videopoem, "Re:Solution," won best performance prize at the Vancouver Videopoem Festival. Her "poem for peace in many voices" has been translated and recorded in ninety languages.

Claudia Lucotti was born in Argentina but has lived in Mexico since 1987 where she works at the Universidad Nacional Autónoma de México. Her main fields of interest are women's poetry, translation studies, and Mexican-Canadian issues and she has published a number of translations of Canadian fiction and poetry including *Donde es aqui?* (2002), an anthology of short stories.

Susan McMaster is the author of a dozen poetry collections, including recordings with First Draft, SugarBeat, and Geode Music & Poetry. The founding editor of national feminist magazine *Branching Out,* she has edited the Living Archives series of the Feminist Caucus of the League of Canadian Poets, *Siolence: Women, Violence, and Siolence*, and *Waging Peace: Poetry and Political Action*, the story of "Convergence: Poems for Peace," her project to bring poetry and art from across Canada to all Parliamentarians in 2001.

Nicole Markotic, poet, critic, and fiction writer, teaches at the University of Calgary, and was an editor of the feminist journal, *Tessera*. Her publications include the prose poetry collection, *Connect the Dots* (1994), a fictional biography about Alexander Graham Bell, *Yellow Pages* (1995), as well as poetry, *Minotaurs & Other Alphabets* (1998).

Daphne Marlatt, one of Canada's best known writers, has published more than twenty-five books of poetry, fiction and essays. A founding co-editor of the feminist periodical *Tessera*, she was a co-organizer of the celebrated Women and Words gathering (1983) and of *Telling It: Women and Language Across Cultures* (1988). Her most recent poetry collection, *This Tremor Love Is* (2001), was short-listed for three literary awards. A chapbook, *Seven Glass Bowls* (2003), is the first movement of a long poem/novel-in-progress. She was the 2004-2005 Writer in Residence at Simon Fraser University.

Karen Mulhallen is the author of nine books of poetry, including *Sea Light* (2003), editor of two anthologies of Canadian literature and co-editor of a book on Dennis Lee. Her essays on literature, music and culture have appeared in national and international journals, and she is Editor-In-Chief of *Descant* magazine. She teaches English at Ryerson University in Toronto.

Sharon H. Nelson is the author of nine books of poems and of essays, plays, political analyses, and literary reviews including the recent *This Flesh These Words* (2002). Her work focuses on feminist, Jewish, and social justice themes. She has been employed as a journalist, editor, and writing teacher, and has co-authored computer science texts. Founder of the women's caucus of the League of Canadian Poets, her pathbreaking research into the status of women in the literary institution in Canada, published in *Fireweed* in 1982, became a rallying point for feminist cultural production seeking social change.

P.K. Page, one of Canada's most celebrated poets, has won many honours in a career that spans nearly seventy years, including the Governor General's Award for poetry (1954) and the Order of Canada (1999). She is the author of a novel, selected short stories, a memoir, three books for children and more than ten volumes of poetry, most recently *Planet Earth* (2002) which gathered several new long poems and selections from earlier work. A two-volume edition of her collected poems, *The Hidden Room*, was published in 1997. She has recently completed a libretto for an opera, *What Time is Now?* Under the name P.K. Irwin, her paintings have been exhibited in solo and group exhibitions in Mexico and Canada and are represented in the permanent collections of major Canadian galleries, including the National Gallery of Canada and the Victoria Art Gallery of the city where she now resides.

Rosemary Sullivan, biographer and poet, is a professor at the University of Toronto. She has published ten books, including *Shadow Maker: The Life of Gwendolyn MacEwen* (Governor General's Award, 1995); *The Bone Ladder: Poems Selected and New* (2000); and *Labyrinth of Desire* (2002). She is a Canada Research Chair and Member of the Royal Society of Canada.

Lola Lemire Tostevin has published two novels, a collection of essays and six books of poetry, including the recent *Site-Specific Poems* (2004). Her third novel, *The Other Sister* is forthcoming. In 2004-2005 she was Writer in Residence at the University of Western Ontario.

Jana Skarecky, a Canadian of Czech background, has composed music for a variety of instruments and voices. Her compositions have been performed on four continents, and she has set to music the work of many poets. She also paints with acrylics, and teaches at the Royal Conservatory of Music.

Aritha van Herk has persistently explored feminist issues in her eight books of fiction, creative non-fiction, and essays since her first novel, *Judith*, received the inaugural Seal First Book Prize in 1978. Women's work, geography, melancholia, and picaresque retributions are at the heart of her writing and critical thought. Her recent books are the novel, *Restlessness* (1998), and *Maverick: an incorrigible history of Alberta* (2001).

Betsy Warland, nonfiction writer and poet, was originally trained as a visual artist and writes regularly for visual art publications. A co-organizer of Women and Words (1983), she edited *f/lip*, a journal of experimental feminist writing. She has recently completed her ninth and tenth books—a poetry narrative, *Colour Quartet*, and a collection of essays *Breathing the Page: Writing on Writing*. She teaches in and directs The Writer's Studio at Simon Fraser University.

Carol Ann Weaver is an eclectic composer/pianist whose genre-bending work, ranging from classical to jazz, avant-garde to folk, has been widely performed. Her recent collaboration with leading Canadian vocalist Rebecca Campbell on the CD *Awakenings* has led to concerts in Europe, Hawaii, mainland USA, and Canada. Carol's previous CDs include *Daughter of Olapa*, with both African themes and Di Brandt settings. Carol is a Music Professor at Conrad Grebel University College/University of Waterloo and a member of the Association of Canadian Women Composers.

Janice Williamson writes, teaches and mothers day and night at latitude 53. Feminist literary and cultural studies propelled her auspiciously around the world. Her sixth book, *Crybaby!* (1998), is a study of the poetics of trauma and the politics of telling in memoir form. *Hexagrams for My Chinese Daughter*, a book in process, uses ancient Chinese divination to explore international adoption, transracial mothering and travels with seven-year-old Bao.

Carolyn Zonailo, born in Vancouver, British Columbia of Doukhobor heritage, has lived in Montreal for the past fourteen years. She has published ten books of poetry, the most recent, *The Holy Hours* (2004). Carolyn Zonailo has served on executives of literary organizations and been active as an editor in small press publishing, putting many women writers into print.

References

Blanco, José Joaquín. *Crónica de la poesía mexicana.* Culiacán, Sinaloa: Universidad Autónoma de Sinaloa, 1978.

Bowering, George. "Sheila Watson." *Encyclopedia of Literature in Canada.* Ed. W. H. New. Toronto: U of Toronto P, 2002. 1197-1199.

Bowles, Samuel and Herbert Gintis. "Is Equality Passé? *Homo reciprocans* and the future of egalitarian politics." *Boston Review* 23.6 (December/January 1998-1999): 1-27.

Brewster, Elizabeth. *In Search of Eros.* Toronto: Clark Irwin, 1974.

Butling, Pauline. *Seeing in the Dark: The Poetry of Phyllis Webb.* Waterloo: Wilfrid Laurier UP, 1997.

Cameron, Dan. "An Interview with William Kentridge." *William Kentridge.* Ed. William Sittenfeld. New York: Harry N. Abrams, 2001.

Carrington, Leonora. "Commentary." *Leonora Carrington: A Retrospective Exhibition.* Center for Inter-American Relations. New York City, November 26-January 4, 1976.

_____. "Down Below." *The House of Fear: Notes from Down Below.* New York: E.P. Dutton 1988.

Christakos, Margaret. *Not Egypt.* Toronto: Coach House Press, 1989.

_____. *Other Words for Grace.* Stratford, Ont.: Mercury Press, 1994.

Cogswell, Fred. Interview with Sharon H. Nelson. New Westminster, B.C., April 2003.

Culler, Jonathan. *Structuralist Poetics: Structuralism, Linguistics and the Study of Literature.* London and New York: Routledge, 1975.

Davis, Lennard. "Enabling Texts." *Disability Studies Quarterly.* 17.4 (Fall 1997): 248-50.

Deane, Seamus. "Imperialism/Nationalism." *Critical Terms for Literary Study.* Eds. Frank Lentricchia and Thomas McLaughlin. Chicago: U of Chicago P, 1995. 354-68.

Downes, G.V. Interview with Sharon H. Nelson. Victoria, B.C., April 2003.

Duras, Marguerite. *Practicalities.* trans. Barbara Bray. New York: Grove Press, 1992.

"Elizabeth Brewster." *Dictionary of Literary Biography: Canadian Writers Since 1960.* Vol. 60. 2nd Series. Ed. W.H. New. Detroit: Gale Research, 1987.

Fiamengo, Marya. *White Linen Remembered.* Vancouver: Ronsdale Press, 1996.

Flores, Angel and Kate Flores, eds. *Poesía feminista del mundo hispánico: Desde la edad media hasta la actualidad. Antologica crítica.* Mexico: Siglo Veintiuno editores, 1984.

Frank, Robert and Henry Sayre, eds. "Introduction." *The Line in Postmodern Poetry.* Urbana: U of Illinois P, 1988.

Geddes, Gary and Phyllis Bruce, eds. *15 Canadian Poets.* Toronto: Oxford UP, 1970.

Geddes, Gary, ed. *15 Canadian Poets X 2.* Toronto: Oxford UP, 1990.

Godard, Barbara. "'Between One Cliché and Another': Language in *The Double Hook.*" *Studies in Canadian Literature 3* (1978): 149-65.

Godzich, Wlad and Jeffrey Kittay. *The Emergence of Prose: an essay in prosaics.* Minneapolis: U of Minnesota P, 1987.

Hamburger, Michael. *La verdad de la poesía. Tensiones en la poesía moderna de Baudelaire a los años sesenta.* Mexico: Fondo de Cultura Económica, 1991.

Hertz, Joseph H., ed. and trans. *Sayings of the Fathers, or Pirke Aboth.* New York: Behrman House, 1945.

Hoogland, Cornelia. "In the meantime: Elizabeth Smart poems." *Marrying The Animals.* London: Brick Books, 1995.

Jitrik, Noé. *Las contradicciones del modernismo.* Mexico: Fontamara, 2000.

Jones, Alun R. *The Life and Opinions of T.E. Hulme.* Boston: Beacon Press, 1960.

Kaplan, Janet. *Unexpected Journeys: The Art and Life of Remedios Varo.* New York: Abbeville, 1988.

Keith, W.J. "Elizabeth Brewster." *Oxford Companion to Canadian Literature.* Ed. William Toye. Don Mills: Oxford UP, 2001.

Kilcup, Karen L. *Robert Frost and Feminine Literary Tradition.* Ann Arbor: U. of Michigan P, 1998.

Kroetsch, Robert and Diane Bessai. "Death is a Happy Ending: A dialogue in thirteen parts." *Figures in a Ground.* Eds. Diane Bessai and David Jackel. Saskatoon: Western Producer Prairie Books, 1978.

Lewis, Wyndham. *The Vulgar Streak.* New York: Jubilee Books, 1973.

Livesay, Dorothy. *The Phases of Love.* Toronto: Coach House Press, 1983.

_____. *The Self-Completing Tree: Selected Poems.* Victoria: Press Porcépic, 1986.

_____. *The Woman I Am.* Erin: Press Porcépic, 1977.

Macpherson, Jay. *The Boatman.* Toronto: McClelland and Stewart, 1957.

Mallinson, Jean. "Introduction." *D'Sonoqua: An Anthology of Women Poets of British Columbia.* Ed. Ingrid Klassen. Vol. 1. Vancouver: Intermedia, 1979.

Mandel, Miriam. *Lions at her Face.* Edmonton: White Pelican, 1973.

Marlatt, Daphne. "musing with mothertongue." *Touch to My Tongue.* Edmonton: Longspoon, 1984.

Marriott, Anne. *Aqua.* Toronto: Wolsak and Wynn, 1991.

_____. *Calling Adventurers.* Toronto: Ryerson, 1941.

_____. *The Circular Coast: Poems New and Selected.* Oakville: Mosaic, 1981.

_____. *Countries.* Fredericton: Fiddlehead, 1971.

_____. *Letters From Some Islands.* Oakville: Mosaic, 1985.

_____. *The Wind Our Enemy.* Toronto: Ryerson, 1939.

McLellan, Marya. Personal correspondence and emails with Sharon H. Nelson, 28 February, 5 and 31 March, 2 April 2003.

McMaster, Susan. *(m)Othêr Tonguès* 2 (Winter 1991): 34-35.

_____. *Pass This Way Again.* Toronto: Underwhich, 1983.

Milosz, Czeslaw. *The Witness of Poetry.* Cambridge, Mass.: Harvard UP, 1983.

Morrison, Philip. Review of Steven Pinker's *The Language Instinct. Scientific American* 27. 4 (October 1994).

Nelson, Sharon H. "Bemused, Branded and Belittled: Women and Writing in Canada." *Fireweed* 15 (December 1982): 64-102.

_____. "Circus Animals On The Commons/Green." *Other Voices* 13 (December 2000): 79-80.

_____. *The Work of Our Hands.* Dorion: Muses, 1992.

_____. *This Flesh These Words.* Victoria: Ekstasis, 2002.

Page, P.K. *Evening Dance of the Grey Flies.* Toronto: Oxford UP, 1981.

_____. *The Glass Air: Poems Selected and New.* Toronto Oxford UP, 1985.

_____. *Hologram.* London: Brick, 1994.

_____. *Planet Earth: Poems Selected and New.* Erin: Porcupine's Quill, 2002.

Perloff, Marjorie. "Linear Fallacy." *Georgia Review* 35.4 (Winter 1981): 855-69.

Scott, Gail. *Main Brides: Against Ochre Pediment and Aztec Sky.* Toronto: Coach House Press, 1993.

Sedgwick, Eve Kosofsky. *Touching Feeling: Affect, Pedagogy, Performativity.* Durham: Duke UP, 2003.

Skarecky, Jana. *Green and Gold: Cycle of Songs for Soprano and Piano.* 2001. Poems by P.K. Page.

_____. *Planet Earth: For Soprano and Piano.* 2002. Poems by P.K. Page.

Smart, Elizabeth. *Autobiographies.* Ed. Christina Burridge. Vancouver: Tanks, 1987.

_____. *By Grand Central Station I Sat Down and Wept.* 1945. Otttawa: Deneau, 1981.

_____. *In the meantime: A collection of poetry and prose.* Ottawa: Deneau, 1984.

_____. *Necessary Secrets: The Journals of Elizabeth Smart.* Ed. Alice Van Wart. Ottawa: Deneau, 1986.

_____. *On the Side of Angels.* Ed. Alice Van Wart. London: Harper Collins, 1994.

Spears, Heather, ed. *Line by Line.* Victoria: Ekstasis, 2002.

St. George, Elyse Yates. *White Lions in the Afternoon.* Regina: Coteau Books, 1987.

Stewart, Susan. *On Longing: Narratives of the Miniature, the Gigantic, the Souvenir, the Collection.* Durham: Duke UP, 1993.

Sullivan, Rosemary. *By Heart, a life.* Toronto: Viking, 1991.

_____. Interview with Leonora Carrington. Mexico City 1994.

_____. Interview with P.K. Page. Victoria, B.C. 1994.

Suzuki, Shunryn. *Zen Mind, Beginner's Mind.* New York and Tokyo: Weatherhill, 1970.

Szumigalski, Anne. *On Glassy Wings.* Regina: Coteau Books, 1997.

Valdés, Héctor, ed. *Antología de poetisas mexicanas del siglo XX.* Mexico: Universidad Nacional Autónoma de México, 1976.

Varo, Remedios. *De Homo Rodans.* Mexico: Calli-Nova, 1970.

Venuti, Lawrence, ed. *Rethinking Translation. Discourse Subjectivity Ideology.* London and New York: Routledge, 1992.

Waddington, Miriam. *Driving Home: Poems New and Selected.* Toronto: Oxford UP, 1972.

Warland, Betsy. *Bloodroot: Tracing the Untelling of Motherloss.* Toronto: Second Story Press/Sumach Press, 2000.

_____. "Colour Quartet." Unpublished manuscript.

Warner, Marina. *Leonora Carrington: A Retrospective Exhibition.* Serpentine Gallery, London 1991.

Watson, Sheila. *Deep Hollow Creek.* Toronto: McClelland and Stewart, 1992.

_____. *The Double Hook.* Toronto: McClelland and Stewart, 1959.

_____. *Four Stories.* Toronto: Coach House Press, 1979.

_____. "Sheila Watson: A Collection." *Open Letter* 3.1 (1974).

Webb, Phyllis. *Hanging Fire.* Toronto: Coach House Press, 1990.

_____. "Mesage Machine." *Language in Her Eye: Views on Writing and Gender by Canadian Women Writing in English.* Eds. Libby Scheier, Sarah Sheard and Eleanor Wachtel. Toronto: Coach House Press, 1990. 293-96.

_____. *Nothing But Brush Strokes: Selected Prose.* Edmonton: NeWest, 1995.

_____. *Selected Poems 1954-1965.* Vancouver: Talonbooks, 1971.

_____. *Talking.* Montreal: Quadrant Editions, 1982.

_____. *Wilson's Bowl.* Toronto: Coach House Press, 1980.

_____ and Smaro Kamboureli. " Seeking Shape, Seeking Meaning: Phyllis Webb interviewed by Smaro Kamboureli." *Dream Interviews with Canadian Poets.* Ed. Beverley Daurio. Toronto: Mercury Press, 2000. 187-214.

Woolf, Virginia. "Women and Fiction." Ed. Michèle Barrett. *Virginia Woolf: Women and Writing.* London: Women's Press, 1979.

Zonailo, Carolyn. "Poems for Women Poets" (Winner). *Giant Canadian Poetry Annual.* Erin: Press Porcépic, 1977.

Acknowledgements

Unless specified otherwise, all poetry in this volume is published by permission of the author.

Dorothy Livesay's *Awakening* Vancouver: Hawthorne Society, 1991, is published by permission of Jay Stewart. Anne Marriott's poems are published by permission of Marya McLellan.

Some of the poems in this volume appeared previously in the same or a different version. We are grateful for permission to republish here selections from Margaret Christakos, *Excessive Love Prostheses* Toronto: Coach House, 2002; Cornelia Hoogland, *Marrying the Animals* London: Brick Books, 1995 ; Susan McMaster, *Until the Light Bends* Windsor: Black Moss, 2004; Sharon H. Nelson, *This Flesh These Words* Victoria: Ekstasis, 2002; P.K. Page, *Evening Dance of the Grey Flies* Toronto: Oxford, 1981; Lola Lemire Tostevin, *Site-Specific Poems* Toronto: Mercury, 2004.

Jana Skarecky's "Green and Gold: 'Evening Dance of the Grey Flies'" (c. 2001) is published by permission of the composer. Thanks to the Laidlaw Foundation for assistance.

We gratefully acknowledge the following for permission to reproduce the visual art.

© Leonora Carrington / SODRAC (Montreal) 2005. *The Ancestor*, 1968. Private collection.
© Leonora Carrington / SODRAC (Montreal) 2005. *Monopoteosis*, 1959. Museo de Arte Contemporaneo, Monterrey.

P.K. Irwin, *The Dance*, 1962. Reproduced by permission of the artist.
P.K. Irwin, *The Garden*, 1961. Reproduced by permission of the artist.

Remedios Varo, *Los amantes* (The Lovers), 1963. Reproduced by permission of Anna Alexandra and Walter Gruen.
Remedios Varo, *Tres destinos* (Three Destinies), 1956. Reproduced by permission of Anna Alexandra and Walter Gruen.

Phyllis Webb, *Cross Word*, 2001. Reproduced by permission of the artist. Courtesy of Smaro Kamboureli.
Phyllis Webb, *Veiled Woman, Afghanistan*, 1997. Reproduced by permission of the artist.

MEMBER OF SCABRINI GROUP

Québec, Canada
2006